Building Bots with Node.js

Automate workflow and internal communication processes and provide customer service without apps using messaging and interactive bots

Eduardo Freitas
Madan Bhintade

Packt>

BIRMINGHAM - MUMBAI

Building Bots with Node.js

First published: January 2017

Production reference: 1240117

Published by Packt Publishing Ltd.
Livery Place
35 Livery Street
Birmingham
B3 2PB, UK.
ISBN 978-1-78646-545-0

www.packtpub.com

Credits

Authors

Eduardo Freitas
Madan Bhintade

Reviewers

Allen O'Neill

Commissioning Editor

David Barnes

Acquisition Editor

Shweta Pant

Content Development Editor

Parshva Sheth

Technical Editor

Prashant Mishra

Copy Editor

Safis Editing

Project Coordinator

Sheejal Shah

Proofreader

Safis Editing

Indexer

Mariammal Chettiyar

Graphics

Abhinash Sahu

Production Coordinator

Melwyn Dsa

About the Authors

Eduardo Freitas currently works as a consultant on software development applied to customer success, mostly related to financial process automation, accounts payable processing, invoice data extraction and SAP integration.

He has provided consultancy services, engineered, advised and supported various projects for global names such as Agfa, Coca Cola, Domestic & General, EY, Enel, Mango and the Social Security Agency among many others. He's also been invited to various companies such as Shell, Capgemini, Cognizant and the European Space Agency. He was recently involved in analyzing 1.6 billion rows of data using Redshift (Amazon Web Services) in order to gather valuable insights on client patterns. He holds an M.S. in Computer Science.

He enjoys soccer, running, traveling, life hacking, learning and spending time with his family. You can reach him at `http://edfreitas.me`.

> *Many thanks to all the people who contributed to this book. All the lovely and amazing team at Packt and also to Madan Bhintade for believing in the project and helping me finalize it.*

Madan Bhintade is an independent solution architect. He is also a developer with focus on cloud based solutions. He enjoys development on AWS, Microsoft Azure & Office 365, SharePoint Server, Angular, and Node.js. He has 16 years of experience building solutions for insurance, financial & banking, and HR industries.

Madan is passionate about what he does and shares what he has learnt through his blog. He also enjoys speaking on what he is exploring in technology area and helps others to adopt the changes in technology. His typical interest areas include UX, Digital Technology Platforms, and artificial intelligence.

He is a C# Corner MVP. His contribution towards C# Corner can be seen at `http://www.c-sharpcorner.com/members/madan-bhintade`. He can be connected with via LinkedIn `https://in.linkedin.com/in/madanbhintade`.

Currently he is working on his startup concept along with his consulting assignments. You can reach Madan on his blog `http://www.madanbhintade.wordpress.com`and follow him on Twitter at `@madanbhintade`.

About the Reviewer

Allen is a chartered engineer with a background in enterprise systems. He is a fellow of the British Computing Society, a Microsoft Insider, and both a CodeProject and C-Sharp Corner MVP. His core technology interests are big data and machine learning, in particular using data science to create intelligent bots/agents for the web, and the Internet of Things. He is also a ball throwing slave to his family dogs.

Allen writes regularly at: Code Project - `https://www.codeproject.com/members/ajson` and C-Sharp Corner - `http://www.c-sharpcorner.com/members/allen-oneill.`

He can be contacted at `www.blox.io` or on twitter `@ajsondev`

www.PacktPub.com

For support files and downloads related to your book, please visit www.PacktPub.com.

Did you know that Packt offers eBook versions of every book published, with PDF and ePub files available? You can upgrade to the eBook version at www.PacktPub.com and as a print book customer, you are entitled to a discount on the eBook copy. Get in touch with us at service@packtpub.com for more details.

At www.PacktPub.com, you can also read a collection of free technical articles, sign up for a range of free newsletters and receive exclusive discounts and offers on Packt books and eBooks.

Mapt

https://www.packtpub.com/mapt

Get the most in-demand software skills with Mapt. Mapt gives you full access to all Packt books and video courses, as well as industry-leading tools to help you plan your personal development and advance your career.

Why subscribe?

- Fully searchable across every book published by Packt
- Copy and paste, print, and bookmark content
- On demand and accessible via a web browser

Customer Feedback

Thank you for purchasing this Packt book. We take our commitment to improving our content and products to meet your needs seriously—that's why your feedback is so valuable. Whatever your feelings about your purchase, please consider leaving a review on this book's Amazon page. Not only will this help us, more importantly it will also help others in the community to make an informed decision about the resources that they invest in to learn. You can also review for us on a regular basis by joining our reviewers' club. **If you're interested in joining, or would like to learn more about the benefits we offer, please contact us**: `customerreviews@packtpub.com`.

Table of Contents

Preface

Bots everywhere! Conversational and chat-enabled apps are well positioned to become the next big platform and how apps are developed. Advances in machine learning, natural conversational APIs have taken off and many high tech and software giants are embracing conversational bots and provide APIs that allow developers to create applications that seamlessly integrate into these conversational platforms, enhancing user's experience. This book explores some of these platforms in and simple and intuitive way, allowing developers to quickly come up to speed with them.

What this book covers

`Chapter 1`, *The Rise of Bots – Getting the Message Across*, introduces and explains the growing importance of bots in today's world and also teaches you how to create an SMS bot app using the Twilio messaging platform.

`Chapter 2`, *Getting Skype to Work for You*, explains how to use the new Microsoft Bot Framework in order to create a Skype bot.

`Chapter 3`, *Twitter as a Flight Information Agent*, teaches you how to create a Twitter bot application that interacts with the Air France KLM API in order to retrieve flight details.

`Chapter 4`, *A Slack Quote Bot*, explains how to create a Slack bot application that sends inspirational quotes to users.

`Chapter 5`, *Telegram-Powered Bots*, shows you how to develop a bot that will provide you the sentiments of messages on Telegram using Telegram APIs.

`Chapter 6`, *BotKit – Document Manager Agent for Slack*, teaches you how to use Slack APIs with BotKit to provide documents at the fingertips of team members collaborating in Slack.

`Chapter 7`, *Facebook Messenger Bot, Who's Off – A Scheduler Bot for Teams*, shows you how to set up a Facebook Messenger Bot that can be used to schedule team meetings, or to see who is off when with the help of the Microsoft Azure platform and services.

`Chapter 8`, *A Bug-Tracking Agent for Teams*, teaches you how to use the IRC platform and DocumentDB for a bug-tracking bot.

`Chapter 9`, *A Kik Salesforce CRM Bot*, explores how to use Force.com API and a Kik to create a Salesforce CRM Bot.

What you need for this book

The following requirements are recommended for maximum enjoyment:

- A good Internet connection
- A fairly modern computer or laptop (preferably Windows-based, but not necessarily)
- A fairly good dose of creativity, imagination, and willingness to learn and explore new concepts

Pretty much all software and APIs mentioned in this book are free of charge and can be downloaded from the Internet.

Who this book is for

This book is for anyone that knows some Node.js and would like to explore how a bot can be written with the various existing conversational platforms available today. The book is written in an easy-to-understand way that is suitable for developers of all kinds, from novice to very experienced ones. Some know-how of Node.js is recommended.

Conventions

In this book, you will find a number of text styles that distinguish between different kinds of information. Here are some examples of these styles and an explanation of their meaning.

Code words in text, database table names, folder names, filenames, file extensions, pathnames, dummy URLs, user input, and Twitter handles are shown as follows: "The `session` object contains the information that Skype passes on to the bot app, which describes the session data that has been received and from whom. Notice that the session object contains properties such as `message` and `text`."

A block of code is set as follows:

```
bot.dialog('/', function (session) {
  if (session.message.text.toLowerCase().indexOf('hi') >= 0){
    session.send('Hi ' + session.message.user.name +
     ' thank you for your message: ' + session.message.text);
  } else{
    session.send('Sorry I dont understand you...');
  }
});
```

Any command-line input or output is written as follows:

```
mkdir telegrambot
cd telegrambot
```

New terms and important words are shown in bold. Words that you see on the screen, for example, in menus or dialog boxes, appear in the text like this: "Click on the **Register a bot** option in order to create and register your Skype bot. Once you've done that, you'll see the following screen:"

Warnings or important notes appear in a box like this.

Tips and tricks appear like this.

Reader feedback

Feedback from our readers is always welcome. Let us know what you think about this book—what you liked or disliked. Reader feedback is important for us as it helps us develop titles that you will really get the most out of.

To send us general feedback, simply e-mail `feedback@packtpub.com`, and mention the book's title in the subject of your message.

If there is a topic that you have expertise in and you are interested in either writing or contributing to a book, see our author guide at `www.packtpub.com/authors`.

Customer support

Now that you are the proud owner of a Packt book, we have a number of things to help you to get the most from your purchase.

Downloading the example code

You can download the example code files from your account at `http://www.packtpub.com` for all the Packt Publishing books you have purchased. If you purchased this book elsewhere, you can visit `http://www.packtpub.com/support` and register to have the files e-mailed directly to you.

You can download the code files by following these steps:

1. Log in or register to our website using your e-mail address and password.
2. Hover the mouse pointer on the **SUPPORT** tab at the top.
3. Click on **Code Downloads & Errata**.
4. Enter the name of the book in the **Search** box.
5. Select the book for which you're looking to download the code files.
6. Choose from the drop-down menu where you purchased this book from.
7. Click on **Code Download**.

You can also download the code files by clicking on the **Code Files** button on the book's webpage at the Packt Publishing website. This page can be accessed by entering the book's name in the Search box. Please note that you need to be logged in to your Packt account.

Once the file is downloaded, please make sure that you unzip or extract the folder using the latest version of:

- WinRAR / 7-Zip for Windows
- Zipeg / iZip / UnRarX for Mac
- 7-Zip / PeaZip for Linux

The code bundle for the book is also hosted on GitHub at `https://github.com/PacktPublishing/Building-Bots-with-Nodejs`. We also have other code bundles from our rich catalog of books and videos available at `https://github.com/PacktPublishing/`. Check them out!

Downloading the color images of this book

We also provide you with a PDF file that has color images of the screenshots/diagrams used in this book. The color images will help you better understand the changes in the output. You can download this file from: `https://www.packtpub.com/sites/default/files/downloads/BuildingBotswithNodejs_ColorImages.pdf`.

Errata

Although we have taken every care to ensure the accuracy of our content, mistakes do happen. If you find a mistake in one of our books—maybe a mistake in the text or the code—we would be grateful if you could report this to us. By doing so, you can save other readers from frustration and help us improve subsequent versions of this book. If you find any errata, please report them by visiting `http://www.packtpub.com/submit-errata`, selecting your book, clicking on the Errata Submission Form link, and entering the details of your errata. Once your errata are verified, your submission will be accepted and the errata will be uploaded to our website or added to any list of existing errata under the Errata section of that title.

To view the previously submitted errata, go to `https://www.packtpub.com/books/content/support` and enter the name of the book in the search field. The required information will appear under the Errata section.

Piracy

Piracy of copyrighted material on the Internet is an ongoing problem across all media. At Packt, we take the protection of our copyright and licenses very seriously. If you come across any illegal copies of our works in any form on the Internet, please provide us with the location address or website name immediately so that we can pursue a remedy.

Please contact us at `copyright@packtpub.com` with a link to the suspected pirated material.

We appreciate your help in protecting our authors and our ability to bring you valuable content.

Questions

If you have a problem with any aspect of this book, you can contact us at `questions@packtpub.com`, and we will do our best to address the problem.

1
The Rise of Bots – Getting the Message Across

Nowadays customers are demanding to communicate with brands, companies, and organizations as casually as they talk to their friends, and they expect an immediate response. Providing that level of service is quite impractical, if not rather logistically impossible to achieve for most organizations, without using some form of automation.

Until recently, the limitations of automated technology meant compromising the seamless, robust experience that's been proven to create loyal customers. Running a call center is an expensive undertaking and yet in order to be able to provide that instant communication channel with customers, most brands and companies opted to do this, in order to provide that instant response.

With the advent of **Artificial Intelligence** (**AI**), **Natural Language Processing** (**NLP**), **Machine Learning** (**ML**), and Sentiment Analysis APIs and frameworks, semi-automated or fully automated agents known as bots are radically changing everything we know about customer communication, initiating a revolution in the way customer interaction is done.

With fewer people using their phone to make phone calls anymore, but instead using their phones for anything else but talking, messaging has become the de facto way to communicate.

A great deal of smartphone owners use their devices to make calls, but most use them for text-based communication (texting/SMS, messaging, or chat). The average adult spends a total of 23 hours a week texting. Furthermore over a lifetime, the average Millennial will spend an astonishing 12 years texting.

The reason for the rise of text messaging as a communication platform is that phone calls are interruptive, inconvenient, and inefficient. They don't allow for multitasking–when you're using your smartphone to make a call, it cannot be used for anything else. While in the past we used to just pick up the phone to solve a problem, now we start with text-based messages, and then escalate to voice.

Another significantly important reason for messaging adoption is that customers are demanding interaction where they already are.

Messaging and chat-related apps are rapidly gaining popularity over SMS, especially among younger people. Globally, 6 of the 10 top apps are messaging applications such as Facebook Messenger, WhatsApp, Telegram, and WeChat.

The main reason for this increased usage of messaging apps is that these don't count against monthly SMS limits, and if you're connected to Wi-Fi, these don't use up any data either. Further to that, there's also an emotional component, which enhances the overall conversation. Messaging has the feel of a real-time conversation. You know when your friends are active in the app and even when they're typing a response, which makes it an addictive and highly engaging medium to communicate with.

With this scenario in perspective, creating messaging bots that provide meaningful interaction with customers provides a cutting-edge advantage to any business, by using today's most common communication medium and also being where customers already are, on their messaging apps.

In this book, we'll explore how we can write bots using various platforms, APIs, and SDKs in order to tackle some of today's most interesting business problems, in steps that are easy to follow and at the same time fun to implement. Specifically, this chapter will dig into:

- Why bots matter and why you should get on the train
- Why SMS still matters
- Twilio as an SMS platform:
    - Installing Twilio for Node.js
    - Setting up a Twilio account
    - Bare-bones Twilio Node.js template
- Core bot functionality on Azure
- Receiving SMS bot logic

Let's not wait any further and get into the details. Have fun!

Why bots matter and why you should get on the train

In the broad sense of its definition, a bot is a piece of software that leverages artificial narrow intelligence to perform specific tasks in place of a human. Bots understand language to a certain extent and not just commands. Ultimately, they could learn from their interactions to get smarter and better.

In roughly two years time, 3.6 billion people (yes 3.6 billion) are projected to be using messaging apps–that's 90% of total Internet users, which is more people than could ever be served with a continuous thread of communication compared to more traditional platforms such as e-mail. Refer to the following link for more information: `https://hbr.org/2016/09/messaging-apps-are-changing-how-companies-talk-with-customers`.

Worldwide, consumers are now demanding messaging as a customer service option. It's not sufficient to have a customer service phone number where the customer can call you, but it's becoming almost a must that customers should be able to reach you through some kind of real-time messaging platform as well. Users are demanding fast-paced interaction and quick answers.

Recent studies found that messaging and chat were the highest rated contact methods for customer satisfaction. Refer to `https://onereach.com/blog/45-texting-statistics-that-prove-businesses-need-to-start-taking-sms-seriously/`.

According to recent polls (`http://customerthink.com/7-data-backed-reasons-why-you-should-let-customers-text-customer-service/`), almost two-thirds of consumers are likely to have a positive perception of an organization that offers messaging or chat as a service channel. Nevertheless, by the end of 2016, roughly 40% of customer service centers will still be missing that opportunity to impress their customers. This translates not only into failing to impress your customers, but also as a loss of business opportunities. Customers are likely to be more loyal and stay with those organizations that are capable of interacting and engaging with them in faster and smarter ways. Refer to `https://blog.kissmetrics.com/live-chat/`.

Consider your organization (corporate) has a messaging app that allows your customers to interact with you. Even though your app might be a great communication gateway, there's still no room for that communication channel to be lost. Say, for instance, a user forgets to turn on notifications or accidentally deletes the app. The ability to seamlessly and easily communicate is suddenly gone.

However, using a personal messaging app (such as Skype, Facebook Messenger, WhatsApp, and so on) eliminates most roadblocks, allowing for companies to become part of the communication framework that users already know and love.

With messaging apps, there are no forms, no downloads, no new platforms. The customer can use the interface that they are already familiar with to instantly engage with your organization. The user can use natural language to purchase a ticket, download a boarding pass, or ask a question. Moreover, given that the user is highly unlikely to stop using the messaging app, your organization can follow up with updates, surveys, and other notifications through the messaging app that the user already knows and loves.

In order to understand this better, say when a consumer asks a question, the bot should be able to:

- Use natural language processing to understand the intent of the question
- Gather relevant details from the company's website, FAQs, or knowledge base, or even trusted external sites
- Sift through that information to find the most likely answer to the customer's intent of the question
- Respond back to the customer more or less in a similar way as a human would

There will surely be cases where bots might encounter situations that require the nuance and analytical thinking of a human. When they do, they can escalate to an agent, passing along the context they've gathered during the interaction to ensure a seamless customer experience. In principle, this should be totally transparent for the end user.

As technology continues to advance, Gartner predicts that by 2018, bots should be able to recognize customers by face and voice rather seamlessly.

Bots could also be able to:

- Allow customers to make purchases without leaving the messaging app
- Offer personalized product suggestions
- Link users to relevant web pages such as customer product reviews
- Initiate new interactions to re-engage users
- Follow up with cart reminders and customer cases

- Overall, help your organization to create an exceptional customer experience by providing robust data and actionable insights

Why SMS still matters

Smart phones are becoming more important in today's world. Arguably, they are almost an extension of yourself. If you lose your phone today, you are in trouble. Everything from e-mails, calendar, messaging, banking, and even your wallet are somehow linked to your phone.

In today's vibrant, dynamic, and always connected society, having access to vast amounts of information at your fingertips through your phone can be a blessing, but it can also be a curse.

Busy professionals nowadays have to deal with hundreds of e-mails on a daily or weekly basis, plus also many messages and notifications from social networks such as Twitter and LinkedIn. Keeping up with this sheer volume of messages can be overwhelming.

But what if phones could actually help us alleviate some of this information overload by notifying us of important things or allowing us to perform custom actions based on SMS or voice commands? Imagine if we were able to automate certain processes through messaging or voice. Wouldn't that be awesome?

Before social networks took off, **Short Message Service** (**SMS**) was the most common way to exchange short messages between people.

According to Wikipedia, even though SMS is still strong and growing, social networking messaging services such as Facebook Messenger, WhatsApp, Skype, and Viber, available on smart phones, are increasingly being used to exchange short messages.

Generally speaking, SMS and voice enabled solutions are platform specific and cannot be customized; however, there's a platform that was designed from the ground up with developers in mind, which allows anyone with development skills to create custom messaging and voice enabled solutions. Welcome to Twilio! refer to `https://www.twilio.com/`.

Twilio as an SMS platform

Twilio is a messaging, voice, video, and authentication API for every application. It has helper libraries or SDKs in many different programming languages that help developers create apps that can leverage the power of voice and messaging.

Despite that, SMS is still very strong and widely used in enterprise development for things such as marketing, **Customer Relationship Management** (**CRM**) automation, real-time alert notifications, and two-step verification of a user's identify.

The significance of SMS usage in the business world is incredibly important given that the technology is considered mature, widely spread, proven, and reliable.

Twilio's services are accessed over HTTP(S) through a RESTful API or helper libraries. Its services are billed based on usage. The platform is based on **Amazon Web Services** (**AWS**) to host its telephony infrastructure and provide connectivity between HTTP and the **Public Switched Telephone Network** (**PSTN**), through its APIs.

Twilio has recently extended its API support to Facebook Messenger, which coincides with the social networking company's introduction of support for bots on its Messenger platform.

In this chapter, we'll explore how to interact with Twilio's REST API using the Node.js helper library in order to build an SMS Messaging bot.

Installing Twilio for Node.js

Twilio provides a REST API, which allows developers to interact with its platform services, such as SMS. Even though the REST API is a great way to interact with Twilio services, there are official helper libraries for the most common programming languages of today, such as: PHP, ASP.NET (C#), Ruby, Python, Java, Salesforce (Apex), and, last but not least, Node.js.

The Twilio Node.js helper library can be obtained from `https://www.twilio.com/docs/libraries/node`. In order to get started, let's get Node.js installed.

Open your browser and navigate to `https://nodejs.org` and there on the main page you can download the version of Node.js that corresponds to your platform.

The steps that follow will be based on installing Node.js on a Windows 64 Bit operating system.

Once you have selected a version, just run the installer and follow the installation steps. You'll first be presented with a Welcome screen and then you can click on the **Next** button.

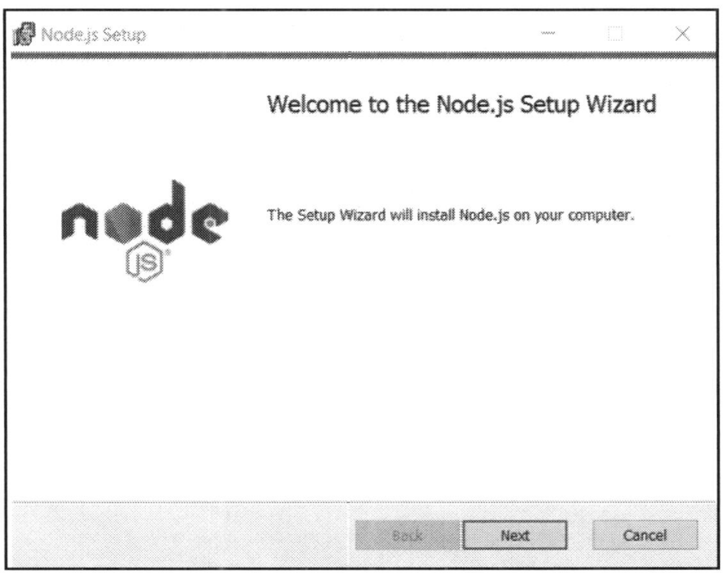

You'll be requested to accept the license terms and then click on the **Next** button again.

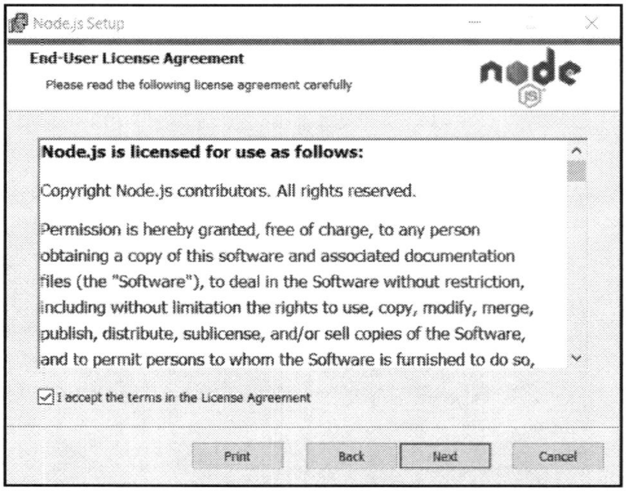

Following that, the installer displays the default installation path, which you may opt to change or not.

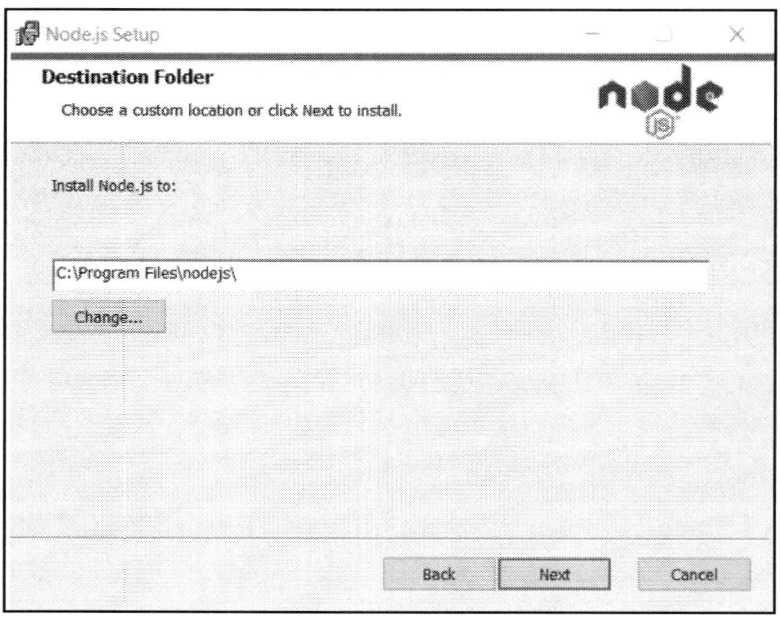

Once the installation path has been defined, simply click on the **Next** button. The next step is to select what features will be installed.

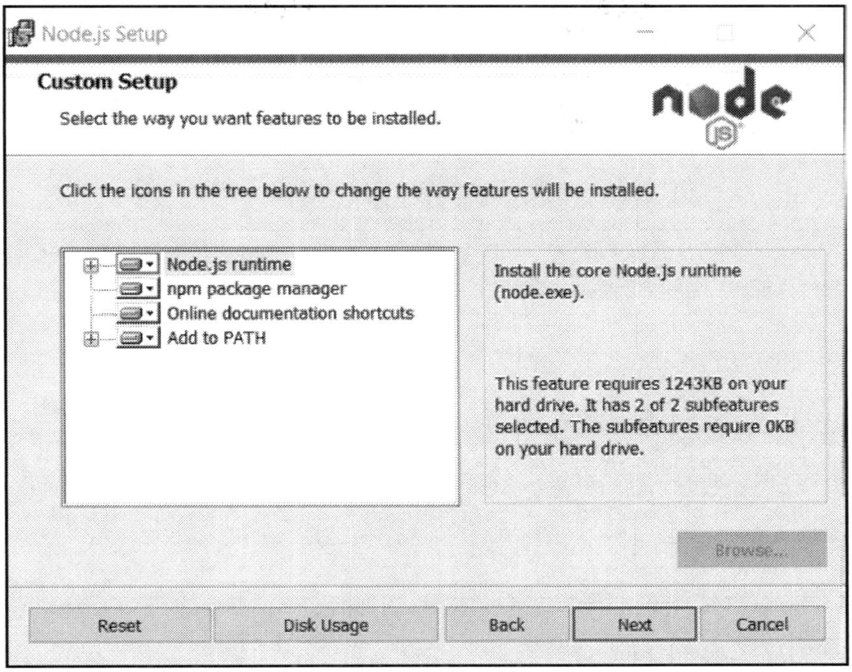

It is highly recommended to leave all the features selected so everything can be installed. The npm package manager will be later required in order to install the Twilio Node.js helper library.

Finally, click on the **Next** button and then the **Install** button, in order to finalize the installation process.

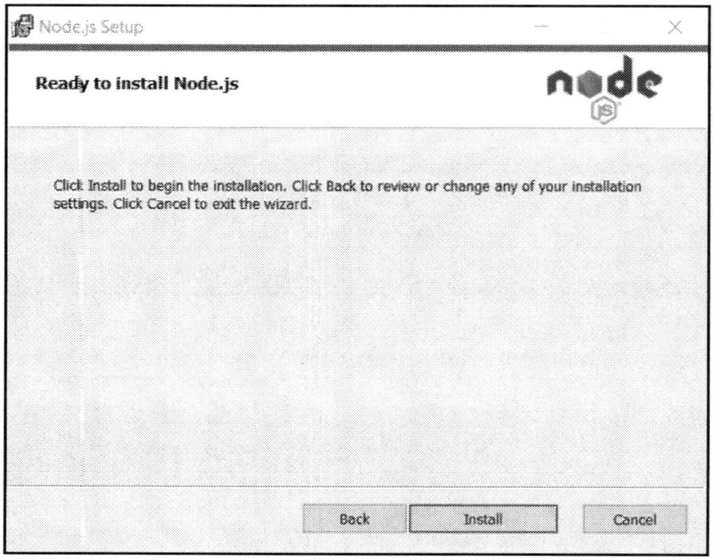

If there was a previous version of Node.js installed on your system, the installer will remove previous older files and then update the system with the newest files.

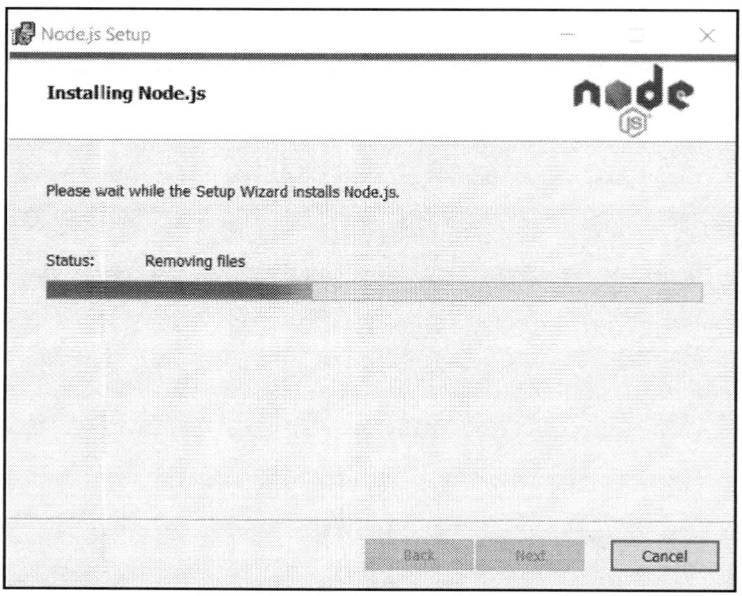

Please note that on other platforms (`https://nodejs.org/en/download/package-manager/`), the installation process and screens might differ (such as on a Mac); however, it should be pretty straightforward and easy to follow along by going through the installation steps.

Once Node.js has been installed, the next thing to do is to get the Twilio Node.js helper library installed.

In order to do this, create a folder anywhere on your PC for this project, browse to this folder, and then open the Command Prompt or shell and type this command:

```
npm init
```

Just follow the steps requested. This will create the `package.json` file (you can refer to `https://docs.npmjs.com/files/package.json`) required for our project.

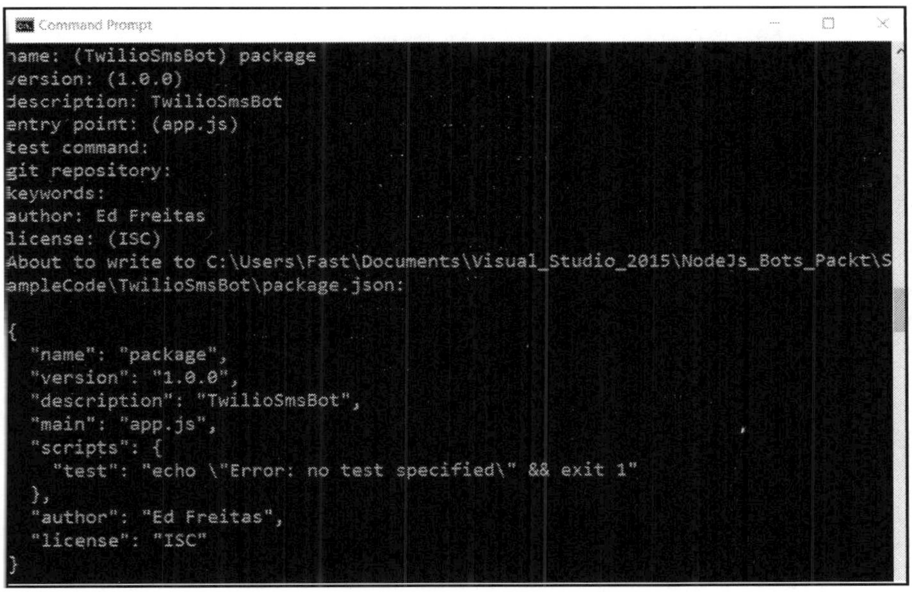

Once the `package.json` file has been created, type in the following command:

```
npm install twilio --save
```

This will install the Twilio Node.js helper library and all its dependencies and save the reference on our `package.json` file. The Twilio library will be installed under the `node_modules` folder within the folder where your `package.json` file resides. We'll be using the awesome Atom editor (`https://atom.io/`) throughout this book. You may use any other editor of your choice, such as Sublime or Visual Studio Code.

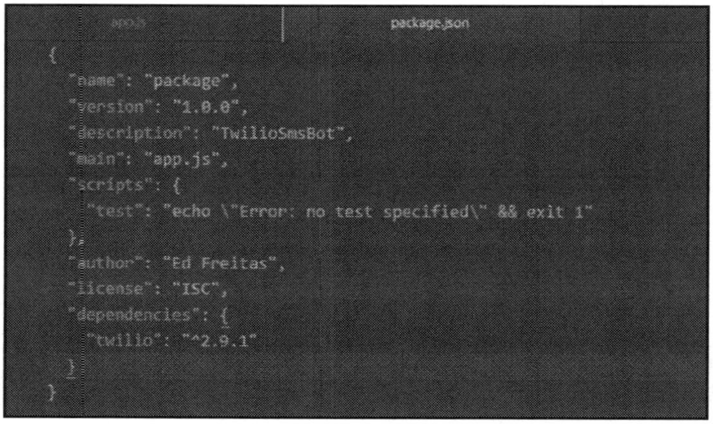

With this in place, we can technically start writing code. However, we first need to sign up for a Twilio account and get all set up with Twilio before we can send our first SMS. Let's explore how we can get this done.

Setting up a Twilio account

In order to be able to send SMS using the Twilio API and Node.js helper library, we need to get a Twilio account set up and also purchase a disposable Twilio number.

Twilio is a pay-as-you-go service, which means that you'll need to set up an account and provide your credit card details in order to have enough credit, which will be used to pay for every SMS you send.

You'll also need to purchase a Twilio number, which is a regular but disposable phone number that will be used to send your messages.

Twilio numbers are available for many countries. They look like any other valid phone number you can think of. They are real phone numbers that you can dispose of when you no longer need them.

In order to set up a Twilio account, from your browser access the following site `https://www.twilio.com/`. Then, click on the **SIGN UP** button.

The sign-up process is fairly straightforward, and is super easy to follow and complete. Just fill in a few fields that are required and you're done.

Once your Twilio account has funds, you'll need to purchase a disposable phone number.

You'll need to go to this location, `https://www.twilio.com/user/billing`, in order to add funds to your account. In order to do that, click on the **Ad Funds** link in red. Make sure that you have logged into Twilio before accessing this URL.

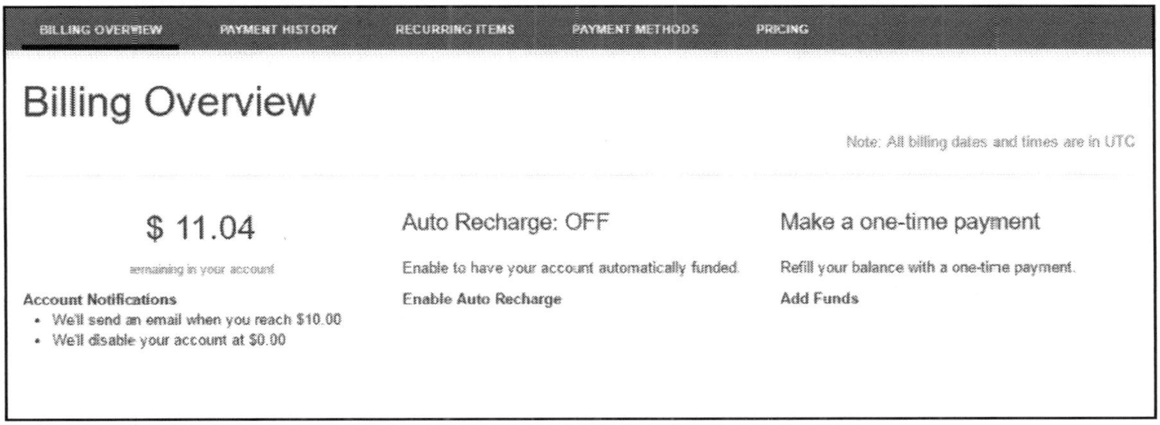

With funds in your account, let's set up a Twilio number. This will be a real phone number, which you can delete at any moment. You may choose from which country and city your number will belong to.

Then click on the **Buy a Number** button.

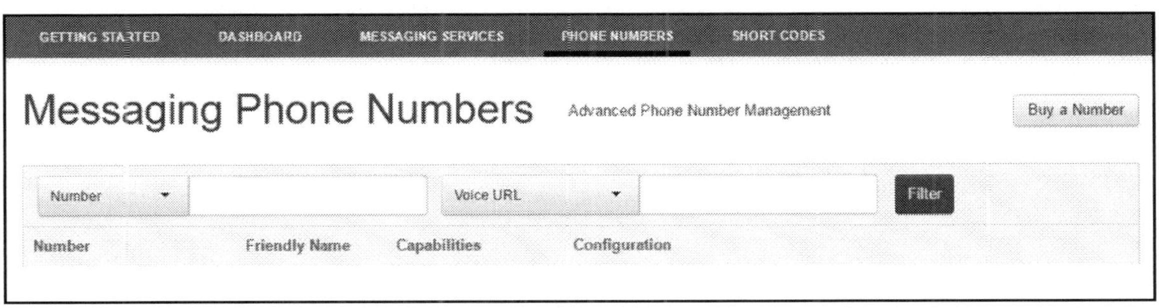

Once you have clicked on the **Buy a Number** button, the following pop-up screen will be shown:

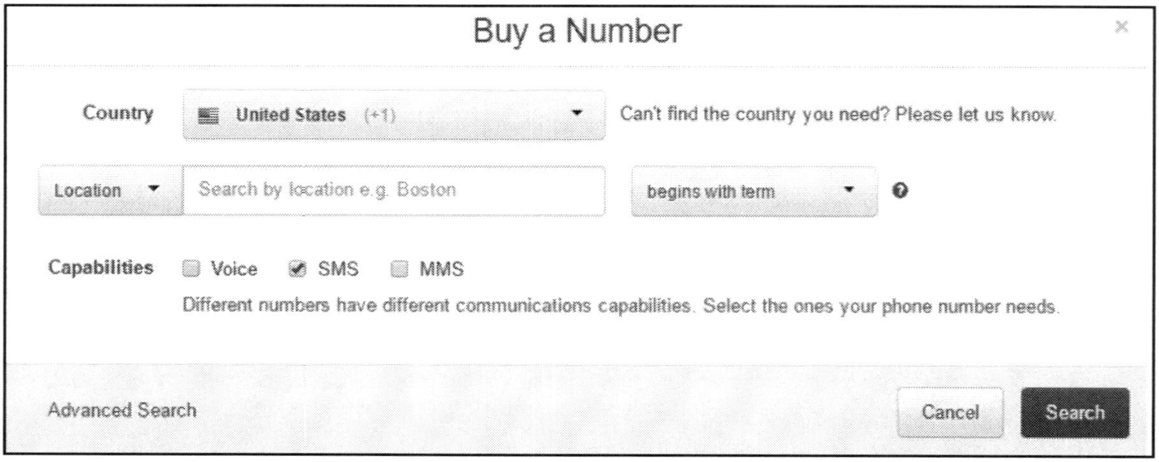

On this screen, you have the option to choose which country you would like to get the number from and also from which geographical location.

The number could be used for **Voice**, **SMS**, and even **MMS**. For now, we are simply interested in making sure that the **SMS** option is ticked.

Once you have purchased your Twilio number, you will see the following screen:

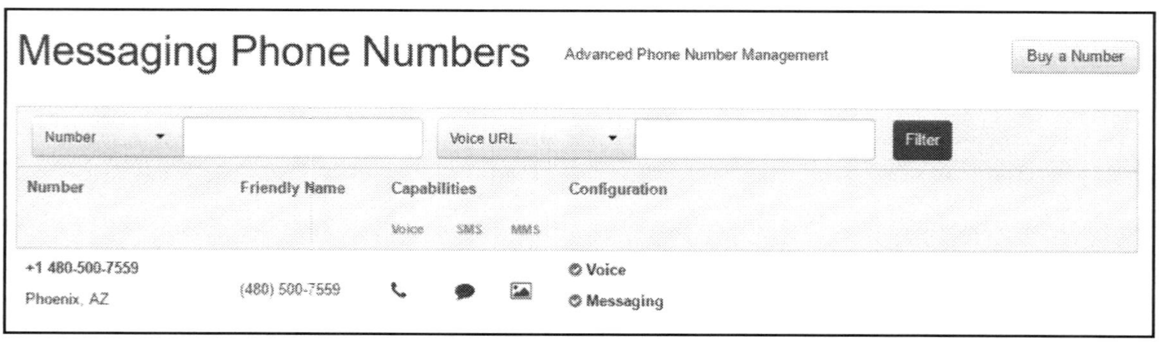

With this in place, we are ready to start writing our Node.js code.

Bare-bones Twilio Node.js template

In order to start writing our code, let's create a new file in the same location as our `package.json` file called `app.js`. You may create this new file directly from the editor you are using.

Once the file has been created, we'll need to include a reference to the Twilio Node.js library that we installed through npm:

```
var twilio = require("twilio");
```

In the Node.js world, this is the equivalent of an import in Java or using statements in C#. Now let's move on to see how we can actually send an SMS using the Twilio Node.js helper library:

```
var accountSid = '<< your twilio account sid >>';
// Your Account SID from www.twilio.com/console

var authToken = '<< your twilio auth token >>';
// Your Auth Token from www.twilio.com/console
```

We'll need two variables to store our Twilio **Account SID** and our **Auth token**. Both values can be obtained when you log in to your Twilio account and browse to the developer console: `https://www.twilio.com/console`.

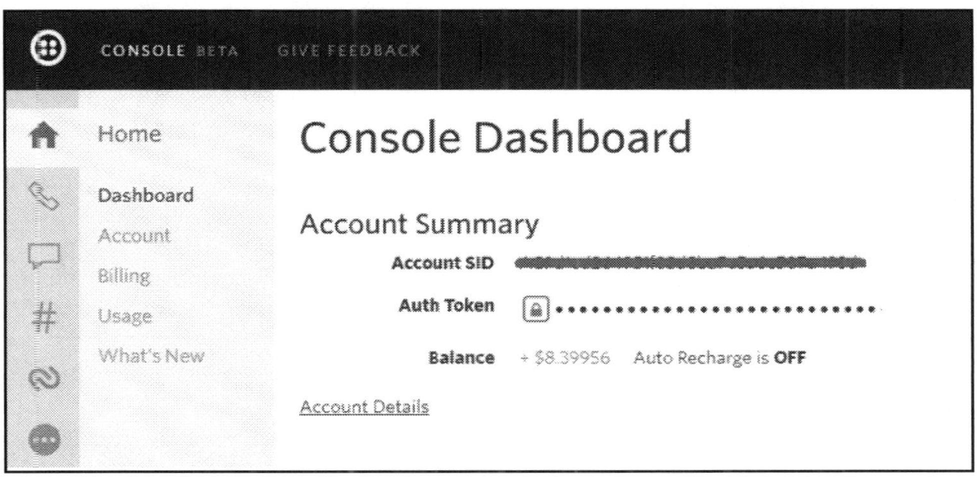

Once we have provided the correct values to the `accountSid` and `authToken` variables, we'll need to create an instance of the `twilio.RestClient` class in order to be able to send an SMS:

```
var client = new twilio.RestClient(accountSid, authToken);
```

With our instance created, we can go ahead and send our SMS using Twilio:

```
client.messages.create({
    body: 'Greetings earthling, this is the TwilioSmsBot ;)',
    to: '+12345678901',  // Number that receives the SMS
    from: '+12345678901' // Purchased Twilio number that send the SMS
},
function(err, message) {
    console.log(message.sid);
});
```

Basically, the SMS is sent by invoking the `messages.create` method from the Twilio `client` instance.

This method expects an object that describes the properties of the SMS, such as the `body`, `to` (receiver number), `from` (sender number), call back function which describes an error `err` (if an error actually happens), and the contents of the posted `message`.

This is all that is required in order to send an SMS using Twilio. Let's have a look at all the code now:

```
var twilio = require("node_modules/twilio/lib");

var accountSid = '<< your twilio account sid >>';
var authToken = '<< your twilio auth token >>';

var client = new twilio.RestClient(accountSid, authToken);

client.messages.create({
    body: 'Hello from Node',
    to: '+12345678901',
    from: '+12345678901'
},
function(err, message) {
    console.log(message.sid);
});
```

In order to execute this code, execute this command from the Command Prompt:

```
node app.js
```

This will send the SMS to the number indicated. We can see the `message.sid` of the SMS sent (which was sent back as a response from the Twilio service) by looking at the Command Prompt.

```
C:\Users\Fast\Documents\Visual_Studio_2015\NodeJs_Bots_Packt\SampleCode\TwilioSm
sBot>node app.js
SM6344d84ce7c84bfbbfe020146692cad3
```

Please notice that if the destination number you will be messaging is an international (non-US) number, you'll need to enable certain permissions to allow Twilio to perform that action.

These permissions can be checked and configured at this URL: `https://www.twilio.com/console/voice/settings/geo-permissions`.

Core bot functionality on Azure

Now that we've implemented and have a working Twilio Node.js template, which can send SMS, let's have a look at expanding our code to do more.

We'll need to be able to somehow hook and listen to incoming SMS and have some very basic **Natural Language Processing (NLP)**, in order to send answers based on the input received.

Listening to incoming SMS requires setting up in our Node.js app a URL that can be configured within your Twilio account as a Request URL. This Request URL will be used by Twilio to push incoming messages on your purchased Twilio number, to our Node.js bot app.

To make our bot publicly available, we'll publish it on Azure websites. Let's create a REST endpoint for our Node.js app, which we will use for listening to new messages. We'll be using the Express framework (`http://expressjs.com/`) to do this.

Express is a minimal and flexible Node.js web application framework that provides a robust set of features for web and mobile applications. It provides a thin layer of fundamental web application features such as routing and middleware.

Let's first install the Express framework by running this command from the command line prompt:

```
npm install express --save
```

A handy utility to have installed is Nodemon (`http://nodemon.io/`). This allows you to make changes to your code and it automatically restarts the Node.js app. You can install Nodemon by running this command from the prompt:

```
npm install nodemon --save
```

Instead of running the app with the node, you can now run it as follows:

```
nodemon app.js
```

With the Express framework installed, let's expand our current code to create a REST endpoint, which we can then use to hook up Twilio to push incoming messages:

```
var express = require('express');

var app = express();

app.get('/receive', function (req, res) {
  res.send('Hi, this is the TwilioBot listening endpoint!');
});

app.listen(8080, function () {
  console.log('TwilioBot listening on port 8080.');
});
```

Before we can hook up our bot app to Twilio in order to process incoming messages, let's first get all the tooling wired up, so that we can publish our app as it is to Azure websites.

We'll need to install the Azure **Command Line Interface (CLI)** (`https://azure.microsoft.com/en-us/documentation/articles/xplat-cli-install/`) in order to push our app to Azure. We'll also need to sign up for Azure if we don't have an account.

You can do that by visiting: `https://azure.microsoft.com`.

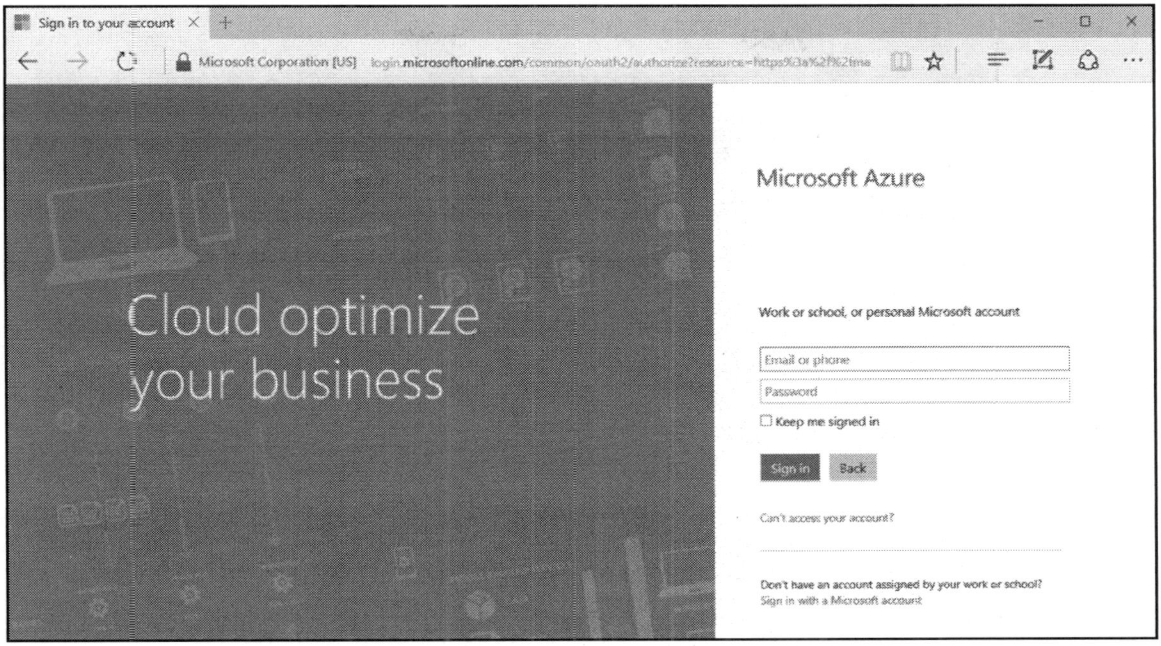

Once you have your account set up with Azure, you may install the Azure CLI using the respective installer for your platform or as an npm package following these instructions.

Using npm, the Azure CLI can be installed as follows:

```
npm install azure-cli -g
```

Once you have installed the Azure CLI, let's deploy the app as it is to Azure in order to make sure all our tooling is correctly wired up.

In order to do that, run the Azure CLI and `login` to Azure:

```
azure login
```

Once the command has been executed, you'll see the following welcome message where you'll be asked to enable data collection:

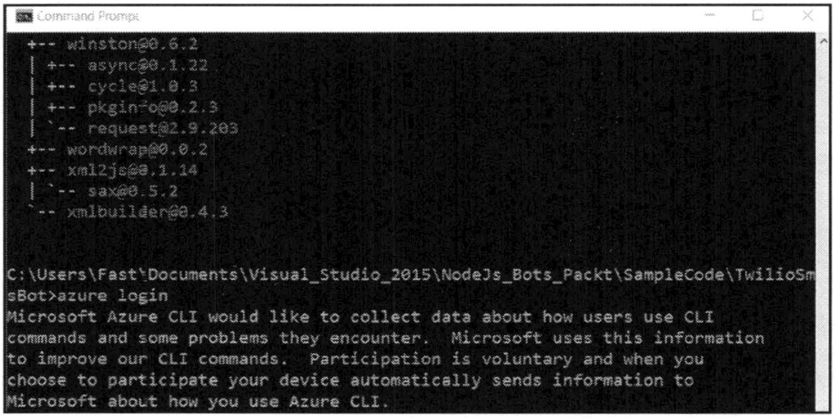

You may opt-in or not, the choice is yours and this doesn't affect your bot app development or usage of Azure at all.

Once you've chosen your option, you'll be prompted to enter the code displayed on the command line on this URL, `http://aka.ms/devicelogin`, and then authenticate with your Microsoft Account, as follows:

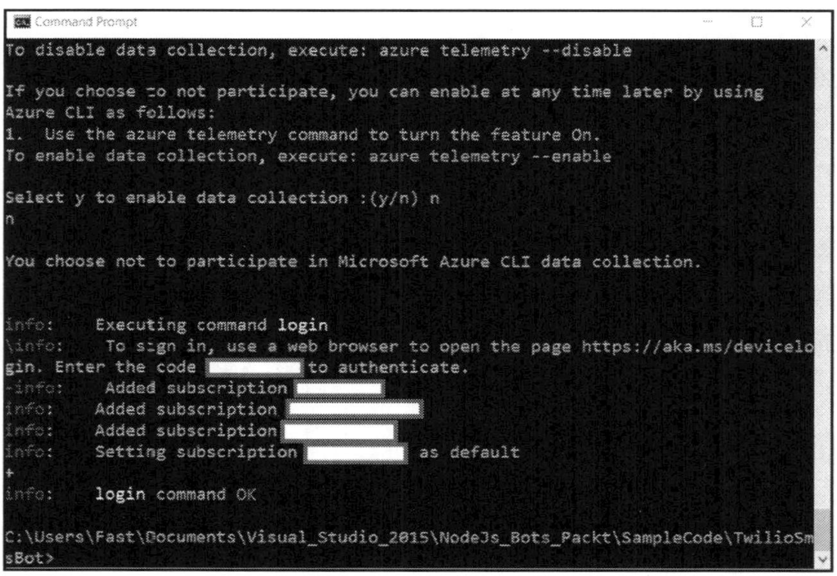

In the preceding screenshot, I've blanked out the Azure subscription keys and information that corresponds to my Azure account.

With this in place, your Azure CLI is all set. The next thing to do is to deploy the app to Azure using the CLI. Let's see how this can be done.

Run this command in order to create the website on Azure. Make sure you're still in the root directory of your app. Create the App Service app resource in Azure with a unique app name with the next command. Your web app's URL will be http://<appname>.azurewebsites.net.

In this case, we'll call our App Service app on Azure: NodeBotSite (you are free to choose any other name if this has been taken). Let's enter the following command:

```
azure site create --git nodebotsite
```

You'll be prompted to select the Azure region where your site will be hosted on. Feel free to choose the one closest to your location.

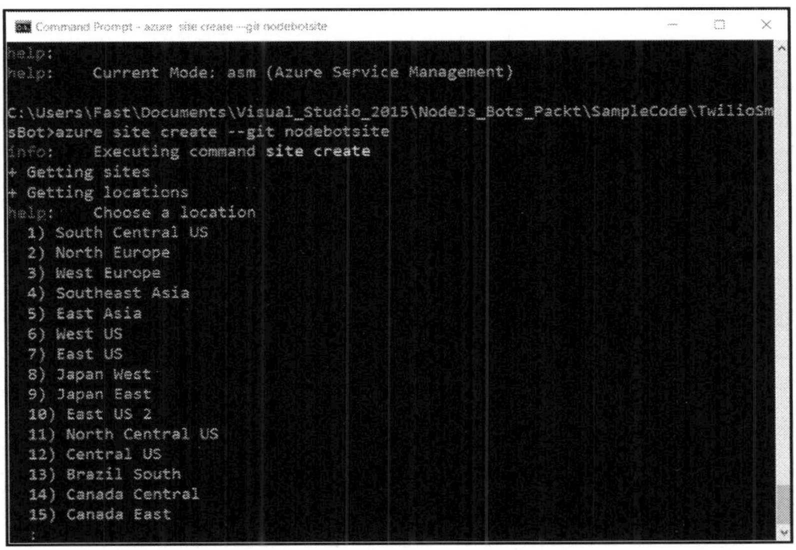

Once you've selected the region, Azure will create your site and you'll see the following details via the command line:

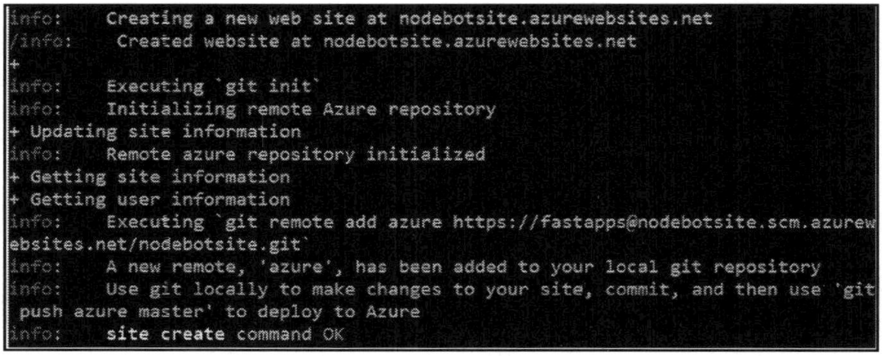

```
info:    Creating a new web site at nodebotsite.azurewebsites.net
/info:    Created website at nodebotsite.azurewebsites.net
+
info:    Executing `git init`
info:    Initializing remote Azure repository
+ Updating site information
info:    Remote azure repository initialized
+ Getting site information
+ Getting user information
info:    Executing `git remote add azure https://fastapps@nodebotsite.scm.azurew
ebsites.net/nodebotsite.git`
info:    A new remote, 'azure', has been added to your local git repository
info:    Use git locally to make changes to your site, commit, and then use 'git
 push azure master' to deploy to Azure
info:    site create command OK
```

Change the port from `8080` within the app to `process.env.port`, as follows:

```
app.listen(process.env.port, function () {
  console.log('Hi, this is the TwilioBot listening endpoint!');
});
```

> Nodemon doesn't seem to play too well with Azure; therefore, if you leave Nodemon as a dependency on your `package.json` file, you might run into problems when deploying the app to Azure. In light of this, remove from your package.json file the dependency that references Nodemon, before deploying to Azure.

Save your changes on both your `package.json` and `app.js` files, and then use the git command to deploy your app to Azure, as follows:

```
git add .
git commit -m "TwilioNodeBot first commit"
git push azure master
```

After you type these commands, if you've never set up git/FTP deployment credentials for your Azure subscription, you'll also be prompted to create them. You can also enter these credentials on the Azure Portal.

Once the git push command has finished, your app will be published on Azure and it is ready to be used.

In order to view it, open your browser and navigate to the site, receive this URL: `http://nodebotsite.azurewebsites.net/receive`. You should then see this:

To make updates to your Node.js web app running on Azure, just run `git add`, `git commit`, and `git push` like you did when you deployed it first.

With Azure all wired up, the next step is to configure this URL: `https://www.twilio.com/console/phone-numbers/incoming`, on your voice number's dashboard within your Twilio account, and then click on your purchased Twilio number. Edit the **Messaging** | **Request URL** for your Twilio number and click on the **Save** button.

Now your Twilio is tied to your Azure app, receive URL, which will be used to receive incoming SMS.

With all these setup steps in place, we can now focus on adding the receive logic for our Twilio bot app.

Receiving SMS bot logic

So far we've implemented the basic bare-bones template for our Twilio bot app and also made all the necessary configurations in order to have our solution wired up with Twilio and also easily deployable to Azure.

Let's now explore how we can make our bot reply to incoming messages. In order to do this, we'll need to have a POST endpoint on our Node/Express app. Let's examine the following code:

```
app.post('/receive', function (req, res) {
  var twiml = new twilio.TwimlResponse();
  twiml.message('Hi, this is TwilioBot');

  res.writeHead(200, {'Content-Type': 'text/xml'});
  res.end(twiml.toString());
});
```

We can see here that in order to reply, we create a **TwiML** response and send that as the response of POST / receive the HTTP endpoint.

TwiML is an XML markup language, which is simply a set of instructions you can use to tell Twilio what to do when you receive an incoming call or SMS.

Twilio makes HTTP requests to your application just like a regular web browser. By including parameters and values in its requests, Twilio sends data to your application that you can act upon before responding. This is what we are actually doing on this, receive endpoint.

Twilio sends the following parameters with its request as POST parameters or URL query parameters, depending on which HTTP method you've configured.

When we receive an SMS or a phone call on our Twilio number, Twilio will fetch the URL associated with that phone number and perform an HTTP request to that URL. This URL will contain an XML response with markup instructions, which indicate what tasks Twilio needs to execute. Some of these tasks can be to record the call, play a message, prompt the caller to enter some digits, and so on.

In this case, what our bot is doing is simply returning a one-line sentence. In short, the preceding example code is simply returning this XML back to Twilio as a response, so that Twilio can actually generate an SMS response out of it, and send it back to the sender's phone:

```
<?xml version="1.0" encoding="UTF-8"?>
<Response>
<Say> Hi, this is TwilioBot.</Say>
</Response>
```

As you can see, it is super simple to tell Twilio to execute a specific action using TwiML. The markup language is made up of verbs highlighted in blue, which represent actions that Twilio will execute.

Some of the TwiML verbs available at the time of the writing are: Say, Play, Dial, Record, Gather, Sms, Hangup, Queue, Redirect, Pause, Conference, Reject, and Message.

Complete details on how to use these TwiML verbs can be found here: `https://www.twilio.com/docs/api/twiml`.

What we've done through the code is to use the Twilio Node.js helper library to generate the TwiML as a response, without explicitly creating the XML response itself.

So our bot starts to finally take shape. It can listen to messages and send a response back. But, how does the bot know how to act to certain inputs? In order to achieve that, the bots need to be able to understand the parameters of the incoming message and be able to act upon it.

Twilio sends several parameters with its request as POST parameters or URL query parameters, depending on which HTTP method you've configured on the Twilio number's dashboard for incoming SMS. Please take a moment to go through and understand this list thoroughly.

Here are some of the prominent properties that Twilio uses:

- **From:** The phone number that sent this message.
- **To**: The phone number of the recipient.
- **Body**: The text body of the message. It can be up to 1,600 characters long.
- **MessageSid**: A 34 character unique identifier for the message. It may be used to later retrieve this message from the REST API.
- **SmsSid**: The same value as MessageSid. It is deprecated and included for backward compatibility.

The full list of parameters can be found here:
`https://www.twilio.ccm/docs/api/twiml/sms/twilio_request.`

So in order to write some logic that acts upon the input of the nature of the messages received, it is necessary to inspect the value of the parameters that are received as part of the `request.body` object. These parameters will have properties on this object.

So for instance, if we want to know from which number the message came from, we would have to do something like this:

```
var from = req.body.From;
```

The actual received text message itself would be obtained as follows:

```
var body = req.body.Body;
```

Knowing from where the message originates and the actual contents, we can then build some logic to internally give the bot some sense of what to do with the input received and act upon it.

So, let's add some core functionality, which for now we will call `BotBrain` and we don't really know what it will do. This will give us an answer based on the input we provide to it, independently of which bot we will be building.

In the next chapter, we'll be creating the logic of this `BotBrain`, and throughout the chapters keep adding subsequent and additional functionality to it, but for now, let's assume this `BotBrain` gives the bot the answer required based on the input received:

```
app.post('/receive', function (req, res) {
  var twiml = new twilio.TwimlResponse();
  var feedback = BotBrains(req.body);
  twiml.message(feedback);

  res.writeHead(200, {'Content-Type': 'text/xml'});
  res.end(twiml.toString());
});
```

As we can see now, the bot will respond to the incoming request based on the results the `BotBrains` will determine, by analyzing the properties of the `request.body` object.

Summary

In this chapter, we've set the foundations on how our bot will be deployed, configured, and set up. We've also created a bare-bones template that we will use throughout the rest of the chapters in this book, in order to add more exciting functionalities.

We've also explored some of the key components that will make it work from an infrastructure point of view and how we can host it on Azure, Microsoft's awesome cloud platform.

Beyond this, we've explained why bots matter and why they are a key component for your business to be aware of and considered in your strategy.

Further to that, we've explored the basics of Twilio as a messaging platform and started to scratch the surface of what is possible to achieve with it.

In the chapters to follow, we'll be adding many more layers and interacting with other APIs and services; however, we'll still use Twilio as a backup messaging provider by also using SMS.

Hopefully you've got an idea of what to expect coming ahead and also this has gotten you excited in our quest to add more layers and logic to our bot.

Thanks for reading!

2

Getting Skype to Work for You

Skype (http://www.skype.com) is an awesome piece of software and a reliable platform that is used by millions of people worldwide in order to make calls, organize meetings, and chat with each other. It is used for both personal communication as well as for business.

One of the great things about Skype is that it allows you make free peer-to-peer VoIP calls with any other user that also has a Skype account. It also allows you to call phone numbers at very cheap rates and even for free to some locations.

Besides that, Skype can also allow you to receive incoming calls on a real phone number or divert them to become text messages. It also allows message forwarding, conferencing, group chatting, file transferring, remote desktop presentation, viewing, and many other features.

So far, it sounds like Skype is a great communication platform, and it is. But what about using Skype as an automated agent that can help to get some work done and could automate some business processes, in order to make our lives easier? Is this even possible?

The good news is that, indeed, it is possible. Skype is now part of Microsoft (https://www.microsoft.com/en-in/) and, recently, at the build developer's event, a framework for creating interactive bots with Skype was unveiled. Skype already has a set of cool and extremely useful APIs, which make it relatively easy for developers to interact with the service, and is great for all sorts of voice and chat-related applications. However, it does not have an API that is solely focused on interactive messaging automation and this is where the **Bot Framework** (https://dev.botframework.com) comes in to fill the void.

In this chapter, we'll explore how to use this framework in order to build a Skype bot that acts like a virtual **Human Resources** (**HR**) assistant, which should be able to provide information about vacation days, notice periods, and other HR-related queries.

Sounds like a lot of fun! Let's get started.

How a Skype bot works

A Skype bot is, in essence, just another Skype contact; the difference is that, instead of talking to another person, it's an automated process that knows how to reply to the input you provide. Bots can do many things, such as fetch the news, check the weather, retrieve photos or information from websites, start a game, or order food or a taxi for you.

Anything that can be turned into a service can be converted into an automated conversation by using a bot. With Skype, bots can have interactive conversations on nearly every platform, at any time, and from anywhere.

Users can send a Skype bot request, and your bot can send back meaningful feedback based on the content received. A Skype bot can also be part of a group conversation and send details to all the parties involved in that group.

The way a Skype bot technically works is that it connects and listens to the bot platform using the Skype bot API directly, or using the C# or Node.js SDK. We'll obviously focus our attention on the Node.js SDK.

When a user sends a message to your Skype bot, we route this activity to a **Webhook** (`https://en.wikipedia.org/wiki/Webhook`) that is defined for the bot. The bot then sends replies back to the bot platform, which passes them on to the user. The Webhooks (which are valid public URLs-HTTP Messaging endpoints) will typically run on a cloud service such as **Microsoft Azure** (`https://azure.microsoft.com`).

Webhooks are called with JSON-formatted requests. Every JSON object indicates some update and looks like this:

```
[
{
    "activity" : "message",
    "from" : "awesomeskypebot",
    "to" : "28:2c967451-ee01-421f-92aa-1a80f9e163dc",
    "time" : "2016-03-30T09:50:01.123Z",
    "id" : "1443805282113",
    "content" : "Hello from a Bot!"
}
]
```

In essence, a bot goes through various stages. Initially the bot can be added to a limited number of users for development, which allows the bot details to be edited, and also allows for previewing features such as group chat or calling. In the example we will build in this chapter, we will focus on chatting (text interaction) and not calling, but it is useful to know that this feature is also possible. Here are the stages:

- Bot creation/editing (initial stage)
- Bot review
- Bot published

Following the creation or editing stage is the review stage, which is just before publishing your bot. Once in review, you cannot edit the attributes of your bot on the portal (such as its name and other properties). It is important to note that a bot cannot be submitted using preview features such as group chat or calling.

Once the review of the bot has been accepted, it goes into the published stage. At this point in time, the bot can be added by any number of users via the bot URL link or button.

Finally, soon after it has been published, the bot is then shown in the Skype bot directory.

Wiring up our Skype bot

With the theory behind us, let's now dig into the details of how we can start using the Bot Framework with Node.js in order to create our Skype HR bot.

In the previous chapter, we saw how to get Node.js installed and also how to deploy our Twilio example to Azure website. For our Skype bot, we'll follow a very similar process.

Let's first start by creating a folder in our local drive from the Command Prompt in order to store our bot:

```
mkdir skypebot
cd skypebot
```

Assuming we have Node.js and npm installed (if not, please refer to the steps in `Chapter 1`, *The Rise of Bots – Getting the Message Across*), let's create and initialize our `package.json`, which will store our bot's dependencies and definitions:

```
npm init
```

When you go through the `npm init` options (which are very easy to follow), you'll see something similar to this. In some cases you might get an `index.js` file created; however, going forward, we'll instead use the name `app.js` as shown in the following screenshot:

In your project folder, you'll see the result, which is your `package.json` file:

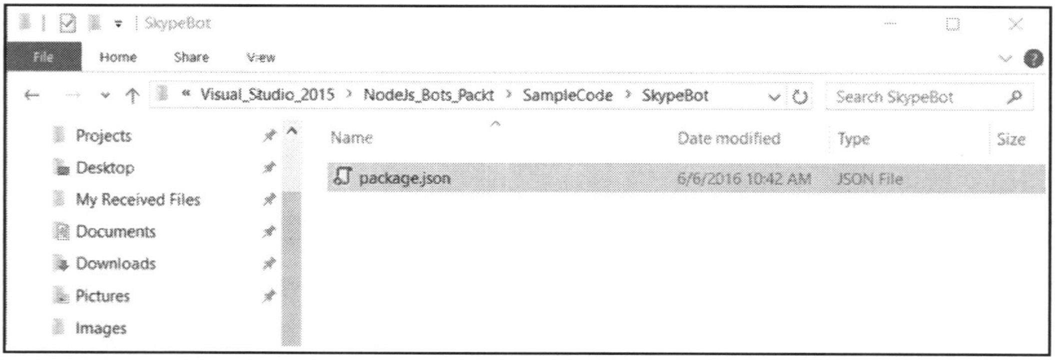

Just like we did in our previous example, we will use **Express** (`http://expressjs.com`) as our **REST** Node.js framework. We'll install it and save it to our `package.json` file, as follows:

```
npm install express --save
```

Once Express has been installed, you should see something like this:

With Express set up, the next thing to do is to install the `BotBuilder` package, which corresponds to the Microsoft Bot Framework Node.js library. Let's do that now.

In order to install it, run this `npm` command:

```
npm install --save botbuilder
```

After BotBuilder has been installed, you should see in your command line a result similar to the following screenshot:

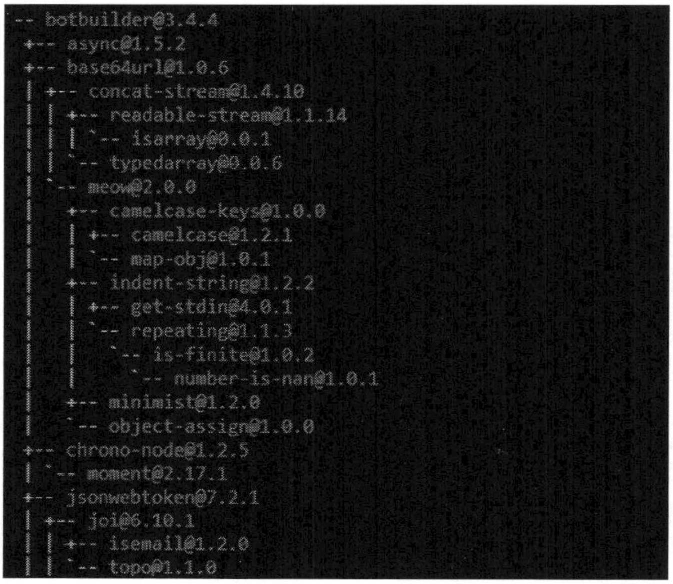

Your package.json should then look similar to mine, as shown in the following screenshot:

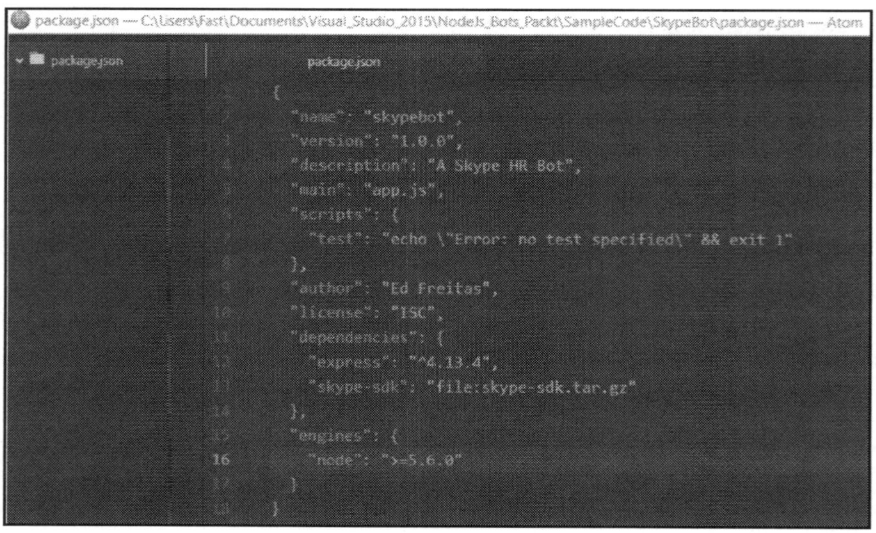

With our bot all wired up, we can then focus on creating the Express endpoints and core logic.

Let's create our `app.js` file, which will be the entry point to our bot. You can create the `app.js` file by using the applicable menu option in the editor of your choice.

Our Skype skeleton bot `app.js` should look like this:

```
var skype = require('botbuilder');
var express = require('express');

var app = express();

var botService = new skype.ChatConnector({
    appId: '',
    appPassword: ''
});

var bot = new skype.UniversalBot(botService);

app.post('/api/messages', botService.listen());

bot.dialog('/', function (session) {
  if (session.message.text.toLowerCase().indexOf('hi') >= 0){
    session.send('Hi ' + session.message.user.name +
     ' thank you for your message: ' + session.message.text);
  } else{
    session.send('Sorry I don't understand you...');
  }
});

app.get('/', function (req, res) {
  res.send('SkypeBot listening...');
});

app.listen(process.env.port, function () {
  console.log('SkypeBot listening...');
});
```

Now let's break this into smaller chunks. The first thing we do is to reference the Bot Framework we previously installed using npm:

```
var skype = require('botbuilder');
```

Once we've indicated this, we need to reference the Express framework, as follows:

```
var express = require('express');
```

Once we have our references all set up, we can proceed to create the `botService` object and wire it up an `HTTP POST` endpoint, hosted on Azure websites, which the Skype bot service will push incoming messages to for our bot to reply to.

Please note that the `botService` object requires `APP_ID` and `APP_SECRET` variables that we will get from the Bot Framework once we have registered it with on the bot developer portal, for which we will go through the steps shortly.

The `botService` object is created as follows:

```
var APP_ID = '';
var APP_SECRET = '';

var botService = new skype.ChatConnector({
    appId: APP_ID,
    appPassword: APP_SECRET
});

var bot = new skype.UniversalBot(botService);
```

With the `botService` object created, it needs to be wired up so that the Skype bot knows where to `POST` the incoming message requests, so they can be processed by the bot. This is achieved by adding this to `app.js`, as shown in the following:

```
app.post('/api/messages', botService.listen())
```

This basically registers the `botService` object on the publicly accessible `/api/messages` HTTP endpoint exposed through the Azure website where this Node.js will be running.

Finally, the Node.js app is exposed by listening on the port `process.env.port` as follows, by adding this to `app.js`:

```
app.listen(process.env.port, function () {
  console.log('SkypeBot listening...');
});
```

Registering our Skype bot app

In order to for this to work, we'll need to register our bot within the Bot Framework Developer Portal. In order to do this, sign in with your Microsoft account at `https://dev.botframework.com/`. You'll be presented with this screen:

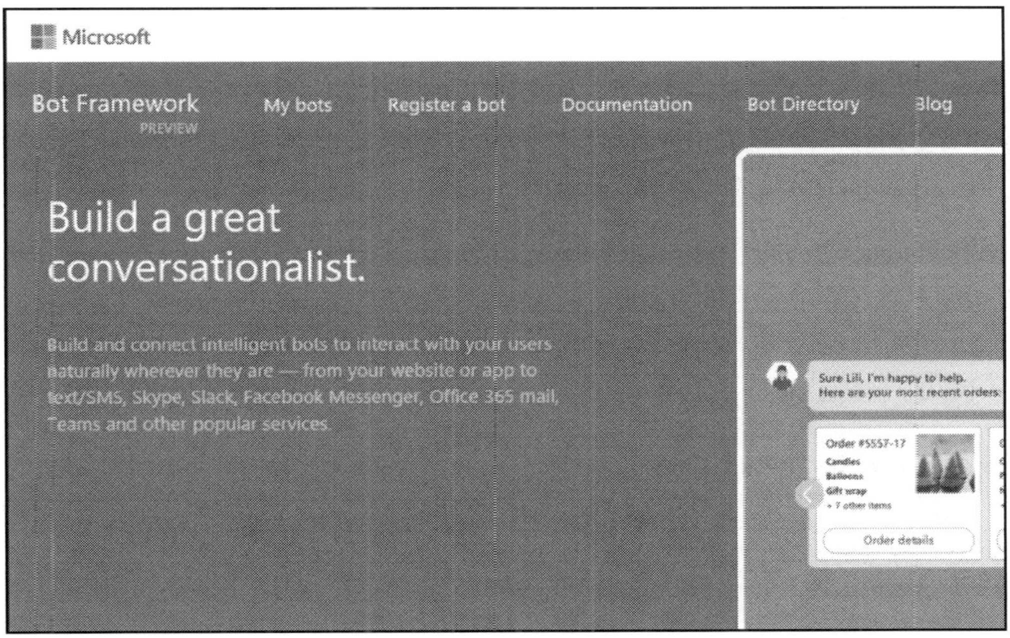

Click on the **Register a bot** option in order to create and register your Skype bot. Once you've done that, you'll see the following screen:

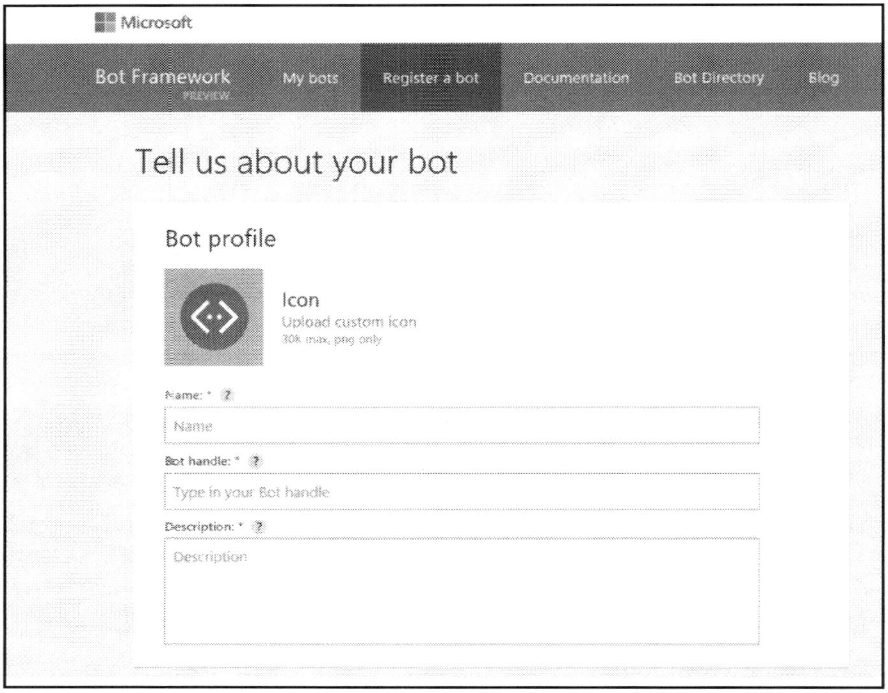

As you can see, there are three basic fields that are mandatory. The first field represents the bot's name, which will be used to identify the bot within the bot directory (if we later decide to make it public). It cannot be longer than 35 characters.

The second field is the bot's handle, which will be used as part of the bot's public URL. It only allows alphanumeric and underscore characters, and it cannot be changed after registration.

The third field is the bot's description. The first 46 characters are displayed on the bot's card on the bot directory and the rest of the description is displayed under the bot's details.

If we scroll down the page, we can see that we are also being asked to enter a Messaging endpoint and an App ID. Let's add some details to our bot. Refer to the following screenshot:

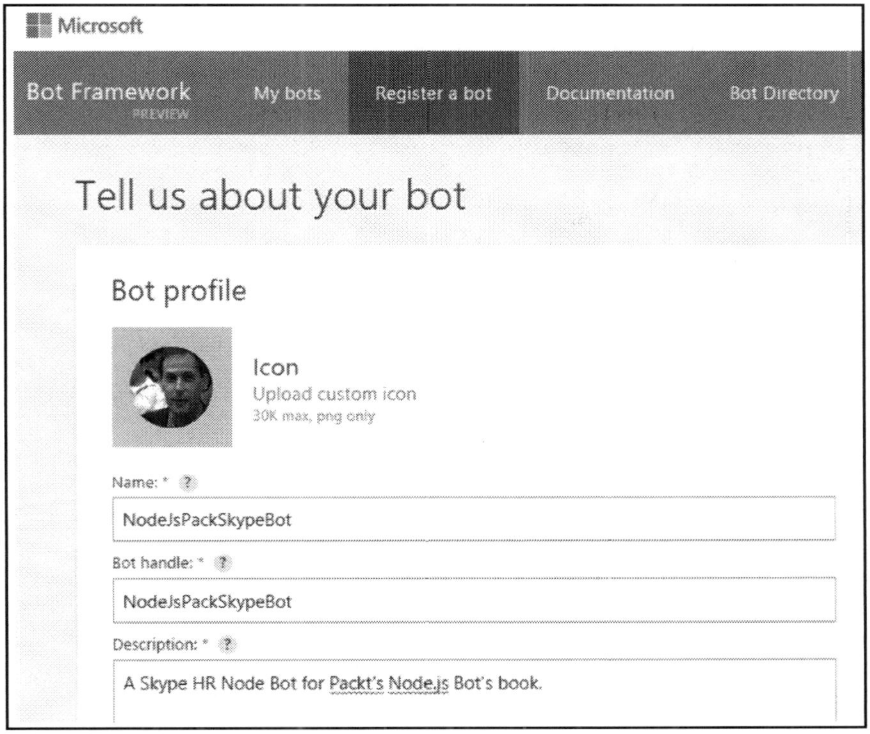

So far, we've added the three initial fields required for our bot. In this case, we'll use the name `NodeJsPacktSkypeBot`; however, you can use any other unique name. I recommend using the same name for both the **Name** and **Bot handle** fields.

So let's scroll down and carry on, in order to add the other required details:

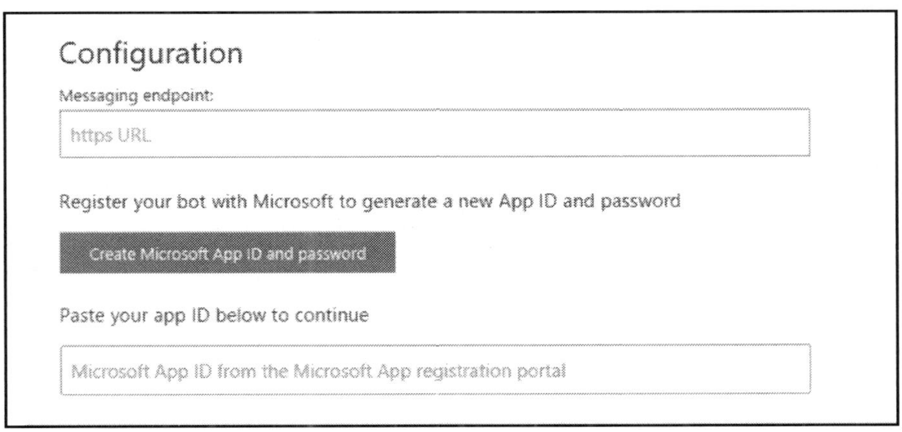

Next we need to add the Messaging endpoint and add the App ID for our bot. So let's click on the **Create Microsoft App ID and password** button in order to get the required App ID.

Once we do this, we get the following result:

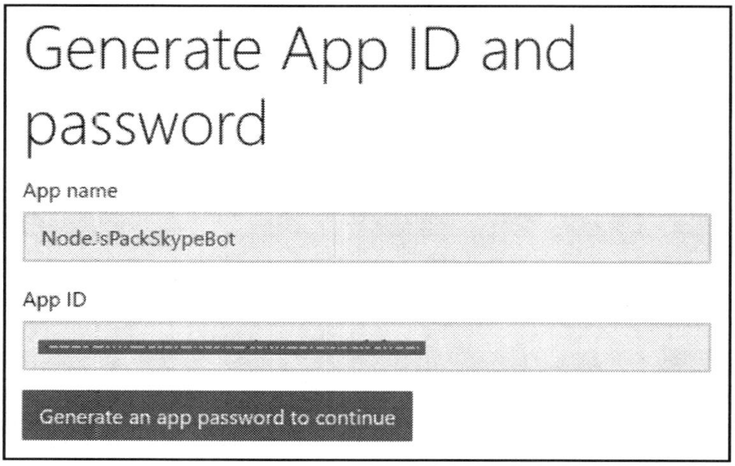

The next thing we need to do is to click on the **Generate an app password to continue** button. Once you do that, you'll see the following screen:

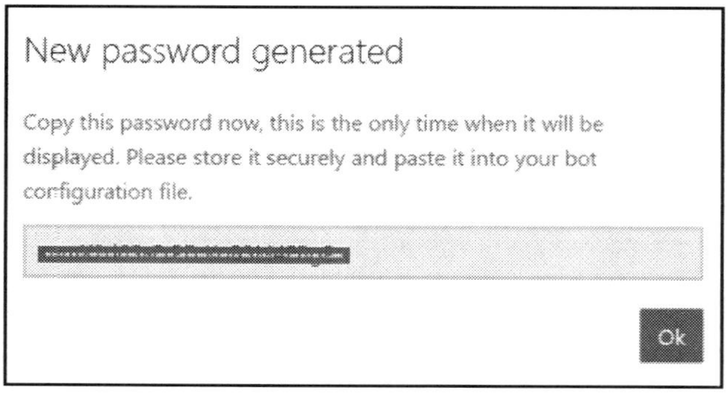

Immediately after, click on the **Ok** button, and this will take you back to the **Generate App ID** and password screen. Once there, click on the **Finish and go back to Bot Framework** button:

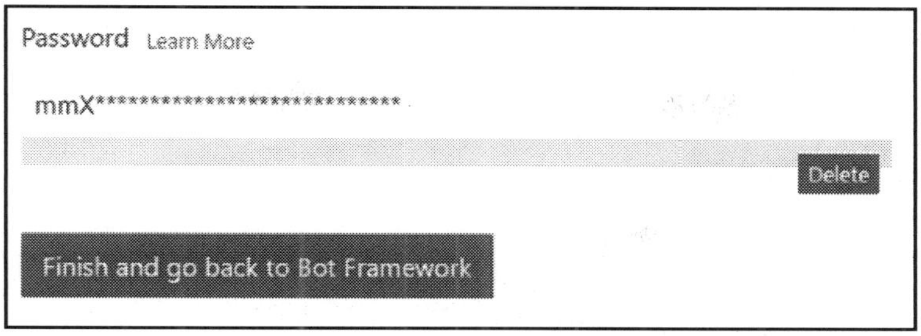

Once you have done that, you'll be back at the main registration screen. The only missing details will be the **Messaging endpoint** and the **Owners** e-mail address fields, as shown in the following screenshot:

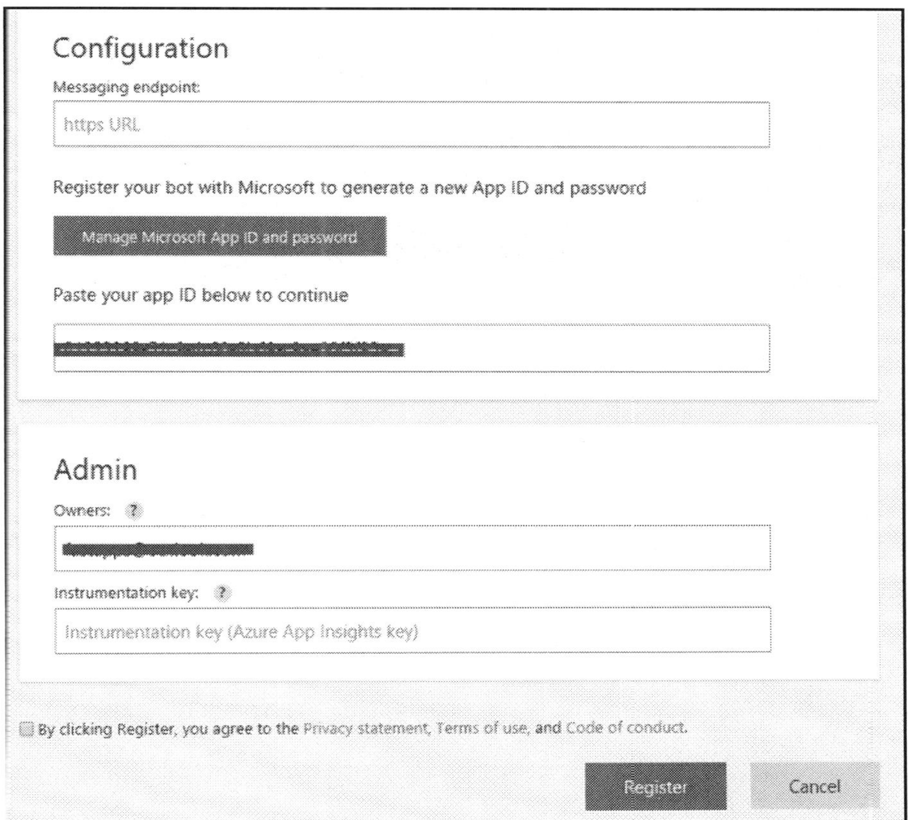

For now, let's leave this as it is (we'll come back to this screen later) because, first, we need to deploy our bot to Azure.

Just like we did in the previous chapter, we can deploy our solution to Azure websites and host our messaging endpoint there. So, before we actually fill in the URL for our Messaging endpoint, let's deploy and push our Skype bot code to Azure websites in order to get a publicly accessible URL.

Assuming you have your Azure account set up and ready (if not please refer to `Chapter 1`, *The Rise of Bots – Getting the Message Across*, for details on how to do this), log in to Azure by executing the following instruction from the Command Prompt:

```
azure login
```

Once that has been done and the credentials provided, you will see a screen similar to the following screenshot:

Open your browser and enter the URL mentioned on the console response. Then enter the code you have been provided with. Once you have done that, you will see the following:

This means that you have successfully logged on to Azure using the command line.

The next thing to do is to actually create the Azure website service that will host the Skype bot code; this can be done by running this command from the prompt:

```
azure site create --git nodeskypehrbotsite
```

When you execute this command, you will be asked to choose the Azure region to which you wish to deploy the bot, as shown in the following screenshot:

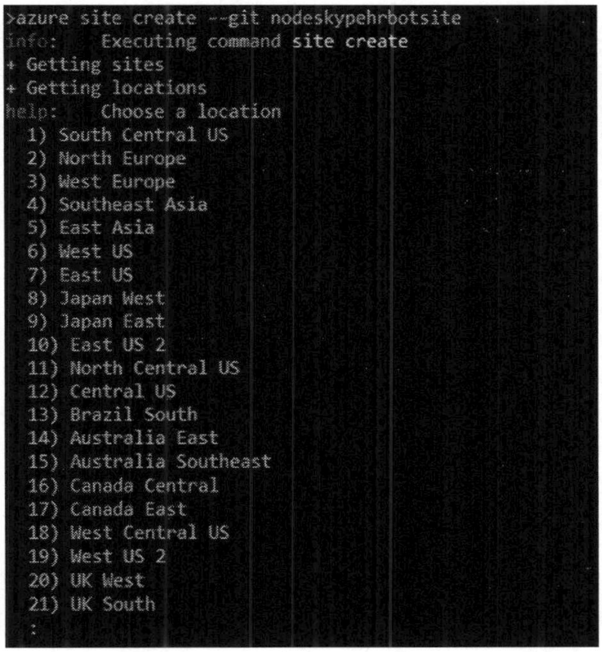

Select the region that is closest to where you are located by typing in the appropriate number. After this has been done, you'll see the following information, indicating that the site has been successfully created:

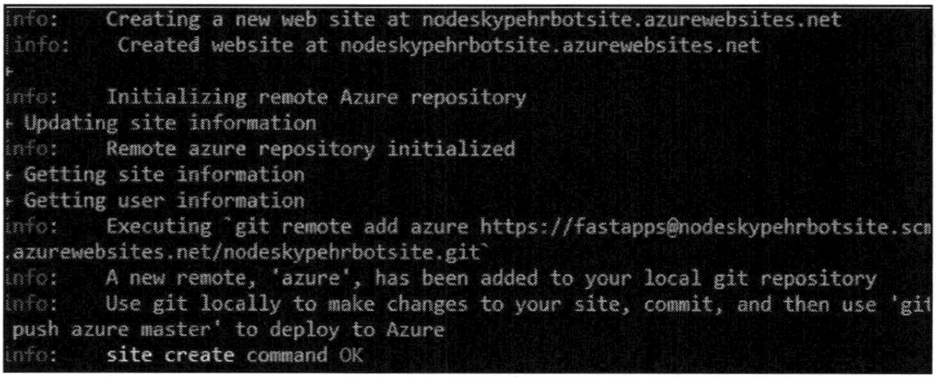

Before deploying the bot's code to Azure, first log in to the **Azure Portal** (`http://portal.azure.com`) with your account, and specify an **FTP/deployment** username and **password**.

This can be done by going into **All resources**, selecting the **nodeskypehrbotsite**, then opening the **Deployment credentials** blade, and, finally, entering the **FTP/deployment username** and **Password**, as seen in the following screenshot:

Once the username and password have been entered, click on the **Save** button at the top of the blade.

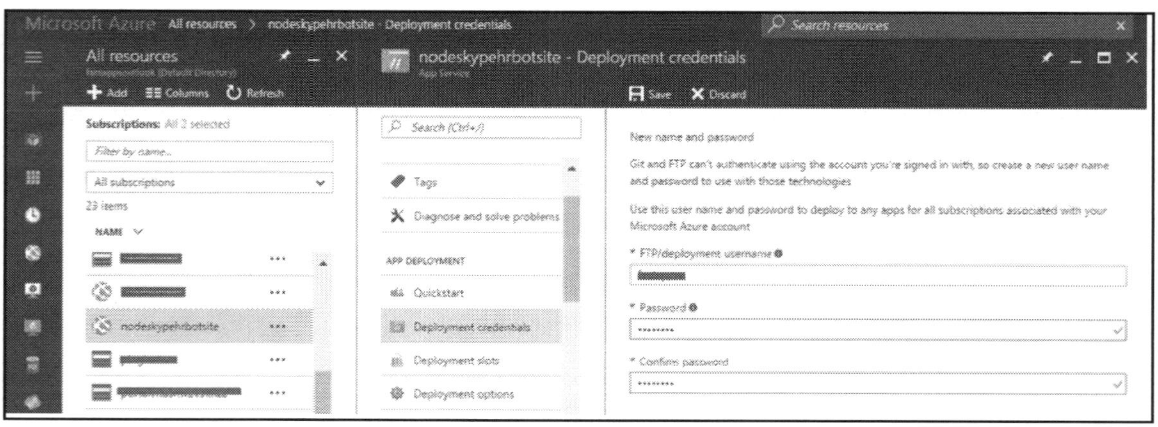

Once this has been done, wait for a couple of minutes. Then we can deploy the code to Azure websites as follows:

```
git add .
git commit -m "SkypeNodeBot first commit"
git push azure master
```

Once these commands have been executed, the bot's code will be deployed to the Azure website and you should see some responses similar to the following:

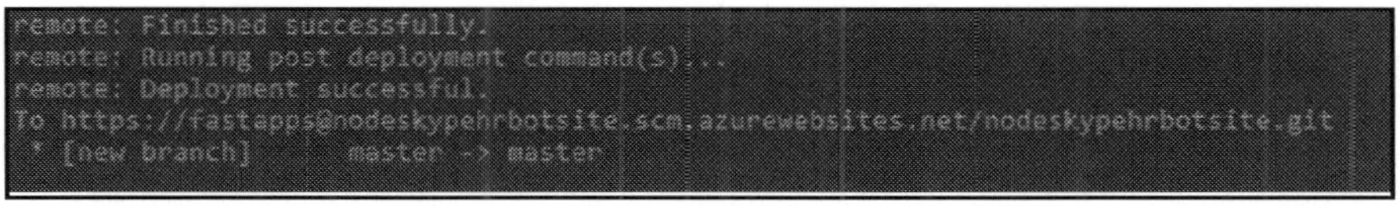

With our site deployed, we can finally get the publicly accessible URL, which in our case will be `https://nodeskypehrbotsite.azurewebsites.net/api/messages`, given that in our code we have defined a `POST` endpoint that our bot will be listening on.

This is the URL that we need to specify as the **Messaging endpoint**.

We can then go back to the bot **Registration** website screen where we recently entered the bot's APP ID and we can now enter the **Messaging endpoint**, as shown in the following screenshot:

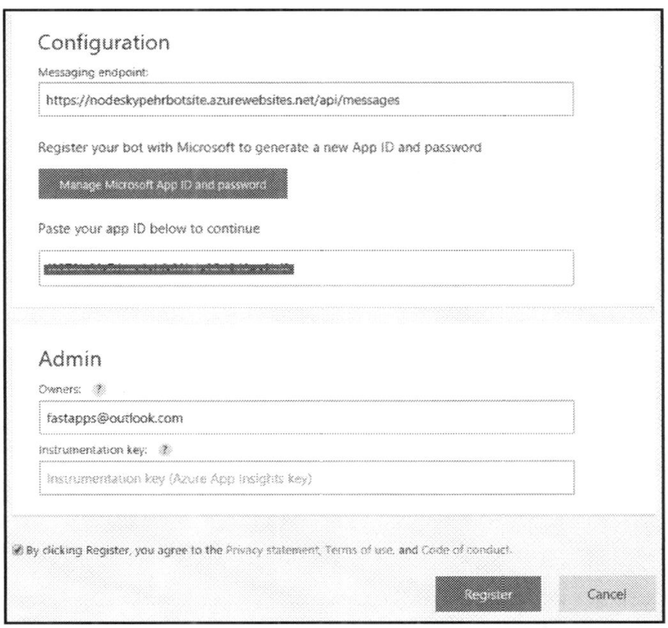

Make sure to check the option for **Privacy statement**, **Terms of use**, and **Code of conduct**, then click on the **Register** button, as shown in the following screenshot:

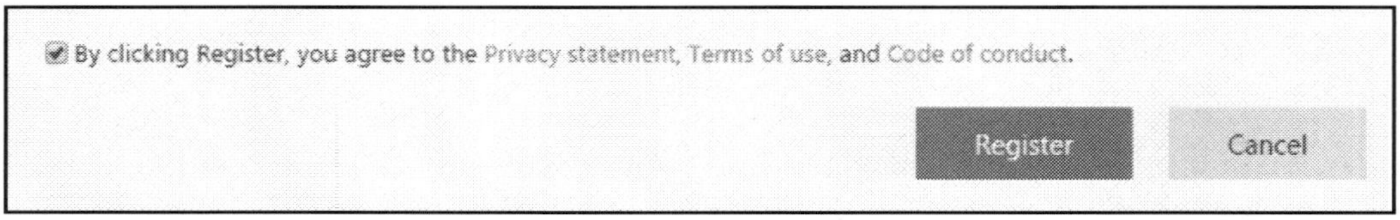

Once you have clicked on the **Register** button, you'll receive a popup dialog that will say that the bot has been created, as shown in the following screenshot:

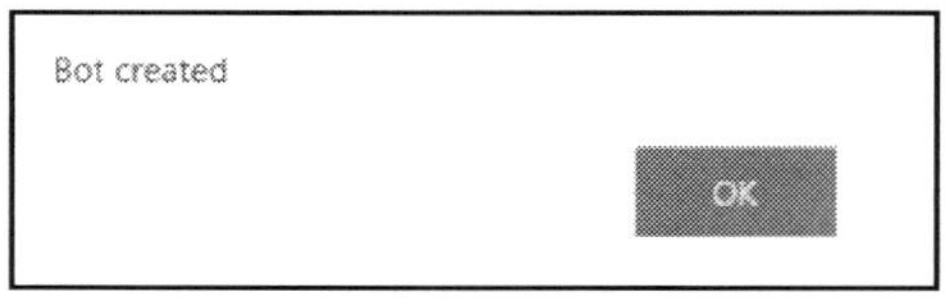

Click on the **OK** button in order to continue. Once you have clicked on **OK**, then you'll be redirected to the following web page:

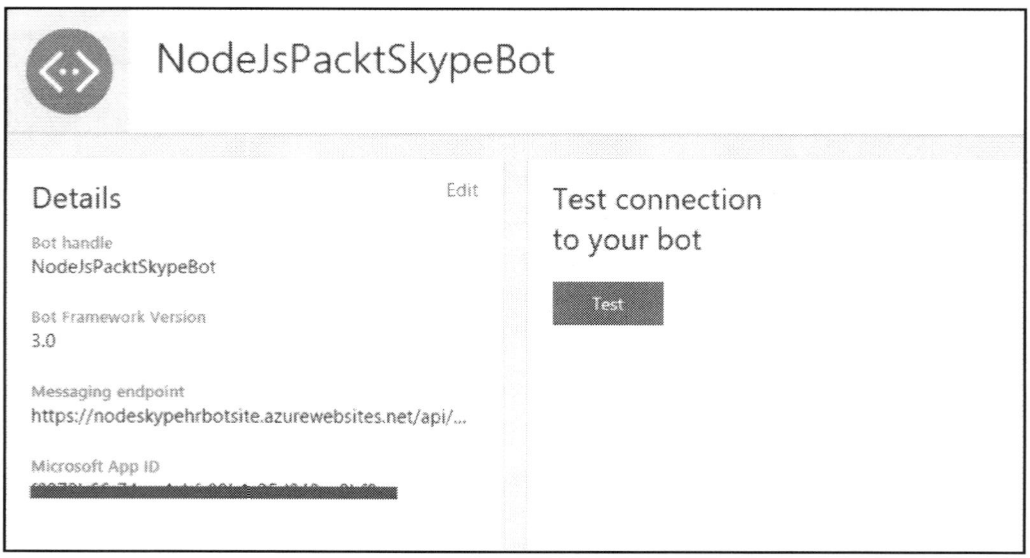

There, you can quickly test the connection to the bot by clicking on the **Test** button.

As we don't want to make the bot public, there is no need to **Publish** it to the Skype bot directory.

If you scroll down a bit, you'll find the channels that are enabled by default. One of them is **Skype**, as shown in the following screenshot:

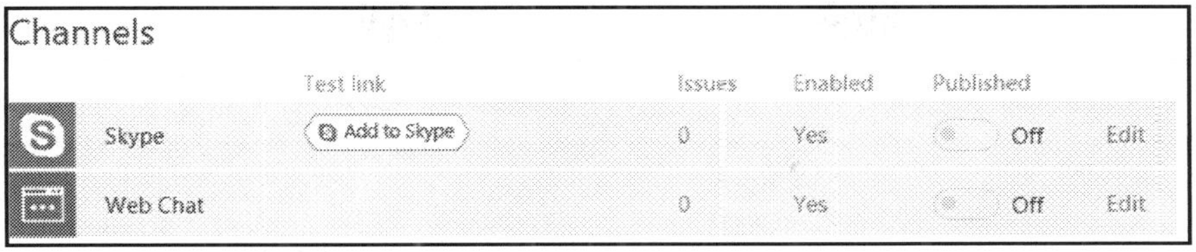

Let's go ahead and click on the **Add to Skype** button in order to add the bot to our Skype contact list. Once we do that, a new browser tab or window will open, and we'll be presented with the following screen:

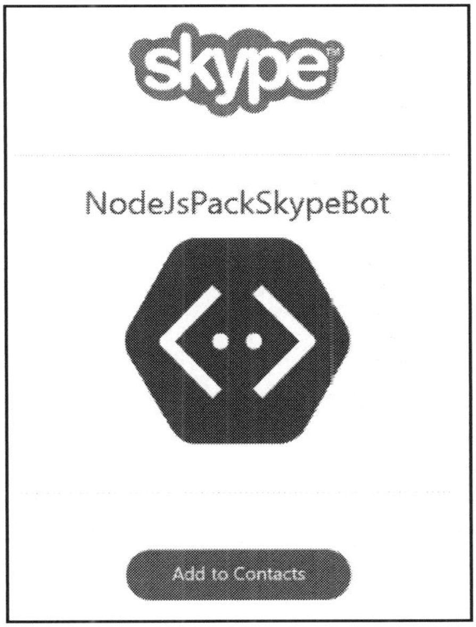

In order to add the bot to Skype, click on the **Add to Contacts** button. This will launch the Skype application and add it to our contacts list.

If your Skype account is not the same as your Azure account (and if you are logged on with your Azure account), then it will be requested that you sign out and then sign in with your Skype account, in order to add the bot to your contacts list.

With all the setup behind us, let's modify our code in order to add our bot ID, Application ID, and application secret. The bot ID and the Application ID that we'll need to add to our code are the same, which is the one entered when registering the bot. Once we've done this, we can re-publish it to Azure websites and test it.

Our Skype bot `app.js` should now look like this:

```
var skype = require('botbuilder');
var express = require('express');

var app = express();

var botService = new skype.ChatConnector({
    appId: '<< Your Application Id >>',
    appPassword: '<< Your Application Password >>'
});

var bot = new skype.UniversalBot(botService);

app.post('/api/messages', botService.listen());

bot.dialog('/', function (session) {
  if (session.message.text.toLowerCase().indexOf('hi') >= 0){
    session.send('Hi ' + session.message.user.name +
     ' thank you for your message: ' + session.message.text);
  } else{
    session.send('Sorry I don't understand you...');
  }
});

app.get('/', function (req, res) {
  res.send('SkypeBot listening...');
});

app.listen(process.env.port, function () {
  console.log('SkypeBot listening...');
});
```

If we publish the changes to Azure websites and have added our bot to our Skype contacts list, using the URL indicated by the label **Add to Skype**, we should see the following when we send a message to it.

The bot, for now, will reply with the same message that we provided as a response wrapped up with a nice thank you appended to the original message.

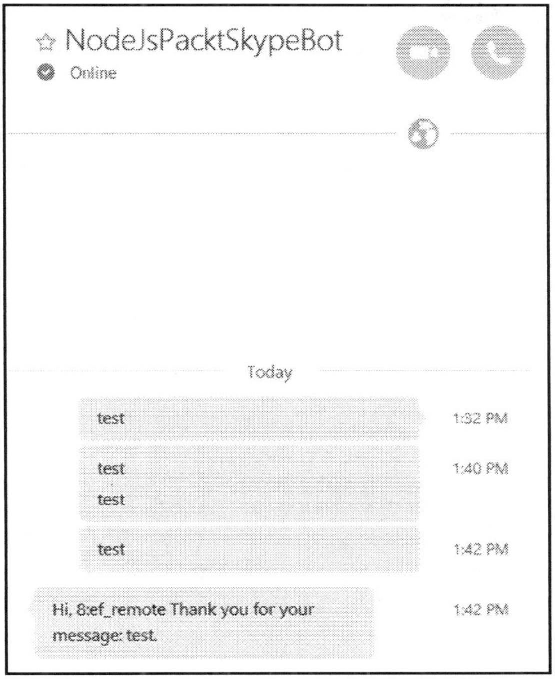

Now, let's explore where the magic actually happens. Notice that **8:ef_remote** is the name of the actual Skype user that sent the message to our bot.

In our code, the part that is responsible for the magic is the `bot.dialog` event.

This event, as its name explicitly implies, gets triggered when Skype sends an `HTTP POST` request when the bot receives a message. Take a look at the following code snippet:

```
bot.dialog('/', function (session) {
  if (session.message.text.toLowerCase().indexOf('hi') >= 0){
    session.send('Hi ' + session.message.user.name +
     ' thank you for your message: ' + session.message.text);
  } else{
    session.send('Sorry I don't understand you...');
  }
});
```

The `session` object contains the information that Skype passes on to the bot app, which describes the session data that has been received and from whom. Notice that the session object contains properties such as `message` and `text`.

HR Skype bot agent

So far, we've been able to create and deploy to Azure a basic Skype bot that essentially responds to any message sent with the same text it received, with an appended thank you message.

In the previous chapter, we briefly mentioned that we would add a `BotBrain` method that will basically be responsible for giving an answer to a particular message input.

Let's now expand our Skype bot in order to create a basic **Human Resources** (**HR**) agent that is capable of answering certain requests, such as checking how many holidays a person has left or requesting a sick leave.

HR is an ample area that covers many topics and, obviously, much more logic could be added to an automated HR agent. However, as the purpose is to illustrate some sort of automated communication, we'll restrict ourselves to simply processing holidays and sick leave requests.

As we are already using Azure, we'll use **Table Storage** (`https://azure.microsoft.com/en-us/documentation/articles/storage-introduction`) in order to define some data and some answers that our bot will provide, depending on the type of message submitted and the type of request provided by the user.

Azure table storage as a backend

The Table Storage service uses a tabular format to store data. Each record represents an entity, and the columns represent the various properties of that entity (fields within a table).

Every entity has a pair of keys (a **PartitionKey** and **RowKey**) to uniquely identify it. It also has a timestamp column that the Table Storage service uses to know when the entity was last updated (this happens automatically and the timestamp value cannot be overwritten; it is internally controlled by the service itself).

Extensive documentation (`https://docs.microsoft.com/en-us/azure/storage/`) about how the Storage and Table Storage services work can be found directly on the Azure website. It is an invaluable resource that is definitely worthwhile checking in order to have a better understanding of both services.

Nevertheless, we'll quickly explore how we can get up and running quickly with Azure Table Storage.

In order to get started with a Storage instance on Microsoft Azure, you'll need to sign in to the Azure Portal with a Microsoft account. You can do that by going to `http://portal.azure.com`. Refer to the following screenshot:

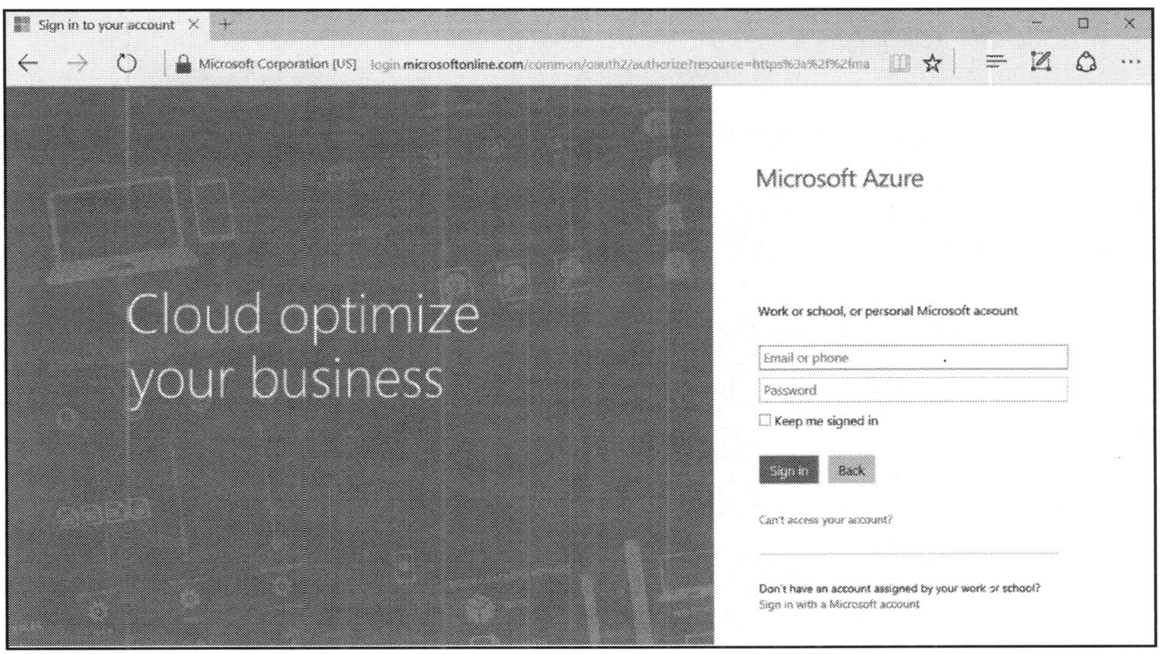

Once you've signed in to the Azure Portal, you can browse through the list of Azure services and select **Storage accounts (classic)**, as shown in the following screenshot:

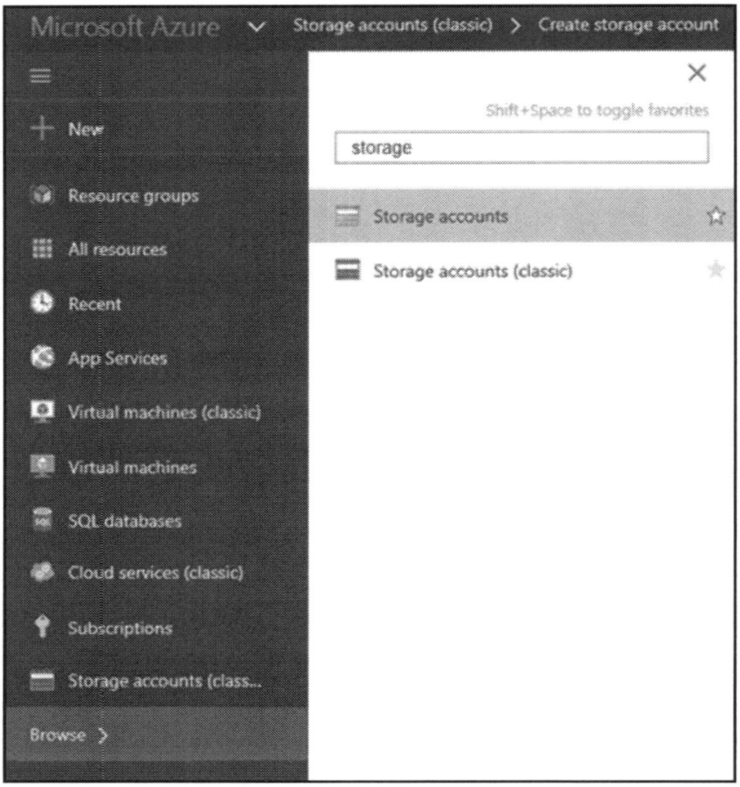

Once you've selected **Storage accounts (classic)**, you'll be presented with the following screen, where you can add a new Storage account:

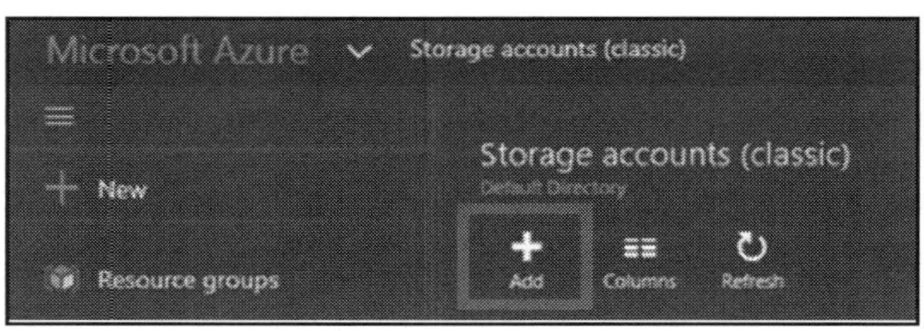

In order to add a new **Storage accounts (classic)**, click on the **Add** button. This will then present a screen where you may add the account's **Name** and select the Azure **Location** in which the account will be hosted, as shown in the following screenshot:

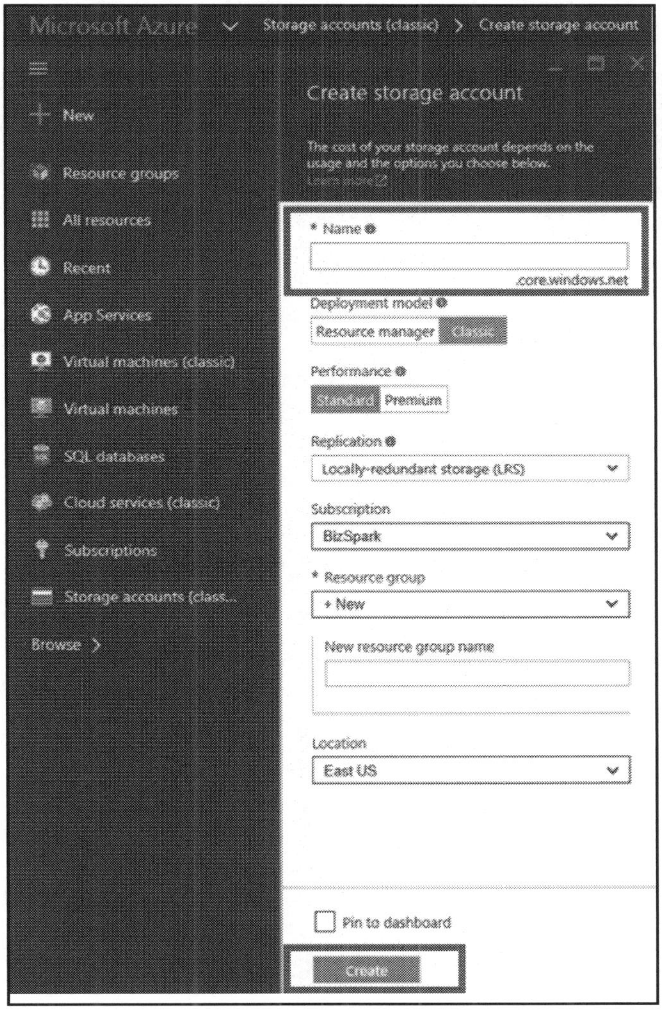

Once you have chosen a name and selected the location nearest to you, click on the **Create** button. Immediately after, Azure will create the Storage account. Once created, it will look as follows. You'll need your access keys in order to interact with the service from your code or any external tool. The keys can be found by clicking on the **Keys** setting, as shown in the following screenshot:

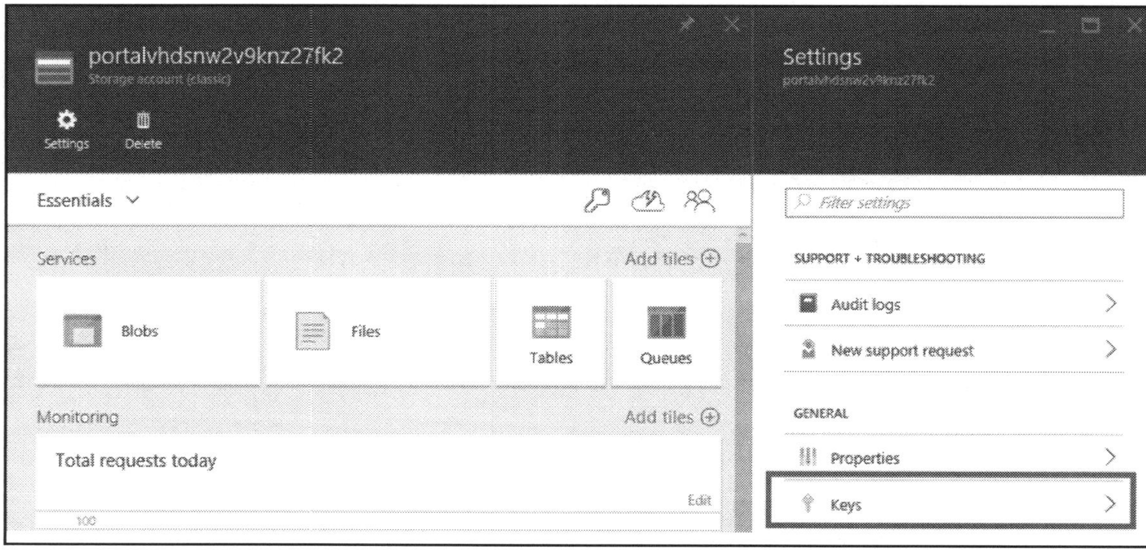

With the Azure Storage account now ready, you can use an open source and very handy tool called **Azure Storage Explorer** (`https://azurestorageexplorer.codeplex.com`), which will allow you to easily connect to your Storage account and create, update, delete, and view any storage tables and data:

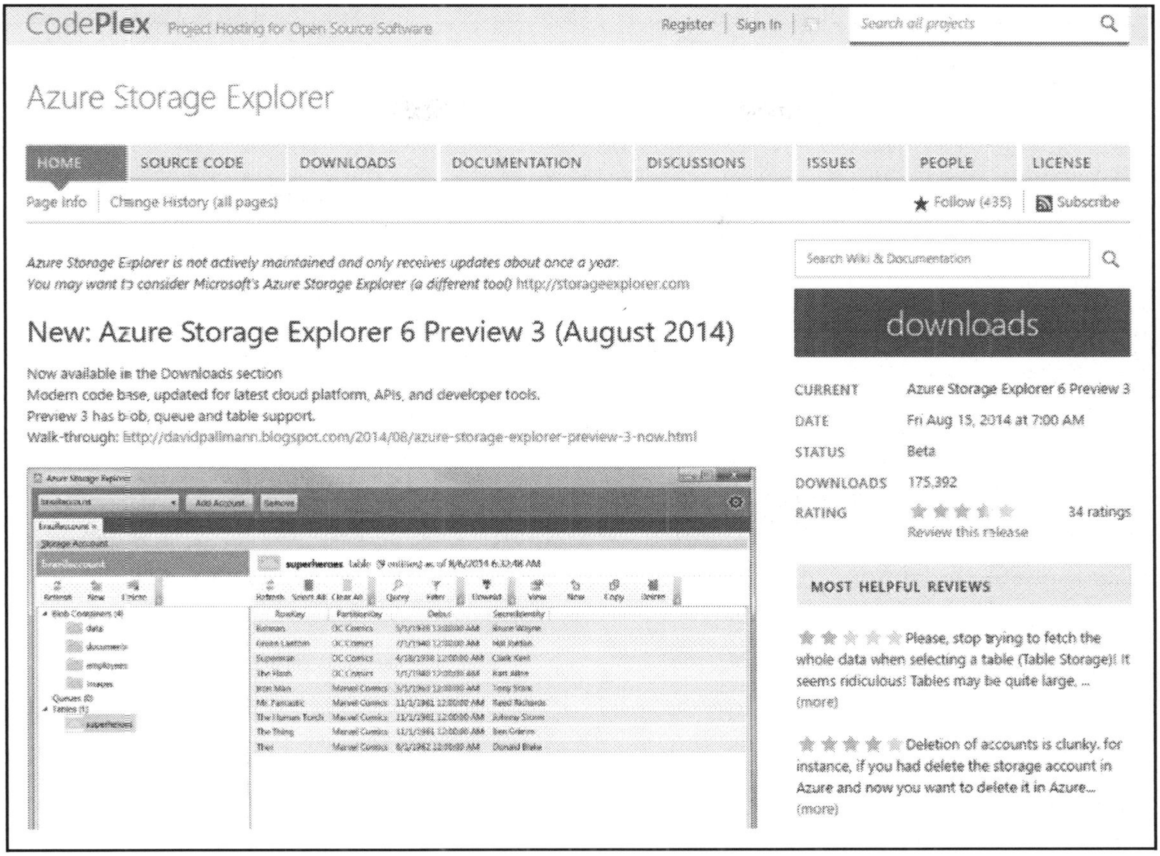

Once you've downloaded the ZIP file from CodePlex, after you unzip it, you'll find an executable that you can run in order to install the tool.

The installation wizard is super easy to follow and self-explanatory, requiring just a few clicks. Please note that the Azure Storage Explorer application only works on Windows. Once installed, you'll see the following files:

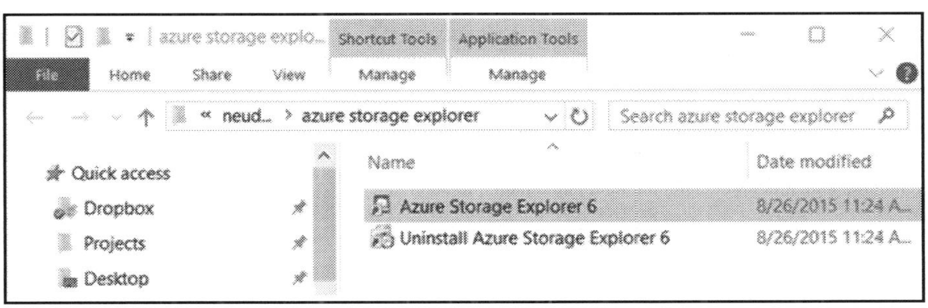

In order to run the tool, double-click on the **Azure Storage Explorer** shortcut. Once the application is running, you'll need to connect your Azure Storage account to it. This can be done by clicking on the **Add Account** button:

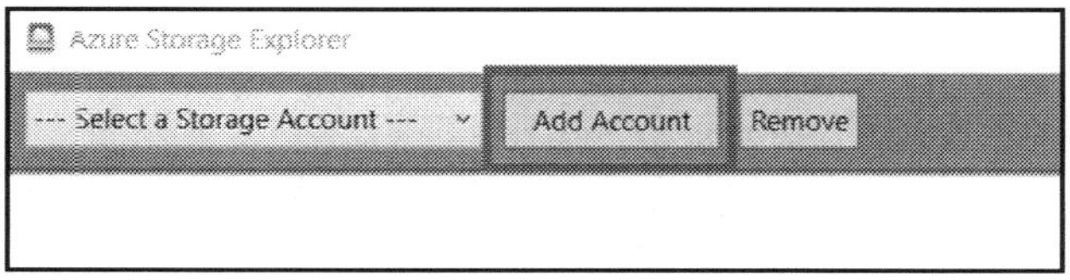

Once you click on the **Add Account** button, it'll be requested that you add your **Storage account name** and key, as follows:

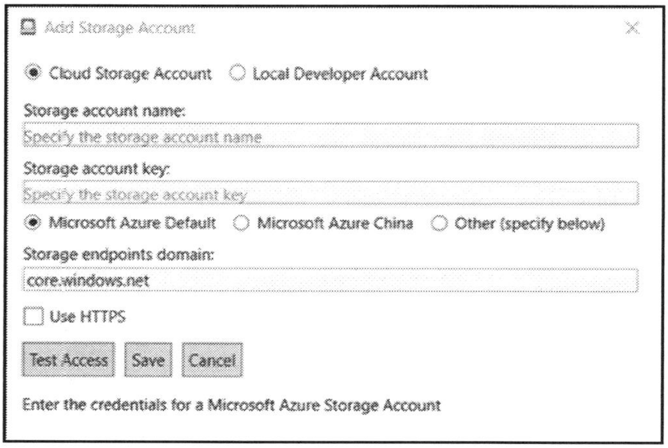

After entering the requested details, you should click on the **Test Access** button in order to check if the connection works. If that is successful, you may click on the **Save** button.

With these details stored, next time you open the Azure Storage Explorer application, you'll be able to access your Storage account from the dropdown next to the **Add Account** button.

HR agent guidelines

Having set up our Azure Table Storage account and seen how to use Storage Explorer in order to connect to it, let's now create a table with some data that our Skype bot will use in order to interpret requests and function as an automated HR agent. Sounds exciting, so let's roll up our sleeves and get started.

We'll create a table called `HolidaysHRBot`, which will contain as its `PartitionKey` the name of the Skype user and as its `RowKey` the full name of the person in the form of `FirstName-LastName`. Both the `PartitionKey` and `RowKey` fields are strings. It will also have a third field called `DaysLeft`, which will be an integer and represent the number of vacation days that a person has left to use.

Let's assume that `DaysLeft` will start with a value of 25 (representing 25 days of vacation available to use). Finally, we can add another field that will indicate the number of sick days used. Let's call this field `DaysSick` and define it as an integer, which will be initially set to zero.

So, let's create the table using Storage Explorer and add some data. Refer to the following screenshot:

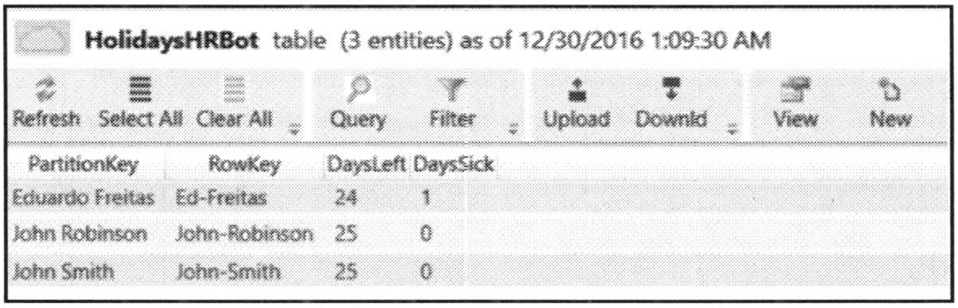

The way the logic of our HR agent will work is that, once a user has been verified, and a holiday or sick request has been placed, the bot will reply back with the option selected.

So, having defined these basic rules, let's develop the `BotBrain` method that can take care of this. Looks like a lot of fun!

Accessing the Azure table through code

So, let's see how we can connect to Azure Table Storage through Node.js, read the information on the database table, and, furthermore, update it.

In order to get started, the first thing to do is to add Azure Storage to our project as an npm package. This can be done, as follows, from the command line:

```
npm install azure-storage --save
```

This will update our `package.json` file, adding a reference to the Azure Storage library. Once the package has been installed, let's add a reference to it in our code:

```
var azure = require('azure-storage');
```

With the reference added, we can go ahead and create the `tableSvc` object that we will be using to connect to and communicate with our `HolidaysHRBot` table. It is necessary to pass the `AZURE_ACCOUNT` and `ACCOUNT_KEY`, which can be found on the Azure Portal.

```
var tableSvc = azure.createTableService(AZURE_ACCOUNT, AZURE_KEY);
```

Because we have manually added data to our table using Storage Explorer, in order to retrieve data based on the `PartitionKey` and `RowKey` we'll need to use the `retrieveEntity` method from the `tableSvc` object. Here's how:

```
tableSvc.retrieveEntity('HolidaysHRBot', 'Eduardo Freitas', 'Ed-Freitas',
   function(error, result, response){
  if(!error){
    // result contains the entity
  }
});
```

So, now let's create a small user verification method that takes the first message from the user and checks on the Azure table if the user actually exists, and if so, the bot carries out the rest of the interactive messaging process. This will be the entry point for our `BotBrain` method. Take a look at the following code snippet:

```
userVerification = function(session) {
    session.send('Hey, let me verify your user id ' +
      userId + ' (' + userName + '), bear with me...');

  tableSvc.retrieveEntity(AZURE_TABLE, userId, userName, function
  entityQueried(error, entity) {
    if (!error) {
      authenticated = true;
      userEntity = entity;

      session.send('I have verified your id, how can I help you?' +
        ' Type a) for Holidays, b) for Sick Leave.');
    }
    else {
      session.send('Could not find: ' + userName +
      ', please make sure you use proper casing :)');
    }
  });
};
```

What we've done here is to basically wrap up the `retrieveEntity` function into a method for which, depending on what result is fetched from the `AZURE_TABLE`, a given `session.send` is sent back to the user.

If, for the user, there is a matching record for the `userId` (PartitionKey) and `userName` (RowKey) specified, then the state is set to authenticated and the entity `retrieved` (record) is copied to the `userEntity` object.

HR agent bot logic

Now let's close the loop and tie all this up by outlining the bot's full code, as follows:

```
var skype = require('botbuilder');
var express = require('express');
var azure = require('azure-storage');

var app = express();

var APP_ID = '<< Your App ID >>';
var APP_SECRET = '<< Your App Password >>';

var AZURE_ACCOUNT = '<< Your Azure Account ID >>';
var AZURE_KEY = '<< Your Azure Account Key >>';
var AZURE_TABLE = 'HolidaysHRBot';

var tableSvc = azure.createTableService(AZURE_ACCOUNT, AZURE_KEY);

var authenticated = false;
var holidays = false;
var sick = false;
var userId = '';
var userName = '';
var userEntity = undefined;

var botService = new skype.ChatConnector({
    appId: APP_ID,
    appPassword: APP_SECRET
});

var bot = new skype.UniversalBot(botService);

app.post('/api/messages', botService.listen());

userVerification = function(session) {
  session.send('Hey, let me verify your user id ' + userId + ' (' +
    userName + '), bear with me...');

  tableSvc.retrieveEntity(AZURE_TABLE, userId, userName,
  function entityQueried(error, entity) {
    if (!error) {
```

```
        authenticated = true;
        userEntity = entity;

        session.send('I have verified your id, how can I help you?' +
          ' Type a) for Holidays, b) for Sick Leave.');
      }
      else {
        session.send('Could not find: ' + userName +
          ', please make sure you use proper casing :)');
      }
    });
  };

  cleanUserId = function(userId) {
    var posi = userId.indexOf(':');
    return (posi > 0) ? userId.substring(posi + 1) : userId;
  };

  BotBrain = function(session) {
    var orig = session.message.text;
    var content = orig.toLowerCase();
    var from = session.message.user.name;
    if (authenticated) {
      if (content === 'a)') {
        holidays = true;
        session.send('Please indicate how many vacation days' +
          ' you will be requesting, i.e.: 3');
      }
      else if (content === 'b)') {
        sick = true;
        session.send('Please indicate how many sick days' +
          ' you will be requesting, i.e.: 2');
      }
      else if (content !== 'a)' && content !== 'b)') {
        if (holidays) {
          session.send(userName + '(' + userId + ')' +
            ', you have chosen to take ' + content +
            ' holiday(s). Session ended.');
          sick = false;
          authenticated = false;
        }
        else if (sick) {
          session.send(userName + '(' + userId + ')' +
            ', you have chosen to take ' + content +
            ' sick day(s). Session ended.');
          holidays = false;
          authenticated = false;
        }
```

```
      else if (!holidays && !sick) {
        session.send('I can only process vacation or sick leave requests.'
+
          ' Please try again.');
      }
    }
  }
  else {
    authenticated = false, holidays = false, sick = false;
    userId = '', userName = '', userEntity = undefined;

    if (content === 'hi') {
      session.send('Hello ' + cleanUserId(from) +
        ', I shall verify your identify...');
      session.send('Can you please your provide your FirstName-LastName?' +
        ' (please use the - between them)');
    }
    else if (content !== '') {
      userId = cleanUserId(from);
      userName = orig;

      if (userName.indexOf('-') > 1) {
        userVerification(session);
      }
      else {
        session.send('Hi, please provide your FirstName-LastName' +
          ' (please use the - between them) or say hi :)');
      }
    }
  }
};

bot.dialog('/', function (session) {
  BotBrain(session);
});

app.get('/', function (req, res) {
  res.send('SkypeBot listening...');
});

//app.listen(3979, function () {
app.listen(process.env.port, function () {
  console.log('SkypeBot listening...');
});
```

Given that we already explained some parts of the code when we went through the process of registering the bot with Skype and we also reviewed how to hook up to the Skype API events that allow the bot to receive incoming messages from users, we won't be covering those parts further. Instead, we will focus on the `BotBrain` function and how the actual process flows. Let's analyze this.

The first thing to notice is that, when the `bot.Dialog` event gets triggered, the `BotBrain` function is invoked:

```
bot.dialog('/', function (session) {
  BotBrain(session);
});
```

Another important part is that somehow we need to keep the state in order to be able to determine what stage of the conversation our bot is at with the user.

A relatively simple way to do this is by using variables that keep the state of the conversation or apply it to some parts.

We'll need to know when the user has been authenticated, which basically means that their Skype Id and name have been checked against the data contained within the `AZURE_TABLE`. Further to that, we'll also need to keep the `userId`, `userName`, and `userEntity` (representing the record on the table) for the authenticated user.

It is also important to know if the user has sent a `holidays` request or a `sick` leave request. With these variables, we can keep the state in a very simple way.

Ideally, for multiple users requesting interaction with the bot at the same time, the state should be kept individually for each user logged on or authenticated. However, this is far beyond the scope of this example and we shall not cover this. Take a look at the following code snippet:

```
var authenticated = false;
var holidays = false;
var sick = false;
var userId = '';
var userName = '';
var userEntity = undefined;
```

With the problem of managing the state covered, let's now focus on the internals of the `BotBrain` function. Let's dissect it into smaller chunks.

There are basically two main parts that are important. One is whether the user has already been authenticated (the user has been verified to exist on the AZURE_TABLE) and the other is where the user has yet not been authenticated, which corresponds to the initial stage of the conversation:

```
authenticated = false, holidays = false, sick = false;
userId = '', userName = '', userEntity = undefined;

if (content === 'hi') {
  session.send('Hello ' + cleanUserId(from) +
    ', I shall verify your identify...');
  session.send('Can you please your provide your FirstName-LastName?' +
    ' (please use the - between them)');
}
else if (content !== '') {
  userId = cleanUserId(from);
  userName = orig;

  if (userName.indexOf('-') > 1) {
    userVerification(session);
  }
  else {
    session.send('Hi, please provide your FirstName-LastName' +
      ' (please use the - between them) or say hi :)');
  }
}
```

Here we can see that, in order to start the conversation, the user must write a message including the word hi. Following that, the bot responds and requests that the user enters their name in the form of FirstName-LastName (proper casing should be used).

FirstName-LastName will be used in order to query the RowKey of the AZURE_TABLE and verify if the userId (the user's Skype Id) corresponds to the record that also contains the value specified by FirstName-LastName. This is done within the userVerification function.

Once the user's identity has been verified, then authenticated is set to true and therefore the bot can ask what type of action the user wants to carry out. Let's check this:

```
if (content === 'a)') {
  holidays = true;
  session.send('Please indicate how many vacation days' +
    ' you will be requesting, i.e.: 3');
}
else if (content === 'b)') {
  sick = true;
```

```
        session.send('Please indicate how many sick days' +
          ' you will be requesting, i.e.: 2');
    }
    else if (content !== 'a)' && content !== 'b)') {
      if (holidays) {
         session.send(userName + '(' + userId + ')' +
           ', you have chosen to take ' + content +
           ' holiday(s). Session ended.');
         sick = false;
         authenticated = false;
       }
       else if (sick) {
         session.send(userName + '(' + userId + ')' +
           ', you have chosen to take ' + content +
           ' sick day(s). Session ended.');
         holidays = false;
         authenticated = false;
      }
      else if (!holidays && !sick) {
         session.send('I can only process vacation or sick leave requests.' +
           ' Please try again.');
      }
    }
```

Once the user has been verified and the bot's state has been authenticated, the bot then requests that the user chooses if he or she wants to request some vacation days or sick leave days. Once the user responds, each state is then stored using Boolean variables called `holidays` and `sick`, which are then used by the bot to send back a reply asking how many days the user wants to book. Take a look at the following screenshot:

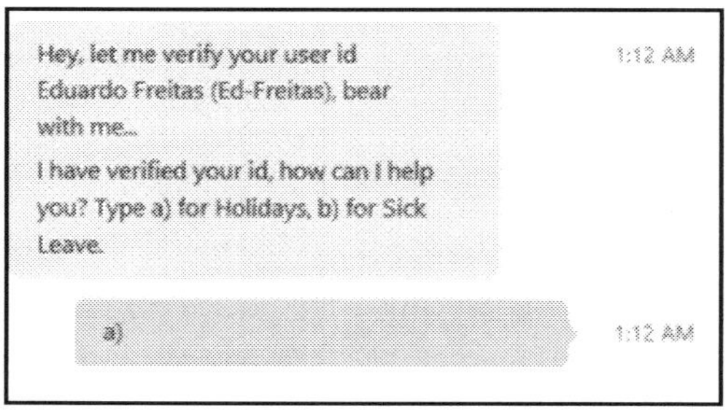

When the user provides the number of days, the bot then replies back confirming the request. The output can be seen as follows:

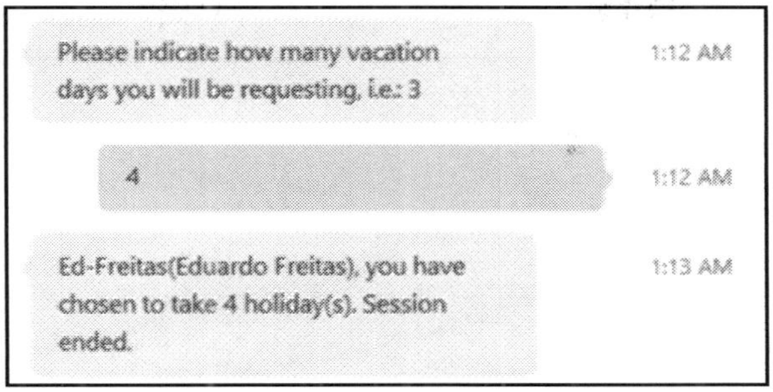

It's important to note that there's room to add additional logic and perform more operations, such as actually changing the values on the `AZURE_TABLE` once the days request has been entered, so there's plenty of opportunity to keep exploring and expanding the functionality of the bot.

Summary

It's been an interesting journey on how to connect and interact with Skype services, and how to create a bot to leverage some basic but interesting and interactive functionality.

We've seen how to get our bot all set up with Skype, how to install the related npm packages, and implement the basic skeleton and structure for our app.

Further to this, you've also learned how to create the bot's brains in order to perform certain tasks and send the right response based on the input received.

If you'd like to expand on this a bit further, something interesting to think about is how to keep the state for multiple users simultaneously and also add more interactive functionality.

Hopefully, this has given you some inspiration, food for thought, and an eagerness to continue exploring many more possibilities for implementing Skype bots. Thanks so much for reading.

3
Twitter as a Flight Information Agent

Twitter is an online social networking service that enables users to send and read short 140 character messages called *tweets*, and has become one of the most prominent ways for people to exchange news and information all over the world.

Twitter's popularity has exploded since its creation, and now it is used for all sorts of things, such as customer service, marketing, news coverage, and many others. It is one of the most popular websites that exist, and it is considered to be the *SMS gateway* of the Internet.

One of Twitter's main uses is for companies to communicate information to their followers. For example, airlines usually tweet about events that are related to the company, as well as those that could affect passengers or their plans.

In this chapter, we'll focus our attention on creating a Twitter bot that is able to provide flight information to passengers, acting like an automated flight information agent.

The examples should be a lot of fun, as well as easy to follow, so let's not wait any longer and get started!

How a Twitter bot works

Just like any other bot, a Twitter bot is, in essence, just another Twitter user account–the difference is that, instead of being manned by another person, the account is controlled by an automated process that knows how to reply to the input you provide. This is possible because Twitter provides an API that allows you to interact programmatically with the service through code.

In essence, anything that can be turned into a service could be converted into an automated conversation by using a bot, and Twitter is no different. Bots can have interactive conversations on nearly every platform, at any time, and from anywhere.

A Twitter bot is typically an application that you write that listens for something to happen on Twitter and then does something in response. In our case, we'll be listening for someone to tweet with a certain hashtag and then tweeting something when that happens. That hashtag will be a flight number, and the bot will be able to provide some feedback based on it.

So, let's get our feet on the ground and get started in building our Twitter bot.

Creating a Twitter app

The first and foremost step in creating a Twitter bot is to actually create a Twitter application. The bot is just a designation we'll be using, but in reality it's really a Twitter application behind the scenes that is able to interact with the Twitter API.

In order to be able to interact with the Twitter API, it is necessary to have a registered Twitter account. Go to the Twitter web page and sign up if you don't have an account. If you have one, sign in.

Once you are signed in, navigate to `https://apps.twitter.com/`. This is where we will register our Twitter application. You'll then see the Twitter **Application Management** welcome page which has a button to create a new application.

To create the Twitter bot, click on the **Create New App** button. Refer to the following screenshot:

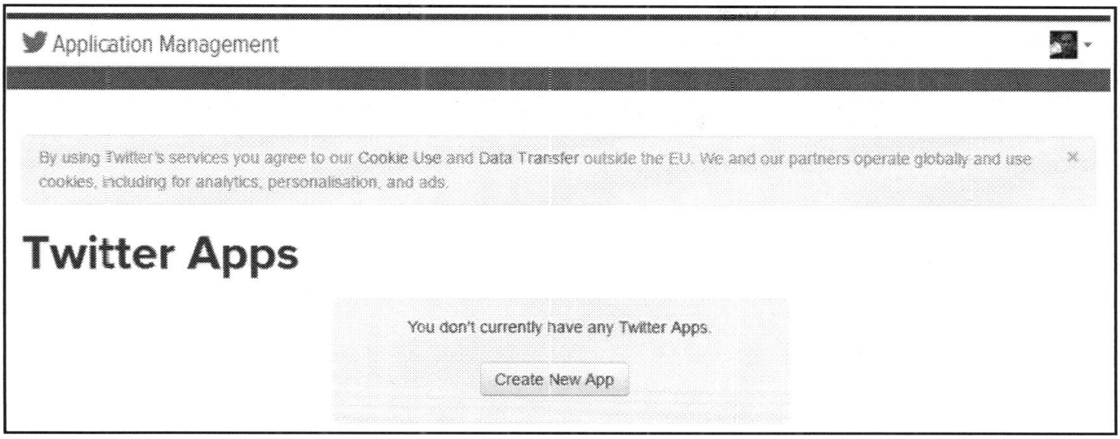

Having done that, the following screen will appear:

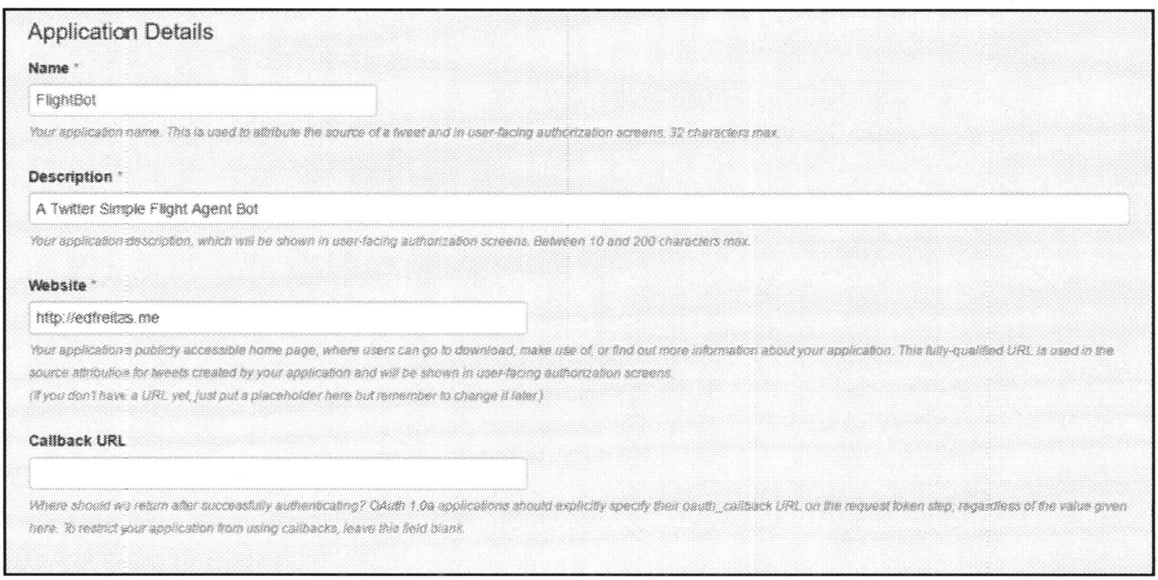

Fill in the required information. Give the application a distinctive name and a description. You are also required to enter a website that will be used as the bot's publicly accessible home page. Once you have entered this data, scroll down and accept the Twitter **Developer Agreement**:

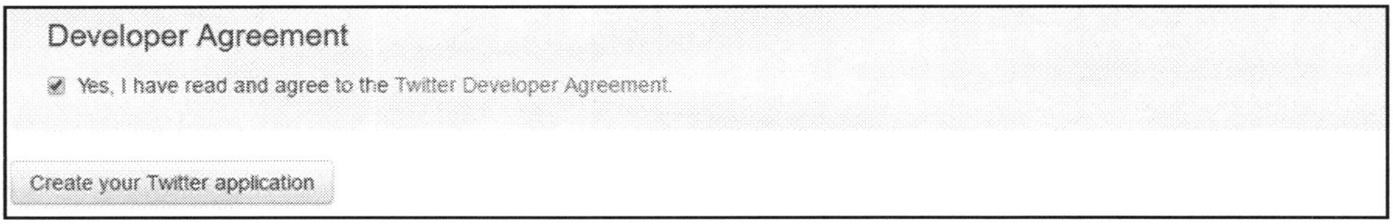

Once you've read the developer agreement, you can click on the **Create your Twitter application** in order to proceed. This will allow Twitter to create your application, and you'll be presented with the following screen once the creation process has finalized:

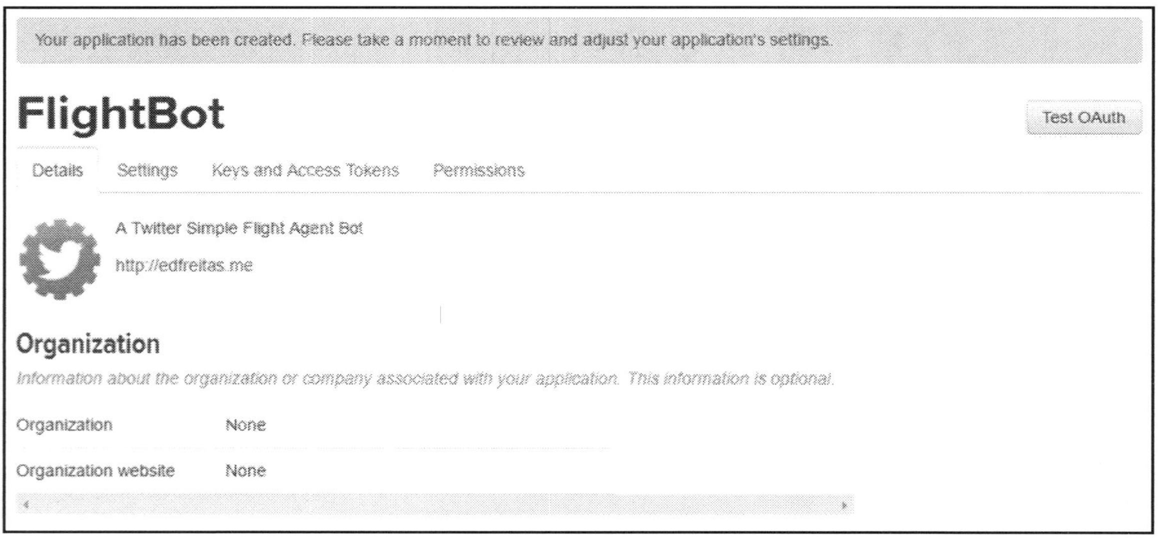

If you scroll a bit, there are also application settings provided that will be needed as soon as we start coding. With the Twitter app created, let's focus on writing some code. So far throughout this book we've been using the Atom editor; however, you are free to use any other editor that you might be comfortable with.

Open the editor and create a new `app.js` file inside a `FlightBot` folder anywhere on your drive. For now, simply add this instruction:

```
console.log('Hi, this is FlightBot');
```

Assuming we have Node.js and npm installed (if not, please refer to the steps in `Chapter 1`, *The Rise of Bots – Getting the Message Across*), let's get some necessary dependencies installed.

Now let's copy the `package.json` (that we used in the previous chapter) and place it in the `FlightBot` folder. Then let's modify it as follows:

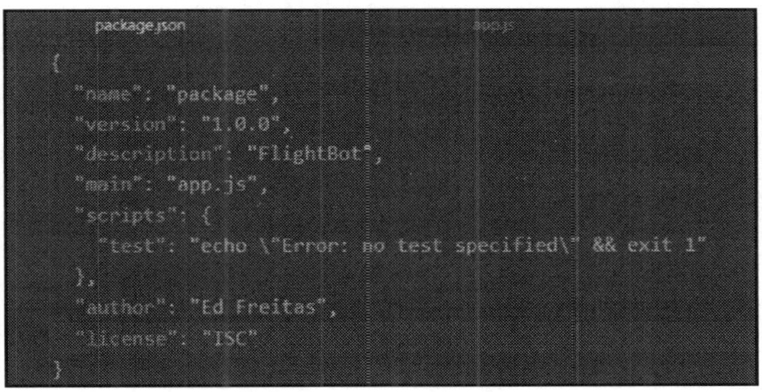

```
{
  "name": "package",
  "version": "1.0.0",
  "description": "FlightBot",
  "main": "app.js",
  "scripts": {
    "test": "echo \"Error: no test specified\" && exit 1"
  },
  "author": "Ed Freitas",
  "license": "ISC"
}
```

Now let's get the dependencies installed, so we can start coding within the `app.js` file:

```
npm install twitter --save
```

This will install the Twitter Node.js SDK, which we will be using to write our app. This will be installed on the `FlightBot` folder as shown in the following screenshot:

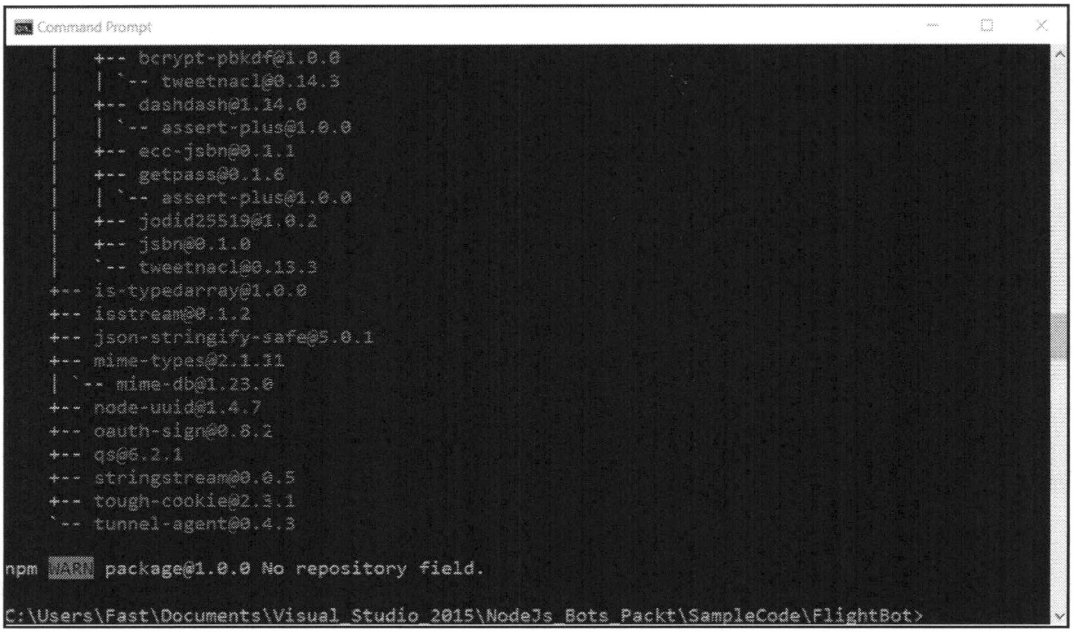

You'll see the updated `package.json` file in your project folder:

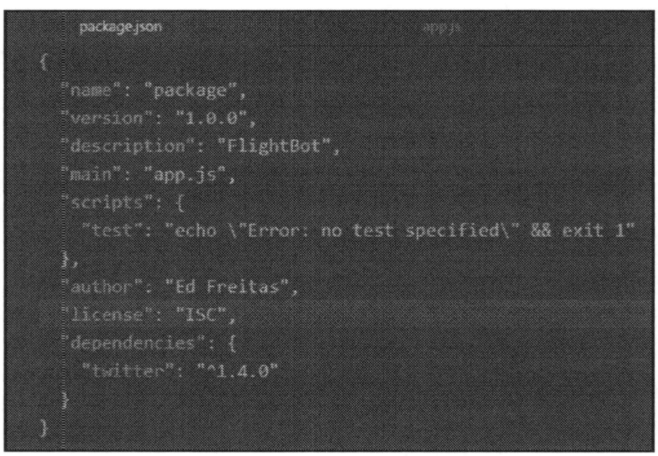

We are now ready to start adding some code in our `app.js` file:

```
var TwitterPackage = require('twitter');
```

What we've done here is to load and import the Twitter package. First, let's get these consumer keys and tokens from the Twitter **Application Management** screen:

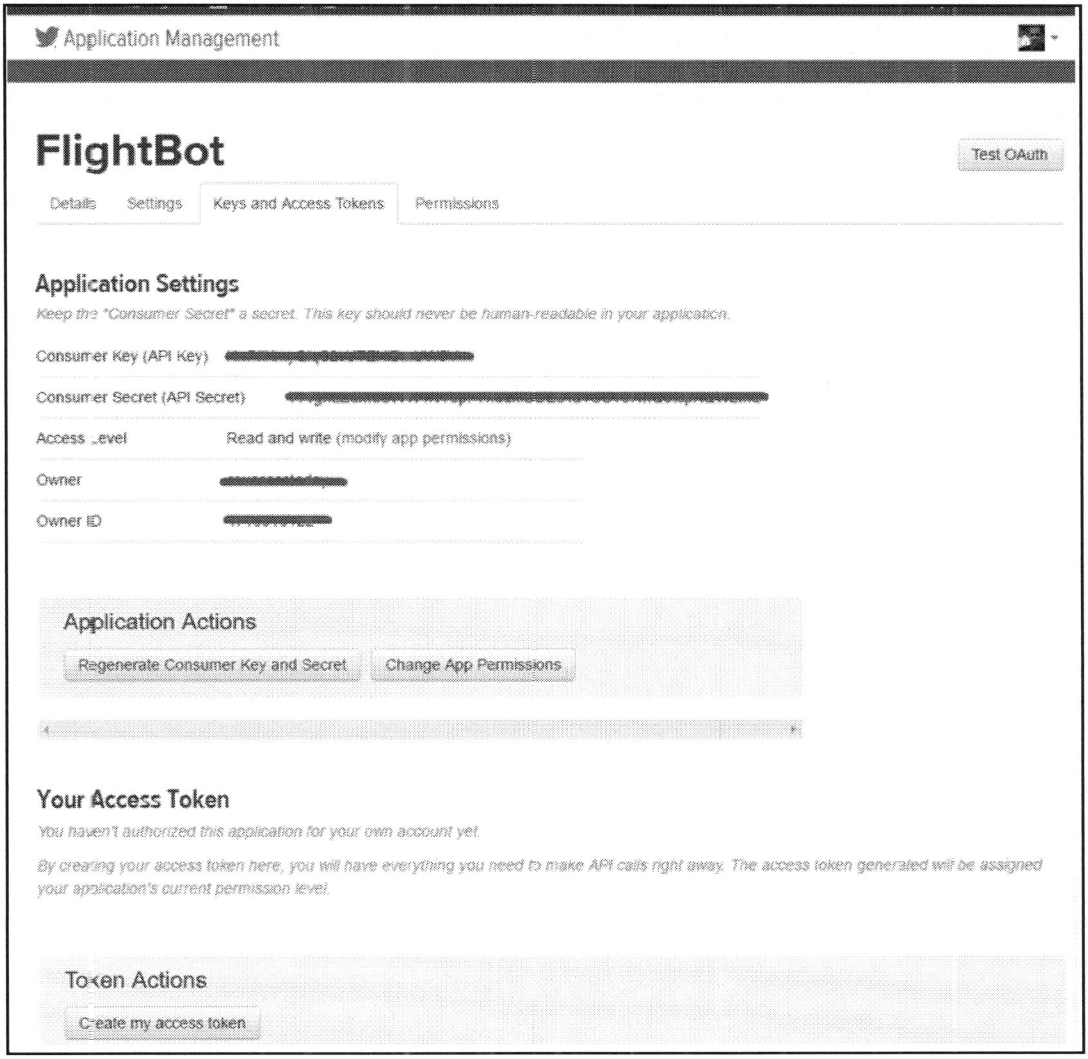

Note how the **Consumer Key** and **Consumer Secret** are available by default, but not the **Your Access Tokens**.

In order to get the **Your Access Tokens**, click on the **Create my access token** button at the bottom of the screen. Once you've done that, you'll see the following screen:

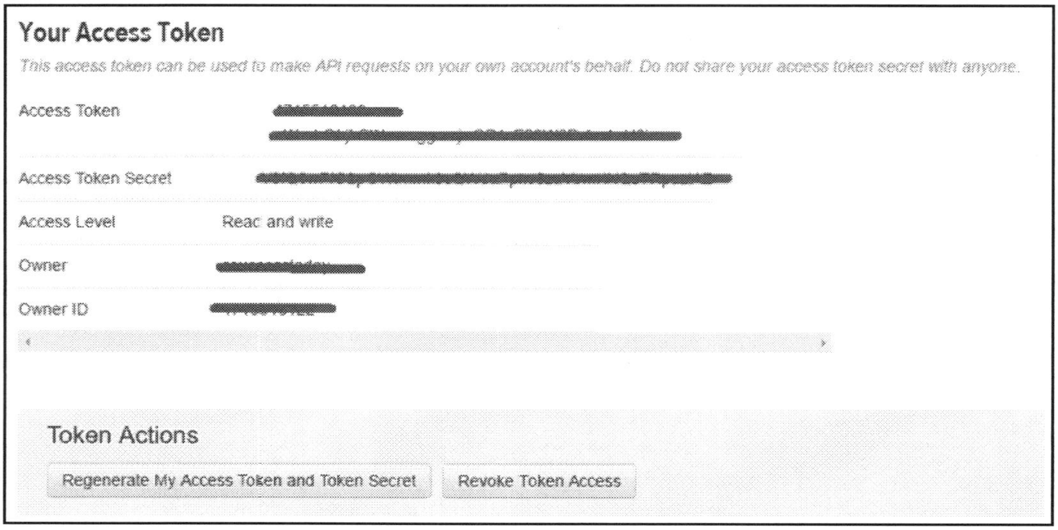

With this done, you can now add the consumer and access tokens to the secret object variable in the code.

We can do this by defining an object variable that will contain the consumer key and secret object, along with the access tokens, as shown in the following code snippet:

```
var secret = {
  consumer_key: 'PUT YOURS',
  consumer_secret: 'PUT YOURS',
  access_token_key: 'PUT YOURS',
  access_token_secret: 'PUT YOURS'
}

var Twitter = new TwitterPackage(secret);
```

Later, we'll store these in a separate `.json` file, but for now let's keep them within our `app.js` file. These will be required in order to authenticate to Twitter.

So at this point, we've pretty much created the app on Twitter and have a very basic structure with tokens and access codes that we can use to authenticate to the Twitter service and start using the API.

With this out of the way, let's move on and start adding some logic to our application.

Posting to Twitter

In order to add our own custom logic, we'll need to make use of Twitter's `REST` API, which will allow us to do several things. One of the things it can do is allow us to post a tweet.

This can be achieved as follows:

```
Twitter.post('statuses/update', {status: 'This is a sample automated
Tweet'},  function(error, tweet, response){
  if(error){
    console.log(error);
  }
  console.log(tweet);  // Tweet body.
  console.log(response);  // Raw response object.
});
```

So let's take a moment to examine this. `Twitter.post` means that we are calling the `post` function in the Twitter object. We pass the `post` function several things–`'statuses/update'` means we want to post a status update (a tweet).

`{status: 'This is a sample automated Tweet'}` is a JavaScript object that we are passing in to this function where we set the status of the tweet being sent out.

Although this contains just the text of the tweet we want to send, there are a whole bunch of other options to set depending on what we want to post to Twitter (such as images, location, and so on). In this case, we are just interested in posting a simple status just so we are familiar with setting the status property.

The last thing we pass in is a function. In JavaScript, you can actually pass functions in to other functions; it is one of the things that makes JavaScript a functional programming language.

In the `Twitter.post` function, you're expected to pass a function in that will be executed after Twitter tries to post the tweet. This is what is known as a callback function. In that function, you'll notice three parameters:

- `error`: This indicates whether there's an error in the process of posting the tweet, in which case this variable will contain an object with information about the error that occurred
- `tweet`: An object that contains all the tweet data
- `response`: An object of the actual response Twitter sends back when you post a tweet

In our code, we'll just post our tweet and then print it out in the console. Now go ahead and remove the `'Hi, this is FlightBot'` line. We don't need it any longer.

Now, save the modified `app.js` file. It should look like this:

```
var TwitterPackage = require('twitter');

var secret = {
  consumer_key: 'PUT YOURS',
  consumer_secret: 'PUT YOURS',
  access_token_key: 'PUT YOURS',
  access_token_secret: 'PUT YOURS'
}

var Twitter = new TwitterPackage(secret);

Twitter.post('statuses/update', {status: 'This is a sample automated
Tweet'},  function(error, tweet, response){
  if(error){
    console.log(error);
  }
  console.log(tweet);  // Tweet body.
  console.log(response);  // Raw response object.
});
```

Now let's go and run the app:

```
node app.js
```

This will produce the following result on the command line console:

If we then inspect Twitter itself, we can see the following:

Really cool! We now have a way to send automatic tweets. However, we don't have a full blown bot yet. Let's explore how we can achieve that.

Listening to tweets

In order to create a functional Twitter bot, it is not enough to be able to simply post something to Twitter. We also need to be able to listen to what gets posted on Twitter.

Twitter has a very useful API called `Streaming` which gives us information about tweets in real time. In other words, when someone tweets something that we care about, we get all the data about that tweet. This is both really useful and really awesome.

So let's re-implement a bit of our code as follows:

```
Twitter.stream('statuses/filter', {track: '#FlightBot'}, function(stream) {
  stream.on('data', function(tweet) {
    console.log(tweet.text);
  });

  stream.on('error', function(error) {
    console.log(error);
  });
});
```

Let's analyze this. The `Twitter.stream` function takes in three parameters:

- The first parameter is a string that tells Twitter that we want to listen for statuses with a certain filter. In this case, we are filtering by using a hashtag.
- The second parameter is where we define that filter with an object. That object contains the property `track` which lets us define a word, hashtag, or phrase that we care to listen for. For this, we will be tracking when someone tweets with the hashtag `'#FlightBot'`.
- The last parameter is a function that gets called when Twitter is done setting up our stream. When it's done setting up our stream, it then passes that stream object in to the function. Within this function, we can set up what happens when we receive a tweet, along with other things, such as error handling, and so on.

Now let's take a closer look at what happens when we receive data:

```
stream.on('data', function(tweet) {
  console.log(tweet.text);
});
```

So, using the `stream` object, it calls the `on` function. Now, with the `on` function, you pass in a string and a function. This means that when a tweet occurs, we call this function with that data. At the moment, we just print out `tweet.text`, which is how you access the actual text of the tweet that was received that used the hashtag `'#FlightBot'`.

Let's now go ahead and comment the `Twitter.post` code so we don't post the same tweet twice. Then, if we save the `app.js` file and then call `node app.js` in the command line, you'll notice that the command line no longer shows you a prompt.

This is because it's running and listening for some sort of data to come in from that stream. If you need to stop it, press *Ctrl* + *C* a few times to return to the prompt.

In order to test this, go to Twitter and tweet something with `'#FlightBot'`, as shown in the following screenshot:

Now check your running command line. You should see the text of your tweet printed out:

```
C:\Users\Fast\Documents\Visual_Studio_2015\NodeJs_Bots_Packt\SampleCode\FlightBot>node app.js
#FlightBot
```

Awesome! We've now implemented a mechanism that can listen to tweets.

The update `app.js` code now looks like this:

```
var TwitterPackage = require('twitter');

var secret = {
  consumer_key: 'PUT YOURS',
  consumer_secret: 'PUT YOURS',
  access_token_key: 'PUT YOURS',
  access_token_secret: 'PUT YOURS'
}

var Twitter = new TwitterPackage(secret);

Twitter.stream('statuses/filter', {track: '#FlightBot'}, function(stream) {
  stream.on('data', function(tweet) {
    console.log(tweet.text);
  });

  stream.on('error', function(error) {
    console.log(error);
  });
});
```

Replying to who tweeted

So far, we've managed to write some code that posts a tweet and we've also written code that acts on tweets that have been written. So what's next?

The next thing to do is to basically combine both parts together into a single code base, as this will be the basic layer of our bot.

One of the things you might want to do is to give the bot the ability to reply to the person who tweeted with your hashtag. To do this, the bot needs to mention them.

You can access the username of the person who tweeted with your hashtag by using `tweet.user.screen_name`.

In order to mention them, concatenate a `'@'` symbol at the beginning by doing this:

```
var mentionString = '@' + tweet.user.screen_name;
```

Then just concatenate that to the string you want to tweet out. We're now replying to the person who tweeted. Cool!

So, let's now look at the complete source code to get a full picture:

```
var TwitterPackage = require('twitter');

var secret = {
  consumer_key: 'PUT YOURS',
  consumer_secret: 'PUT YOURS',
  access_token_key: 'PUT YOURS',
  access_token_secret: 'PUT YOURS'
}

var Twitter = new TwitterPackage(secret);

Twitter.stream('statuses/filter', {track: '#FlightBot'}, function(stream) {
  stream.on('data', function(tweet) {
    console.log(tweet.text);
    var statusObj = {status: "Hi @" +
    tweet.user.screen_name + ", Thanks for reaching out. How are you?"}

    Twitter.post('statuses/update', statusObj, function(error,
    tweetReply, response){

      if(error){
        console.log(error);
      }

      console.log(tweetReply.text);
    });
  });

  stream.on('error', function(error) {
```

```
      //print out the error
      console.log(error);
    });
  });
```

If we now execute the app with `node app.js`, we should be able to pick up any hashtags with the keyword `'#FlightBot'`. Let's have a look:

We now get the following result:

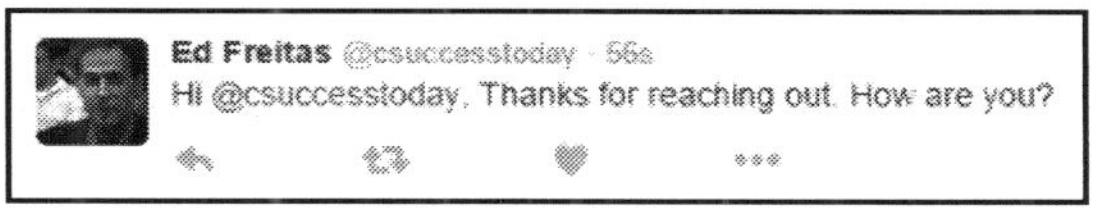

This is really awesome. With just a few lines of code we were able to create a simple Twitter bot. But we are still not done. We haven't added any logic on how to provide basic flight details or data yet .

But before we do that, let's put the `secret` variable object into a `secret.json` file, so we can avoid having the access codes and tokens within our code.

Create a new `secret.json` file and save it in the same folder as the `app.js` file. The `secret.json` file should now look like this:

```
{
  "consumer_key": "PUT YOURS",
  "consumer_secret": "PUT YOURS",
  "access_token_key": "PUT YOURS",
  "access_token_secret": "PUT YOURS"
}
```

This `secret.json` file is then referenced from the code, and it now looks as follows:

```
var TwitterPackage = require('twitter');
var secret = require("./secret");
var Twitter = new TwitterPackage(secret);

Twitter.stream('statuses/filter', {track: '#FlightBot'}, function(stream) {

  stream.on('data', function(tweet) {
```

```
      console.log(tweet.text);
      var statusObj = {status: "Hi @" + tweet.user.screen_name +
      ", Thanks for reaching out. How are you?"}

      Twitter.post('statuses/update', statusObj,
        function(error, tweetReply, response){
        if(error){
          console.log(error);
        }
        console.log(tweetReply.text);
      });
    });

    stream.on('error', function(error) {
      console.log(error);
    });
  });
```

Now that we have the updated code, let's add the necessary logic to send information about flights statuses and information.

Flight APIs

In order to get some flight information, we'll have to rely on a flight API. One that is free and really useful is the one from **Air France-KLM**, which is available at `https://developer.airfranceklm.com/`.

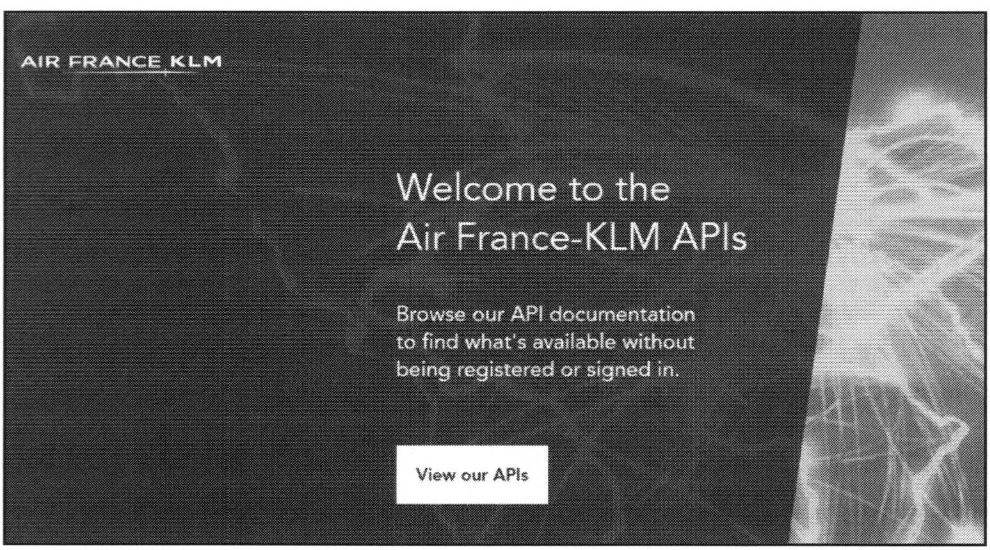

So let's sign up and register an account. There are several APIs (found at `https://developer.airfranceklm.com/Our_Apis`) provided by Air France-KLM such as Reservations, Order, Flight Offer, Flight Status, Location, Contact Information, Ancillary Shop, and Check-in.

We are interested in using the **Flight Status API** (`https://developer.airfranceklm.com/page/Flight_status_API`), which will provided up-to-date and accurate information about specific flight numbers. Let's explore this API a bit.

The Flight Status API provides flight status information–such as scheduled and actual arrival and departure times–of KLM-operated flights, or Delta and Air France-operated flights with a KLM codeshare, flying to and from the Air France-KLM hub in Amsterdam.

The API supports operational decision making, such as notification in case of exceptional situations, like extreme weather conditions.

The great thing about this API is that it doesn't require API keys, and it is available for free. The catch is that it only returns data from the day that you execute the query-that is, it only returns today's data and doesn't return any past flight status information.

There are two ways to search with this API. One is to search using a flight number and the other is to use a route.

Flight status API

When searching using a flight number, the `REST` endpoint will provide the flight status for a given flight, and you must specify the day's date; for example, flight KL1699 on September 16, 2016. The request would look like this:

```
http://fox.klm.com/fox/json/flightstatuses?flightNumber=KL1699&departureDate=20
16-09-16
```

This would return the following JSON response:


```
{ "flights" : [ { "@type" : "OperatingFlight",
        "aircraft" : { "registrationCode" : "PH-BGT" },
        "carrier" : { "code" : "KL" },
        "flightNumber" : "1699",
        "marketingFlights" : [ { "carrier" : { "code" : "KQ" },
              "flightNumber" : "1699"
            },
            { "carrier" : { "code" : "DL" },
              "flightNumber" : "9605"
```

```
            }
          ],
        "operatingFlightLeg" : { "arrivesOn" : { "@type" : "Airport",
                "IATACode" : "MAD"
              },
            "departsFrom" : { "@type" : "Airport",
                "IATACode" : "AMS"
              },
            "flightStatus" : "ARRIVED",
            "legs" : [ { "actualArrivalDateTime" :
"2016-09-16T09:26+02:00",
                  "actualDepartureDateTime" : "2016-09-16T06:59+02:00",
                  "arrivesOn" : { "@type" : "Airport",
                      "IATACode" : "MAD"
                    },
                  "departsFrom" : { "@type" : "Airport",
                      "IATACode" : "AMS"
                    },
                  "scheduledArrivalDateTime" : "2016-09-16T09:35+02:00",
                  "scheduledDepartureDateTime" : "2016-09-16T07:00+02:00",
                  "status" : "ARRIVED"
                } ],
            "scheduledArrivalDateTime" : "2016-09-16T09:35+02:00",
            "scheduledDepartureDateTime" : "2016-09-16T07:00+02:00"
          },
        "remainingFlyTime" : "PT0.000S"
      } ]
}
```

That was easy and fun! Now let's explore the route search API.

Route search API

The Route Search REST endpoint provides a summary of flight statuses for all applicable flights in a given route, such as Amsterdam (AMS) and Paris Charles de Gaulle (CDG).

The request would look like this:

```
http://fox.klm.com/fox/json/flightstatuses?originAirportCode=AMS&destinationAir
portCode=CDG
```

The JSON result would be as follows.


```
{ "flights" : [ { "@type" : "OperatingFlight",
        "_links" : { "detailedInfoLink" :
"http://fox.klm.com/fox/json/flightstatuses
flightNumber=KL1223&departureDate=2016-09-15&originAirport=AMS&destinationA
irport=CDG" },
        "carrier" : { "code" : "KL" },
        "flightNumber" : "1223",
        "operatingFlightLeg" : { "arrivesOn" : { "@type" : "Airport",
                "IATACode" : "CDG"
              },
            "departsFrom" : { "@type" : "Airport",
                "IATACode" : "AMS"
              },
            "flightStatus" : "ARRIVED",
            "scheduledArrivalDateTime" : "2016-09-15T08:00+02:00",
            "scheduledDepartureDateTime" : "2016-09-15T06:45+02:00"
          }
      },
      { "@type" : "OperatingFlight",
        "_links" : { "detailedInfoLink" :
"http://fox.klm.com/fox/json/flightstatuses?flightNumber=KL1227&departureDa
te=2016-09-16&originAirport=AMS&destinationAirport=CDG" },
        "carrier" : { "code" : "KL" },
        "flightNumber" : "1227",
        "operatingFlightLeg" : { "arrivesOn" : { "@type" : "Airport",
                "IATACode" : "CDG"
              },
            "departsFrom" : { "@type" : "Airport",
                "IATACode" : "AMS"
              },
            "flightStatus" : "ARRIVED",
            "scheduledArrivalDateTime" : "2016-09-16T08:40+02:00",
            "scheduledDepartureDateTime" : "2016-09-16T07:15+02:00"
          }
      },
      { "@type" : "OperatingFlight",
        "_links" : { "detailedInfoLink" :
"http://fox.klm.com/fox/json/flightstatuses?flightNumber=GA9240&departureDa
te=2016-09-16&originAirport=AMS&destinationAirport=CDG" },
        "carrier" : { "code" : "GA" },
        "flightNumber" : "9240",
        "operatingFlightLeg" : { "arrivesOn" : { "@type" : "Airport",
                "IATACode" : "CDG"
              },
            "departsFrom" : { "@type" : "Airport",
                "IATACode" : "AMS"
```

```
                },
            "flightStatus" : "ARRIVED",
            "scheduledArrivalDateTime" : "2016-09-16T09:25+02:00",
            "scheduledDepartureDateTime" : "2016-09-16T07:55+02:00"
          }
        }
      ]
  }
```


The response includes the following information–Scheduled Departure Date Time, Scheduled Arrival Date Time, Flight Status, Marketing Flights, Remaining Fly Time, Arrival, and Departure information.

So now that we have an API to query, let's make our bot a bit smarter and allow it to retrieve flight status and route details.

Adding a REST client library

Using the code we already have, which is able to respond back to the person that actually tweeted the `'#FlightBot'` hashtag, let's make some modifications so that it can provide status details about flights and routes using the Air France-KLM APIs.

The first thing that we need to do in order to communicate to the Air France-KLM endpoints is to include a `REST` client library for Node.js in our app.

There are various Node.js REST client libraries out there, and you can choose whichever makes you feel more comfortable. For our example, however, we'll be using the library found at `https://www.npmjs.com/package/request`.

The first thing we need to do is to install it. We can do this from the command line by executing this instruction:

```
npm install request --save
```

After doing this, our `package.json` file will be updated as follows:

```
package.json                                   app.js
{
  "name": "package",
  "version": "1.0.0",
  "description": "FlightBot",
  "main": "app.js",
  "scripts": {
    "test": "echo \"Error: no test specified\" && exit 1"
  },
  "author": "Ed Freitas",
  "license": "ISC",
  "dependencies": {
    "request": "^2.75.0",
    "twitter": "^1.4.0"
  }
}
```

Note how a reference to `request` has been added. This is because we have used the save option when executing the previous instruction.

Making the bot a bit smarter

Now that we have added a `REST` client library, it's time to add some logic to our application in order to interact with the Air France-KLM APIs.

Our bot should be able to provide feedback about flights and routes using the API endpoints previously described.

Let's make some changes to our code to accommodate this. In order to do that, let's add some logic to make sure that the bot is able to process not only the Twitter hashtag but also a flight number.

So we will essentially automate the call to this REST endpoint and parse the response associated with it, returning just some essential bits of that data, but not all of it. Sounds exciting, so let's get started.

We need to automate this endpoint through a `REST` call. We need to make sure that, besides the hashtag, a flight number is also passed as part of the message:

```
http://fox.klm.com/fox/json/flightstatuses?flightNumber=KL1699&departureDate=20
16-09-16
```

Here's the full updated code. Let's have a complete look at it and then dissect it bit by bit to understand the changes that were made:

```
var TwitterPackage = require('twitter');
var secret = require("./secret");
var Twitter = new TwitterPackage(secret);
var request = require('request');

padLeft = function (str, paddingChar, length) {
  var s = new String(str);

  if ((str.length < length) && (paddingChar.toString().length > 0))
  {
      for (var i = 0; i < (length - str.length) ; i++)
        s = paddingChar.toString().charAt(0).concat(s);
  }

  return s;
};

GetDate = function() {
  var dateObj = new Date();
  var month = dateObj.getUTCMonth() + 1; //months from 1-12
  var day = dateObj.getUTCDate();
  var year = dateCbj.getUTCFullYear();

  return year + '-' + padLeft(month.toString(), '0', 2) + '-' +
    padLeft(day.toString(), '0', 2);
};

FlightNumberOk = function(str) {
  var posi = str.indexOf('KL');
  var fn = str.substring(posi);
  return (posi >= 0 && fn.length === 6) ? fn : '';
};

var fd = '';

GetFlightDetails = function(fn) {
  var dt = GetDate();
  var rq = 'http://fox.klm.com/fox/json/flightstatuses?flightNumber=' + fn
+
    '&departureDate=' + dt;

  request(rq, function (error, response, body) {
    if (!error && response.statusCode == 200) {
      fd = body;
    }
```

```
  })
};

Twitter.stream('statuses/filter', {track: '#FlightBot'}, function(stream) {

  stream.on('data', function(tweet) {
    var statusObj = {status: "Hi @" + tweet.user.screen_name +
      ", Thanks for reaching out. We are missing the flight number."};

    var fn = FlightNumberOk(tweet.text);

    if (fn !== '') {
      GetFlightDetails(fn);
    }

    setTimeout(function() {
      console.log ('fd: ' + fd);

      if (fd !== undefined) {
        var ff = JSON.parse(fd);
        statusObj = {status: "scheduledArrivalDateTime: "  +
          ff.flights[0].operatingFlightLeg.scheduledArrivalDateTime};
      }

      Twitter.post('statuses/update', statusObj,  function(error,
tweetReply,
      response) {
        if (error){
          console.log(error);
        }
        console.log(tweetReply.text);
      });
    }, 1500);
  });

  stream.on('error', function(error) {
    console.log(error);
  });
});
```

OK, so there are some changes. The first one is that we have added a reference to the `request` library which we will be using to make the requests to the REST API:

```
var request = require('request');
```

Following that, we've added a `GetDate` function which will return today's date so it can be passed onto the `REST` endpoint as the `departureDate` parameter:

```
GetDate = function() {
  var dateObj = new Date();
  var month = dateObj.getUTCMonth() + 1; //months from 1-12
  var day = dateObj.getUTCDate();
  var year = dateObj.getUTCFullYear();

  return year + '-' + padLeft(month.toString(), '0', 2) + '-' +
    padLeft(day.toString(), '0', 2);
};
```

This `GetDate` function uses a `padLeft` function that is responsible for correctly formatting each of the parts of the date as shown in the following code snippet:

```
padLeft = function (str, paddingChar, length) {
  var s = new String(str);

  if ((str.length < length) && (paddingChar.toString().length > 0))
  {
      for (var i = 0; i < (length - str.length) ; i++)
        s = paddingChar.toString().charAt(0).concat(s);
  }

  return s;
};
```

These two functions cover the `departureDate` part of the REST endpoint. So now let's focus on the `flightNumber` part.

For this, we've written a function called `FlightNumberOk`, which does a quick check to ensure that the flight number is correct:

```
FlightNumberOk = function(str) {
  var posi = str.indexOf('KL');
  var fn = str.substring(posi);
  return (posi >= 0 && fn.length === 6) ? fn : '';
};
```

With the flight number correct, we can then use another function called `GetFlightDetails` to actually perform the call to the `REST` endpoint. The JSON response is represented by the variable `body`, which is then assigned to the `fd` variable, which is later used to tweet a response back to the user. Refer to the following code:

```
GetFlightDetails = function(fn) {
  var dt = GetDate();
```

```
  var rq = 'http://fox.klm.com/fox/json/flightstatuses?flightNumber=' + fn
+
    '&departureDate=' + dt;

  request(rq, function (error, response, body) {
    if (!error && response.statusCode == 200) {
      fd = body;
    }
  })
};
```

Because the `GetFlightDetails` uses the request library to perform an asynchronous request to the `REST` endpoint, we cannot tweet the response until the JSON response is obtained, and to ensure that, the tweet response is executed within a `setTimeout` JavaScript function 1,500 milliseconds after the execution of the `GetFlightDetails` takes place.

So basically our `Twitter.stream` function now looks like this:

```
Twitter.stream('statuses/filter', {track: '#FlightBot'}, function(stream) {
  stream.on('data', function(tweet) {
    var statusObj = {status: "Hi @" + tweet.user.screen_name + ", Thanks
for
      reaching out. We are missing the flight number."};

    var fn = FlightNumberOk(tweet.text);

    if (fn !== '') {
      GetFlightDetails(fn);
    }

    setTimeout(function() {
      console.log ('fd: ' + fd);

      if (fd !== undefined) {
        var ff = JSON.parse(fd);
        statusObj = {status: "scheduledArrivalDateTime: "  +
          ff.flights[0].operatingFlightLeg.scheduledArrivalDateTime};
      }

      Twitter.post('statuses/update', statusObj,  function(error,
tweetReply,
      response) {
        if (error){
          console.log(error);
        }
        console.log(tweetReply.text);
```

```
        });
      }, 1500);
    });

    stream.on('error', function(error) {
      console.log(error);
    });
  });
```

Note how `FlightNumberOk` and `GetFlightDetails` are called before the `Twitter.Post` is called by the `setTimeout` function. This is done to ensure that the flight number is OK, and that the JSON response containing the flight details exists, before sending out the tweet to the user.

The tweet response basically sends out `scheduledArrivalDateTime`, which is obtained by parsing the JSON response using `JSON.parse`. This is accessed as follows:

```
ff.flights[0].operatingFlightLeg.scheduledArrivalDateTime
```

If we execute the program now and tweet `#FlightBot KL1699`, we'll get the following:

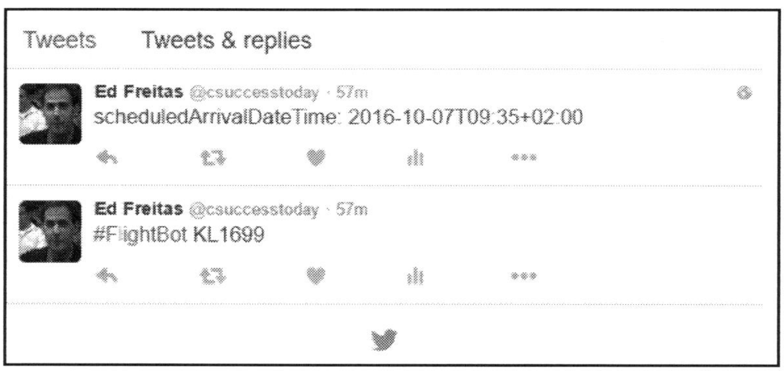

So that's cool, isn't it? Really cool!

Summary

Throughout this chapter, we've seen how to interact with Twitter and also how to query the Air France-KLM API in order to retrieve flight details and respond to tweets.

We've barely scratched the surface of what can be done with these APIs; the possibilities are, frankly, quite endless. All you need is time and a good dose of imagination!

You are encouraged to keep exploring both the Twitter and also the Air France-KLM APIs, as well as other flight data APIs out there. It's definitely an interesting area, and one worth exploring further.

I hope you have enjoyed following these examples. The next chapters will look at other fascinating topics. Have fun!

4
A Slack Quote Bot

If you haven't been living isolated in a galaxy very far away, eons from Earth with no Internet connection during the last year or so, I am sure you have already heard about Slack (`https://slack.com/`), the famous real-time messaging app and collaboration suite for teams.

Slack has been built from the ground up to be easy and fun to use. It offers a broad set of APIs that allows developers to extend its capabilities to make it even more useful.

One of the features I most enjoy from Slack is the Slackbot. It is a friendly bot available in every Slack team to guide users to create their profiles and to explain to them how Slack works.

If you think Slackbot sounds cool, what you'll really love even more is the possibility to build your own custom bots, which can act as automated users that can respond to specific events and help your team do useful things.

Throughout this chapter, we'll explore how we can use the Slack Real Time Messaging API in order to create our own custom Slackbot. We'll walk through the whole process so you can get a really good idea of what is possible.

By the end of this chapter, you should feel right at home with creating your own Slackbot and know a bit more about Slack and how it could help your team and you.

Overall, the process should be a lot of fun and easy to follow, so let's not wait any longer and get started!

Getting started

We are going to be building a bot that gives quotes as responses to the general channel. The idea is to have a bot that inspires your team during their daily activities, and quotes are definitely a great way to get inspired.

The first thing we need to do is to set up our bot with Slack and register it in order to use the Slack API.

In order to do this, we'll be using the Slack Real Time Messaging API (`https://api.slack.com/rtm`), which is a WebSocket-based API that allows us to receive events in real time and send messages to channels, private groups, and users.

The API is really well constructed and the documentation is easy to follow. We won't be using WebSockets directly, but instead a Node.js module (`https://www.npmjs.com/package/slackbots`) that makes development much easier, using JavaScript.

We need to configure our channel extensions and create the new bot. This way we will obtain the API token that is required to authenticate to Slack and get started. So, let's roll up our sleeves and get moving!

Registering a bot on Slack

In order to add the bot into your Slack organization, we'll need to register it at the following URL: `https://yourorganization.slack.com/services/new/bot`.

Notice that you will need to change your organization with the name of your company or team, which you used when registering your Slack account. Once you open up the URL in your browser, you will be redirected to the following screen:

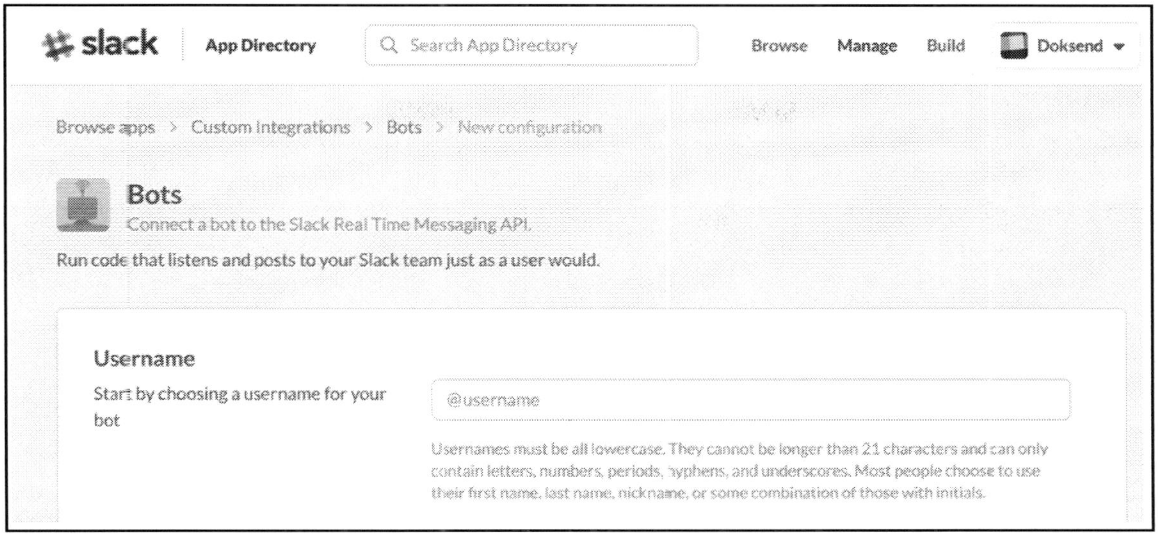

We'll be calling our bot, `quotebot`. This is the value we will fill in our username. Notice how Slack requires that all bot names are all written in lowercase.

Once the name has been entered in the **Username** field, click on the **Add bot integration** button.

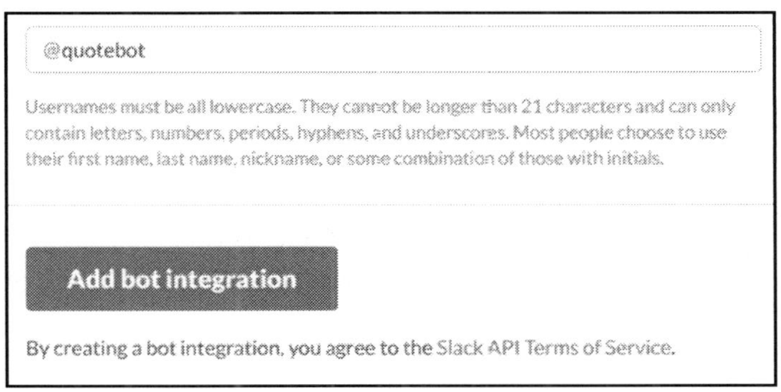

Once that has been done, you will be presented with a screen where the bot can be further customized and features can be added, such as a picture or emoji. This is what this screen looks like:

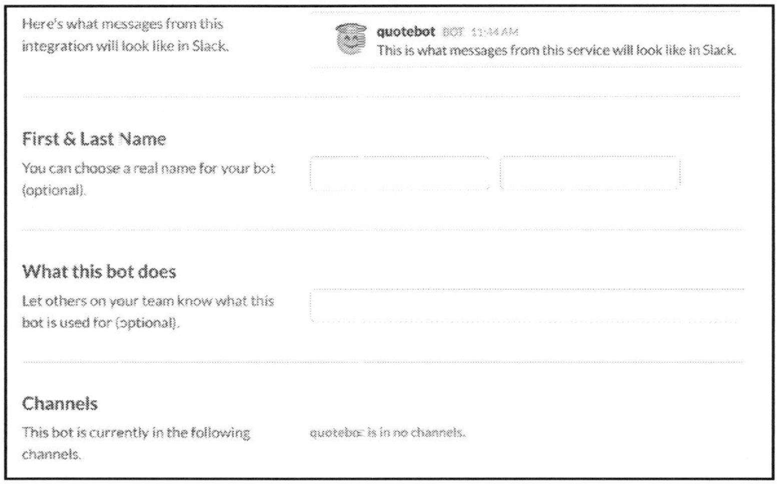

There are further options that are available and can be customized, but they don't fit in a single screenshot, so you'll see them once you reach the end of this screen. Nothing too complicated.

This screen also contains the **API Token**, which we will need to reference in our code.

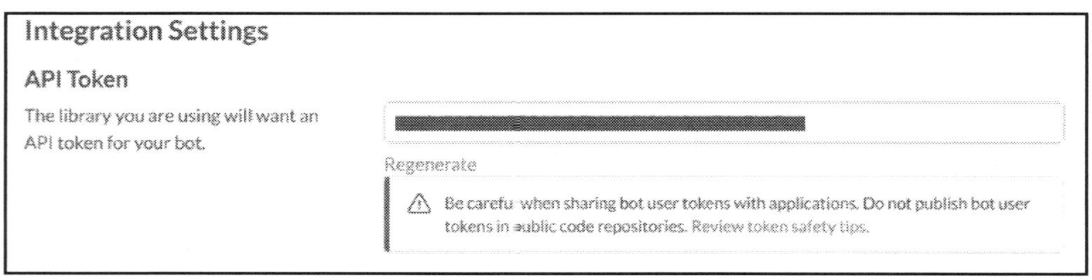

Once you've done the necessary configuration adjustments and changes, click on the **Save Integration** button.

Setting up our Node.js app

Now that we've registered our bot on Slack we are ready to set up our Node.js project in order to start coding.

Let's go ahead and create our `package.json` file. Open the Command Prompt and type the following command:

```
npm init
```

After you have done this, follow the guided configuration procedure, which should look similar to the following screenshot:

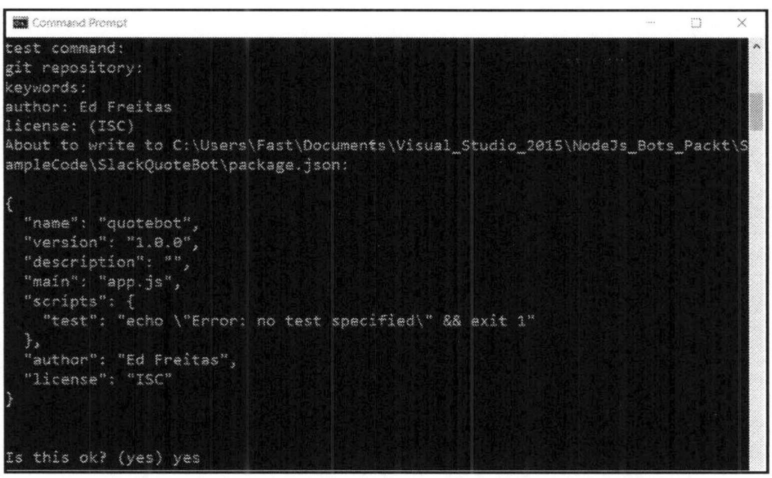

Once you have finished with this configuration, it is time to install the dependencies we will need in order to write our bot.

But before we install any dependencies, let's quickly brainstorm what our bot should do. In short, our bot must be able to retrieve a quote and reply back to the general channel.

There's an awesome site called *They Said So* (`https://theysaidso.com/`), which is a service that provides **Quotes-as-a-Service** (**QAAS**). Quotes from multiple authors can be obtained through an easy-to-use REST API.

As we'll need to access this service using REST, let's include a REST client library for Node.js in our app. Just like we did in the previous chapter, we'll be using this one.

In order to get this library installed, execute this instruction from the command line:

```
npm install request --save
```

Now that this has been done, the next step is to install a library called `slackbots` (`https://www.npmjs.com/package/slackbots`) that will act as an abstraction layer to deal with the Slack Real Time Messaging API:

```
npm install slackbots --save
```

After doing this, our `package.json` file will be updated as follows:

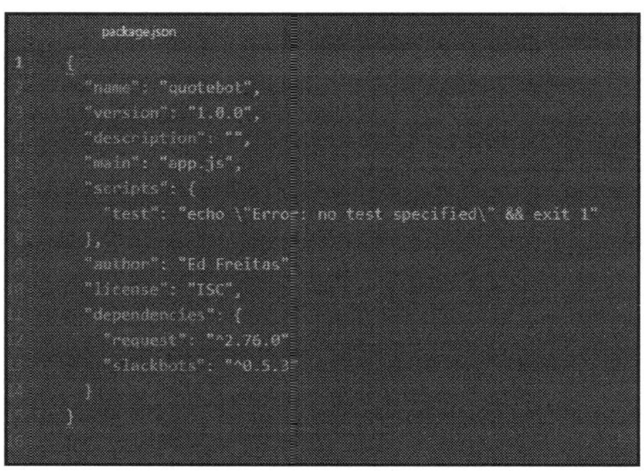

With our Node.js bot settings all wired up, we are now ready to start writing some code.

Slackbots library basics

As mentioned earlier, in order to interact with the Slack Real Time Messaging API, we'll be using a Node.js library (npm package) called `slackbots` (`https://www.npmjs.com/package/slackbots`).

Before we write any code, let's have a look at the main functions offered by this module by looking at the following short example:

```
var Bot = require('slackbots');

var settings = {
    token: 'API TOKEN',
    name: 'quotebot'
};

var bot = new Bot(settings);

bot.on('start', function() {
    bot.postMessageToChannel('channel-name', 'Hi channel.');
    bot.postMessageToUser('a-username', 'Hi user.');
    bot.postMessageToGroup('a-private-group', 'Hi private group.');
});
```

Before you run this code, please substitute the strings `channel-name`, `a-username` and `a-private-group` with your own values, taken from your Slack organization.

You'll also need to replace the `API TOKEN` string with the quotebot token you were given when the bot was created. The code should now look similar to this:

```
var Bot = require('slackbots');

var settings = {
    token: 'xoxb-.........-R7VVJ1FI5Hzfcyt.........',
    name: 'quotebot'
};

var bot = new Bot(settings);

bot.on('start', function() {
    bot.postMessageToChannel('general', 'Hi channel.');
    bot.postMessageToUser('radkiddo', 'Hi user.');
    bot.postMessageToGroup('tisdoksend', 'Hi private group.');
});
```

Once you have replaced those values, you can run the app from the command line as follows:

```
Node app.js
```

If you log in to Slack and open your team's page, you should be able to see this when you browse to the **#general** channel:

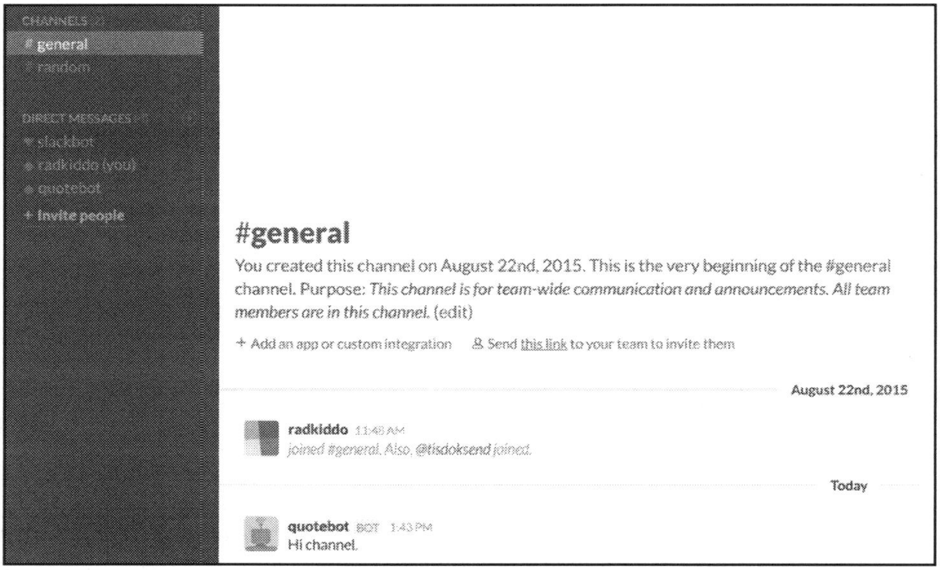

Awesome, our quotebot just came to life with its first ever message! Now let's break the code down into pieces in order to understand it a bit better:

```
var Bot = require('slackbots');
```

As you can see from the preceding code, the first thing we need to do is to require the Slackbot constructor. From there we can instantiate a new `Bot` object and add callbacks to specific events.

On this code, we use the `start` event that is triggered when the bot connects successfully to the Slack server:

```
bot.on('start', function() {
    bot.postMessageToChannel('general', 'Hi channel.');
    bot.postMessageToUser('radkiddo', 'Hi user.');
    bot.postMessageToGroup('tisdoksend', 'Hi private group.');
});
```

Then we can use the methods offered by the library to post a message in a channel using the `postMessageToChannel` method, to a user as a private message using `postMessageToUser`, or in a private group conversation by calling `postMessageToGroup`.

With these fundamentals covered, we can move on to explore the `They Said So` API, which is necessary in order to for us to build our bot.

The They Said So API

The They Said So service has a huge collection of quotes in their database and the **Quotes** API is a great and convenient way to access this data. In order to consume the Quotes API, you'll first need to sign up for the service via this URL: `https://theysaidso.com/register`.

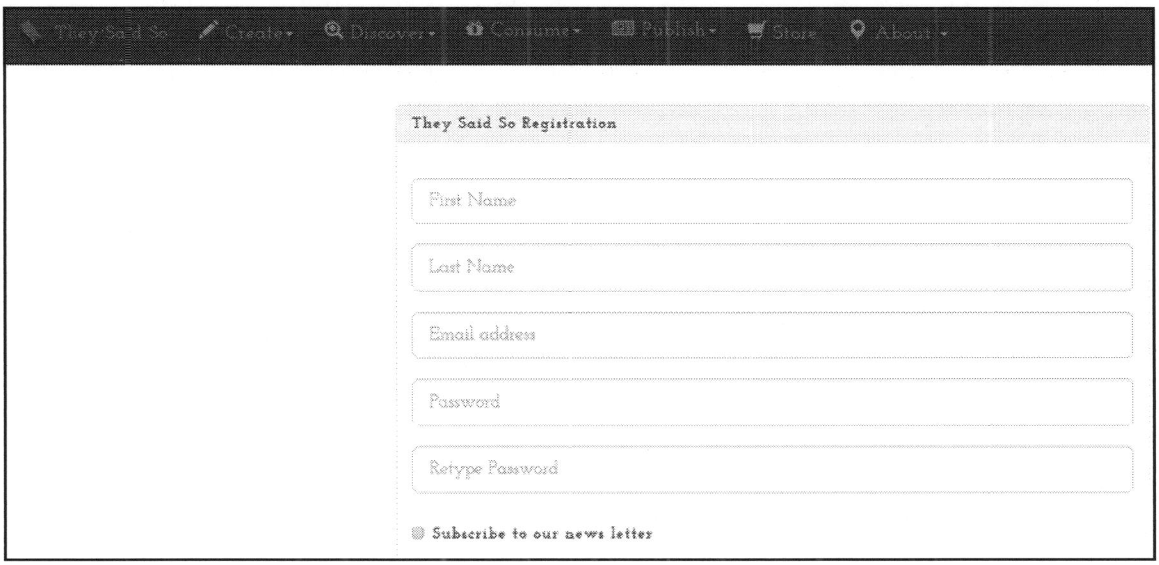

Once you have entered your details and have registered, you will receive an automated verification e-mail, which will look like this:

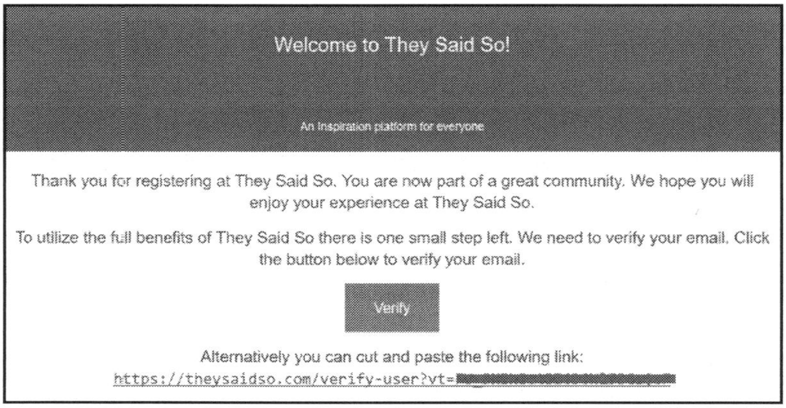

When you receive this, simply click on the **Verify** button in order to validate your newly registered account and start enjoying the service.

Once you've done that, you will shortly receive this e-mail:

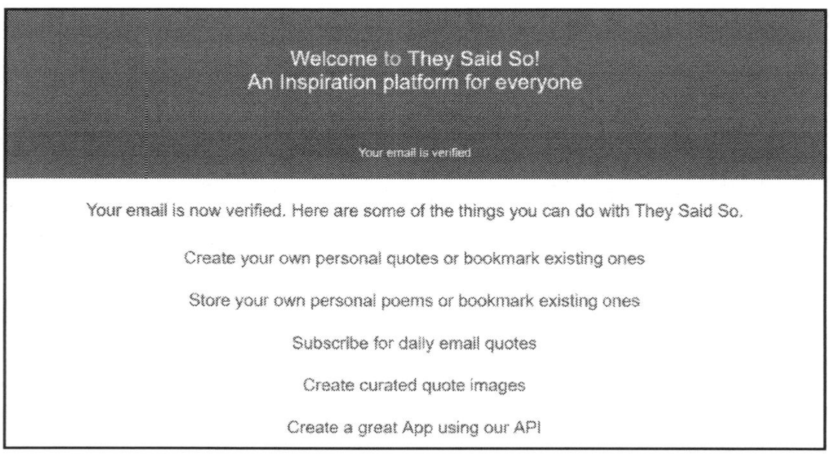

The next step is to subscribe to the Quotes API in order to start consuming it. This can be done by visiting the following URL: `https://theysaidso.com/api/#subscribe` or alternatively clicking on the **Create a great App using our API** link from the e-mail received.

When you open this, scroll to the very bottom of the page and you will see the following API subscription plans on the screen.

In our case, because we are building a demo application, we won't sign up for any specific paid plan, but instead we'll consume the API through **Mashape** (`https://market.mashape.com/orthosie/they-said-so-say-it-with-style/`).

Mashape is a service that helps developers deliver better APIs and microservices. Many third-party APIs are provided through Mashape or similar services.

However, if you wish to get a paid plan, you may **Sign Up** for any of the paid API options that the service offers. The advantage of doing this is that you won't need to sign on to Mashape in order to consume the API.

So when we use the API through Mashape, we can click on the **Consume API** button at the bottom of the screen.

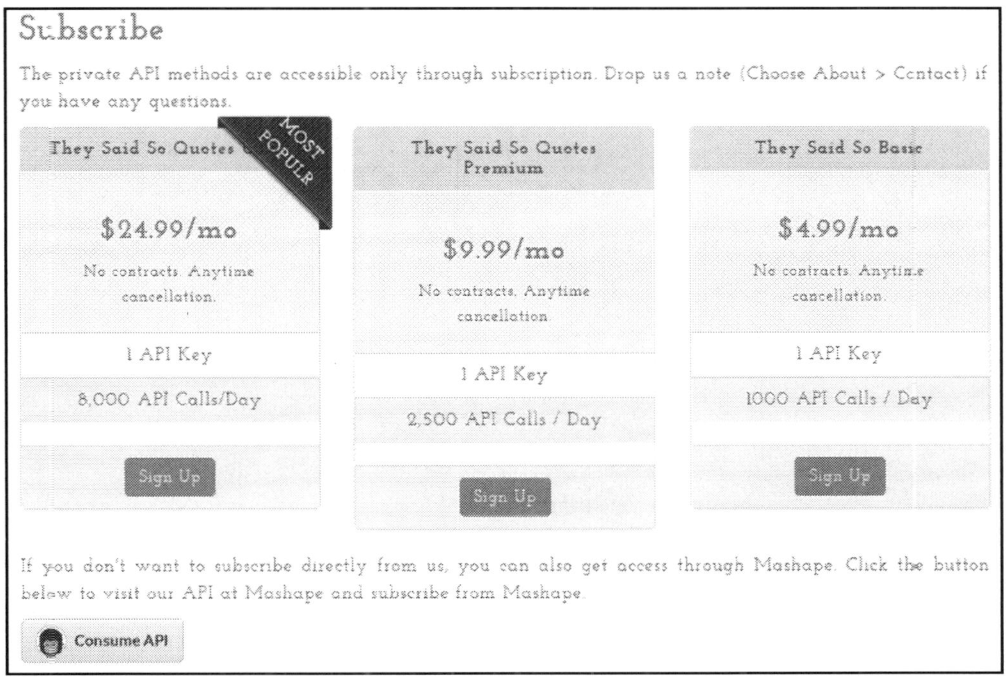

When we click on that button, the next thing we'll see is the following screenshot. Once there, click on the **PRICING** tab.

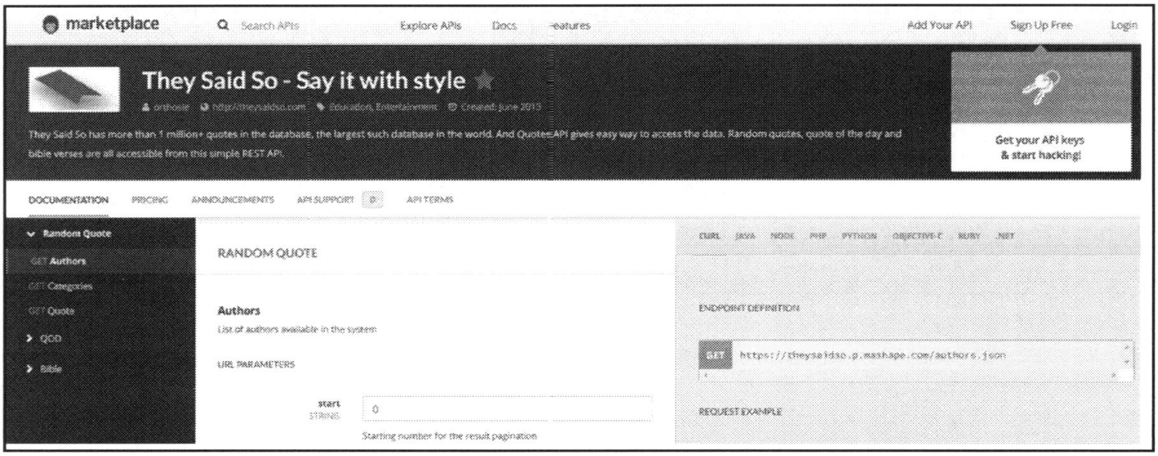

On the **PRICING** tab, under the **BASIC** plan, click on the **SUBSCRIBE** button.

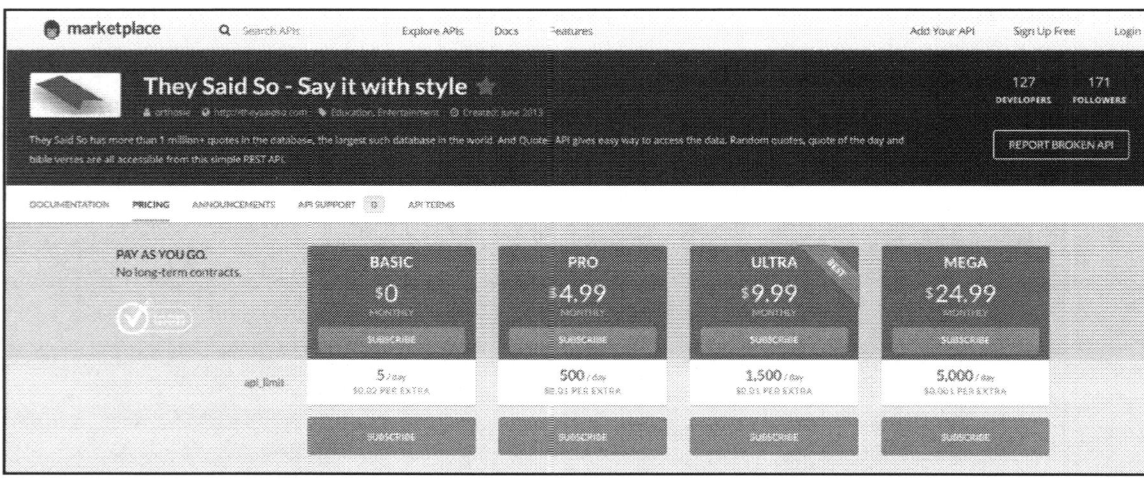

When you click on the **SUBSCRIBE** button, you'll see the following pop-up screen:

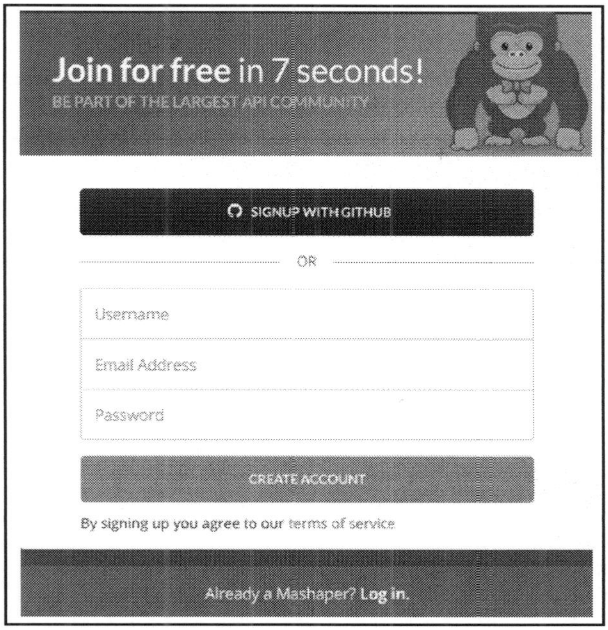

If you have a GitHub or Mashape account, you can simply subscribe to the API by logging into the service with any of those accounts. Otherwise you will have to create an account on Mashape.

The process anyway is very easy and straightforward. Once that's been done, we are ready to start exploring the API and consuming it. You'll see this on your screen:

Simply click on the **Explore public APIs** button and then hit the back button on your browser or navigate to this URL: `https://market.mashape.com/orthosie/they-said-so-say-it-with-style/` to start exploring the API. So let's do that.

From the API, we are interested in the quotes section. We can look at this by clicking on the **GET Quote** link on the left side of the screen.

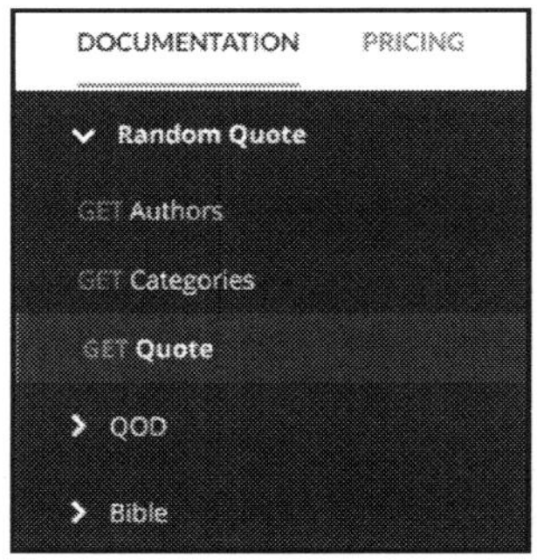

This will take us to the following page, where we can see how to construct an API call in order to get a quote:

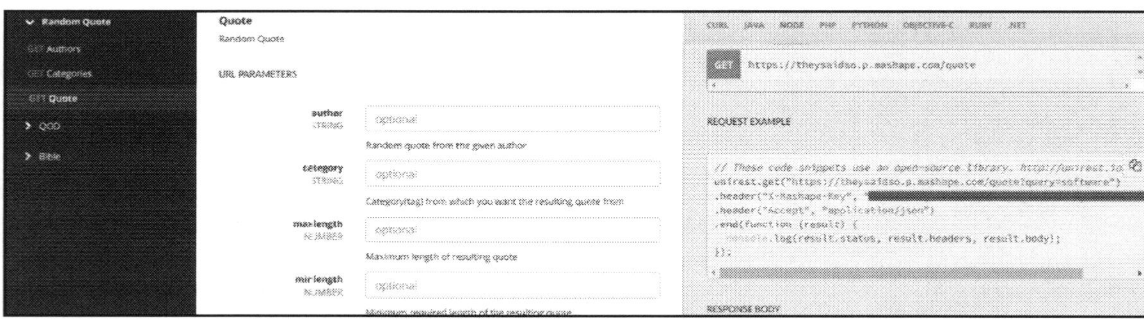

There are also multiple examples in various programming languages, including Node.js, which uses the Unirest library (`http://unirest.io/`) to make HTTP requests. In our application, we'll be using the Request library instead (`https://www.npmjs.com/package/request`).

Notice how on all the sample code, including the Node.js one mentioned on the **GET Quote** documentation page, the API Token key is passed on the header of the HTTP request as the value of the `X-Mashape-Key` parameter.

So let's see how we would be able to write a small example on how to retrieve a quote using the Request library.

Let's create a new file called `TestRequest.js` so we don't mix up this test code with the main quotebot code that we have started to write using `App.js`:

```
var rq = require('request');

var token = 'Your They Said So API Key';

GetQuote = function() {
  var options = {
   url: 'https://theysaidso.p.mashape.com/quote?query=software',
   headers: {
      'User-Agent': 'request',
      'X-Mashape-Key': token
   }
  };

  rq(options, function (error, response, body) {
    if (!error && response.statusCode == 200) {
      console.log(body);
    }
  })
};

GetQuote();
```

Before you can run this, make sure you are subscribed to the **BASIC** plan, which includes five calls per day. You will still have to enter a credit card number, which will be billed if you go over five requests per day.

You can always unsubscribe on this URL: `https://market.mashape.com/orthosie/they-said-so-say-it-with-style/pricing` by clicking on the **Unsubscribe** link under the **BASIC** plan.

Now you may run this script from the command line as follows:

```
Node TestRequest.js
```

This produces the following result:

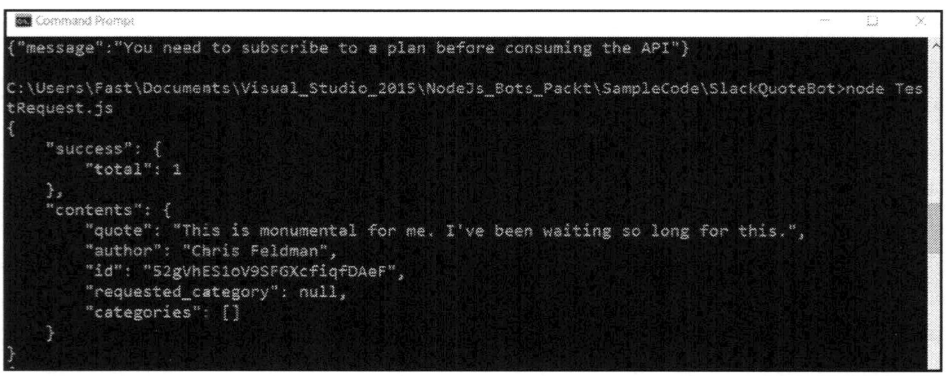

Now that we know how to interact both APIs, we can expand the basic code we initially wrote in order to create a full blown quotebot.

In our previous code snippet, we used the start event. Going forward, we'll also need the message event, which will be used to intercept an incoming message and based on that reply back.

We need to have a function that will intercept every real-time API message that is readable by our bot. This includes pretty much every chat message in any channel where the bot has been installed, and also private messages directed to the bot or other real-time notifications, such as a user typing in a channel, edited or deleted messages, users joining or leaving the channel, and so on.

Real-time API messages are not just chat messages, but any kind of event that occurs within our Slack organization. This is important to keep in mind.

Ideally, we would like the bot to filter all these events to detect public messages in channels that mention getquote or the name of the bot, and then we want to react to this message by replying with a random quote, fetched from the API we have subscribed using Mashape.

Ideally, we want to divide all these checks in a list of operations; this is exactly what we need to do. These are:

- Verify if the event represents a chat message
- Verify if the message comes from a user that is different from quotebot (to circular references and loops)
- Verify if the message mentions getquote

The code would look as follows:

```
onMessage = function (msg) {
    if (isChatMsg(msg) &&
        !isFromQuoteBot(msg) &&
        isMentioningQuote(msg)) {
        replyWithRandomQuote(bot, msg);
    }
};
```

The `onMessage` function receives an `msg` object as a parameter. The `msg` contains all the information that describes the real-time event received through the Slack Real Time API.

Now let's look at each helper function, one by one:

```
isChatMsg = function (msg) {
    return msg.type === 'message';
};
```

This function verifies if a real-time event corresponds to an `msg` sent by a user. With our first helper function in place, let's have a look at the second one:

```
isFromQuoteBot = function (msg) {
    return msg.username === 'quotebot';
};
```

This helper function allows us to see if the `msg` comes from a user who is not the quotebot itself.

Last but not least, our final helper function checks if messages contain the string `getquote`. Without this verification we could potentially end up with an infinite loop of quotes:

```
isMentioningQuote = function (msg) {
    return msg.text.toLowerCase().indexOf('getquote') > -1;
};
```

With all the helper verification functions done, our random quote reply back method would look like this:

```
replyWithRandomQuote = function (bot, oMsg) {
  var options = {
   url: 'https://theysaidso.p.mashape.com/quote?query=software',
   headers: {
      'User-Agent': 'request',
      'X-Mashape-Key': token
   }
  };
  rq(options, function (error, response, body) {
    if (!error && response.statusCode == 200) {
      bot.postMessageToChannel(bot.channels[0].name, body);
    }
  })
};
```

Finally, we tie it all together by passing the `onMessage` callback to the listening event as follows:

```
bot.on('message', onMessage);
```

The full code looks like this.

```
var Bot = require('slackbots');
var rq = require('request');

var token = ' YOUR MASHAPE API TOKEN ';

var settings = {
```

```
    token: 'YOUR SLACK API TOKEN',
    name: 'quotebot'
};

var bot = new Bot(settings);

isChatMsg = function (msg) {
    return msg.type === 'message';
};

isFromQuoteBot = function (msg) {
    return msg.username === 'quotebot';
};

isMentioningQuote = function (msg) {
    return msg.text.toLowerCase().indexOf('getquote') > -1;
};

replyWithRandomQuote = function (bot, oMsg) {
  var options = {
    url: 'https://theysaidso.p.mashape.com/quote?query=software',
    headers: {
      'User-Agent': 'request',
      'X-Mashape-Key': token
    }
  };
  rq(options, function (error, response, body) {
    if (!error && response.statusCode == 200) {
      bot.postMessageToChannel(bot.channels[0].name, body);
    }
  })
};

bot.on('message', function (msg) {
    if (isChatMsg(msg) &&
        !isFromQuoteBot(msg) &&
        isMentioningQuote(msg)) {
        replyWithRandomQuote(bot, msg);
    }
});
```

In order to see this in action, simply message quotebot with the text `getquote` on Slack:

Once you do that, you will receive the following feedback on the **#general** channel:


```
{
  "success": {
    "total": 1
  },
  "contents": {
    "quote": "It is my deliberate opinion that the one essential requisite of human welfare in all ways is scientific knowledge of human nature.",
    "author": "Harriet Martineau",
    "id": "cxYewykgu64xGRQhw_hyQeF",
    "requested_category": null,
    "categories": [
      "humannature",
      "nature"
    ]
  }
}
```


That's awesome! Notice, however, that we have returned the full body response.

This could be further optimized and you could eventually parse the body response and just output the quote and the author, without any of the other details.

This is totally up to you and a nice exercise in order to improve this code. Further to this, you could also add additional code in order to process natural language, interpret more commands, and also to respond to different channels.

The possibilities are frankly endless and all that is needed is time, imagination, and dedication. We leave the challenge open for you to further expand and explore.

Summary

We've seen briefly how Slack is a great collaboration platform and also how incredibly easy it is to interact with its real-time API.

In a matter of minutes, you can have a small demo bot up and running.

In the following chapters, we'll explore other interesting platforms that are also quite popular nowadays and this should also be a lot of fun to play around with.

I hope you have enjoyed following these examples and the upcoming chapters will touch upon other fascinating topics. Keep having fun!

5
Telegram-Powered Bots

Telegram (`https://telegram.org/`) is a free, cloud-based mobile and desktop messaging app. Telegram takes us into a new era of messaging, which focuses primarily on security and the speed of the message delivery.

Telegram has clients for platforms including Windows, OS X, Linux 64 bit, and Linux 32 bit. The Telegram messaging app is available for use as a web version too. When it comes to mobile devices, Telegram has native apps for Android, iOS, and Windows Phone.

With Telegram, you can send messages, photos, videos, and files of any type (doc, zip, mp3, and many more); and you can create groups for up to 5,000 people, or channels for broadcasting your messages and media.

One of the great things about Telegram is that Telegram messages are encrypted and can be set to self-destruct. While chatting or messaging, for those who want more privacy and secrecy, Telegram has secret chats. This means only you and the recipient can see these messages; nobody else can see them, including Telegram. Such messages from this secret chat cannot be forwarded and, more importantly, when you delete such messages from your side, Telegram secret chat also deletes the messages from the other side as well.

In this chapter, we'll explore how to use Telegram. Also, we'll look at how we can build a Telegram powered bot that will act like a virtual assistant for us. This virtual assistant will provide information about the sentiments of our Telegram messages.

Sounds great!! Let's get started.

How a Telegram bot works

A Telegram bot is a special account that does not require an additional phone number to be set up. Users can interact with these bots in two ways:

- Send messages and commands to bots by opening a chat with them, or by adding them to groups. This means of communication is used for typical chat bots.
- Send requests directly from the input field by typing the bot's username and a query. These are called inline bots.

Such bots can enhance Telegram chats with content from external sources, can alert or notify you about news and translations, and can provide relevant information to you. Bots can even connect like-minded people looking for conversation partners within Telegram.

Technically, Telegram bots are third-party applications running inside Telegram. When a user sends a message to a Telegram bot, Telegram's intermediary server takes care of the encryption and communication with the help of Telegram bot APIs.

In this chapter, we will focus on chatting conversations (text interaction) by opening a chat with our bot and not calling it, with our Telegram bot.

Setting up a Telegram account

So far, we are just talking about Telegram and bots within it. In this section, we will actually start setting up our own Telegram account, followed by an account for our Telegram chat bot.

I am using the web version of Telegram to create my own account first. Open the browser window and enter the URL `https://web.telegram.org/#/login`. This will launch a **Sign in** screen, as shown in the following screenshot:

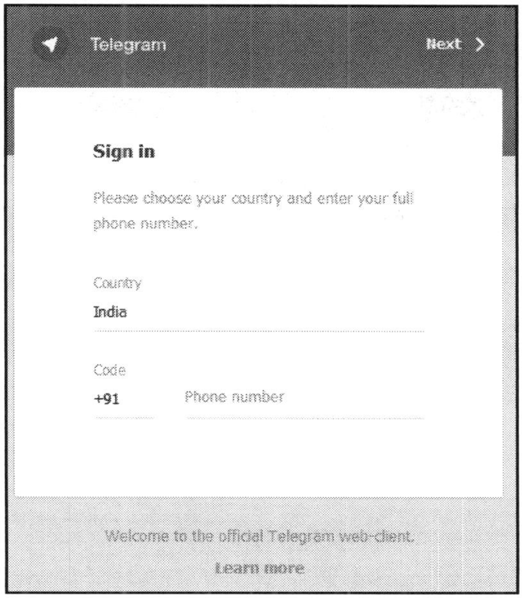

Provide your **Country**, **Code**, and **Phone number**. Click on the **Next >** link in the top-right corner to launch the next step, as shown in the following screenshot:

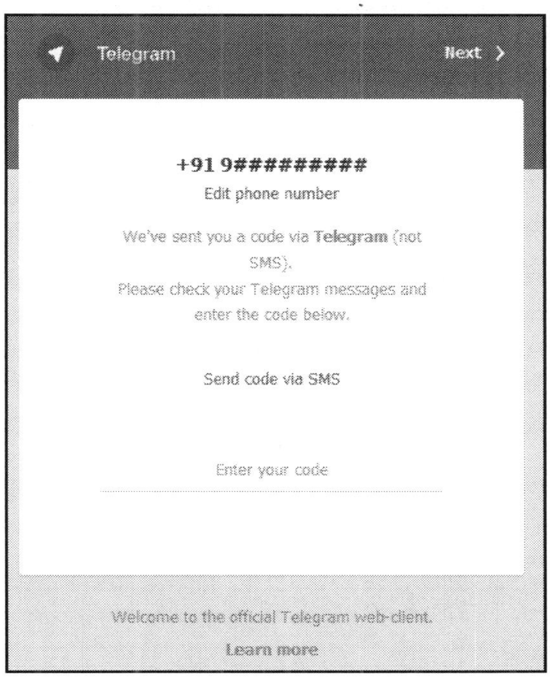

Enter the SMS code you have received, in the space provided, and you are set for your own account for Telegram. Once you enter your profile details, you can start messaging with the help of the following screen:

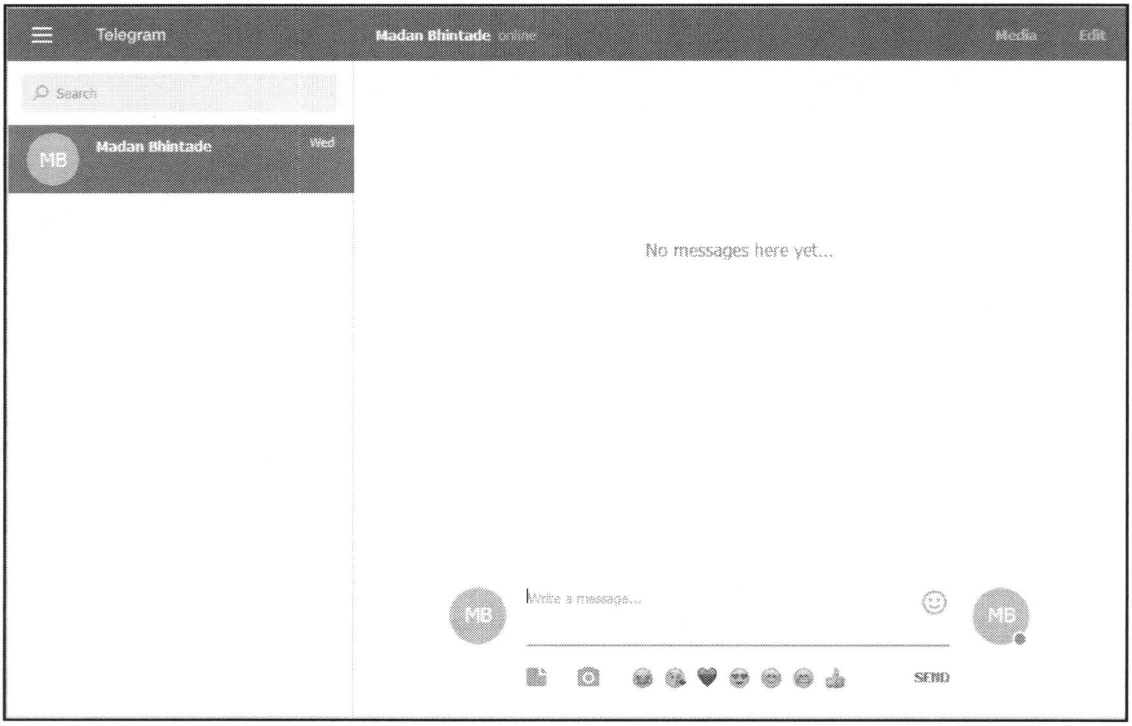

With this, we have now set up our own Telegram account. You can start messaging your colleagues, and search for them as well. In the next section, we will start building Telegram powered bots.

Setting up a bot account using a Telegram bot – @BotFather

Sounds confusing! But this is the easiest way to start with Telegram bots. As I mentioned, Telegram bots are special accounts and, to set up these accounts, we will be using another Telegram bot named *BotFather*.

This is the awesome technique that Telegram has specially provided for developers to create their own bots. Here, we can see the capability of one bot that helps us in creating other bots.

Let's search for `@Botfather` and add it for our conversations, or you can directly open the URL `https://telegram.me/botfather` to start conversations with BotFather. To start, BotFather will introduce itself and will display a **START** button at the bottom for the user.

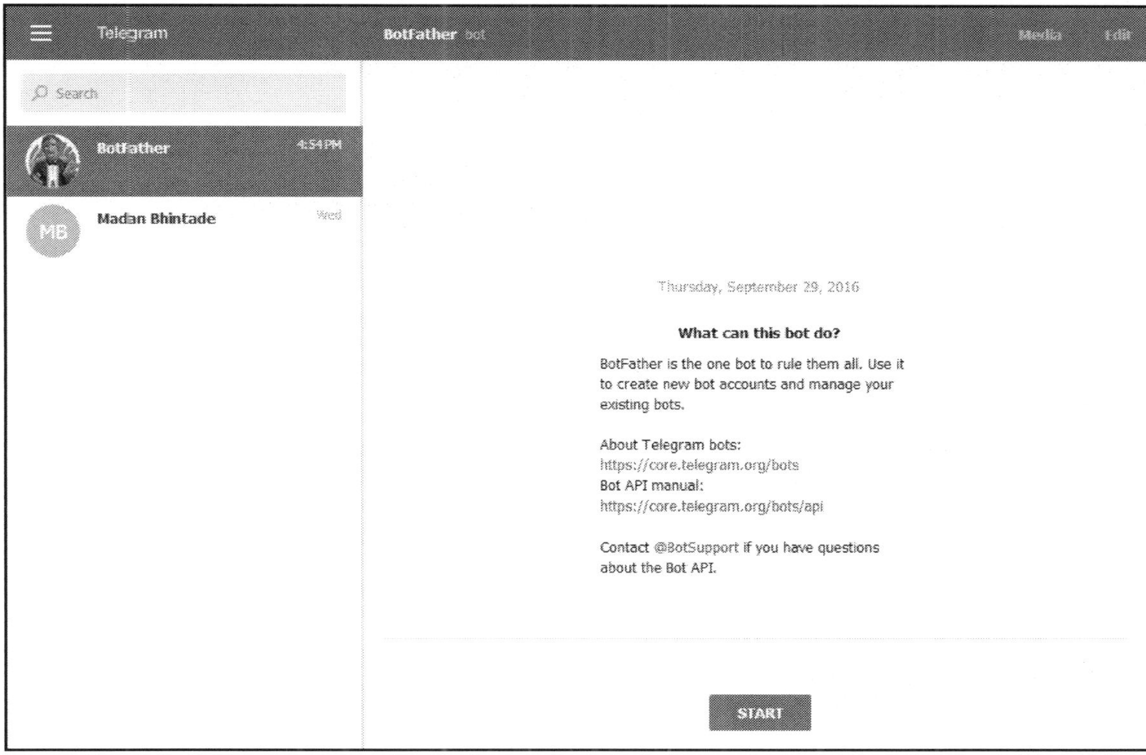

Once you click on the **START** button, **BotFather** will provide you with all the commands that can be used for creating a new bot, as shown in the following screenshot:

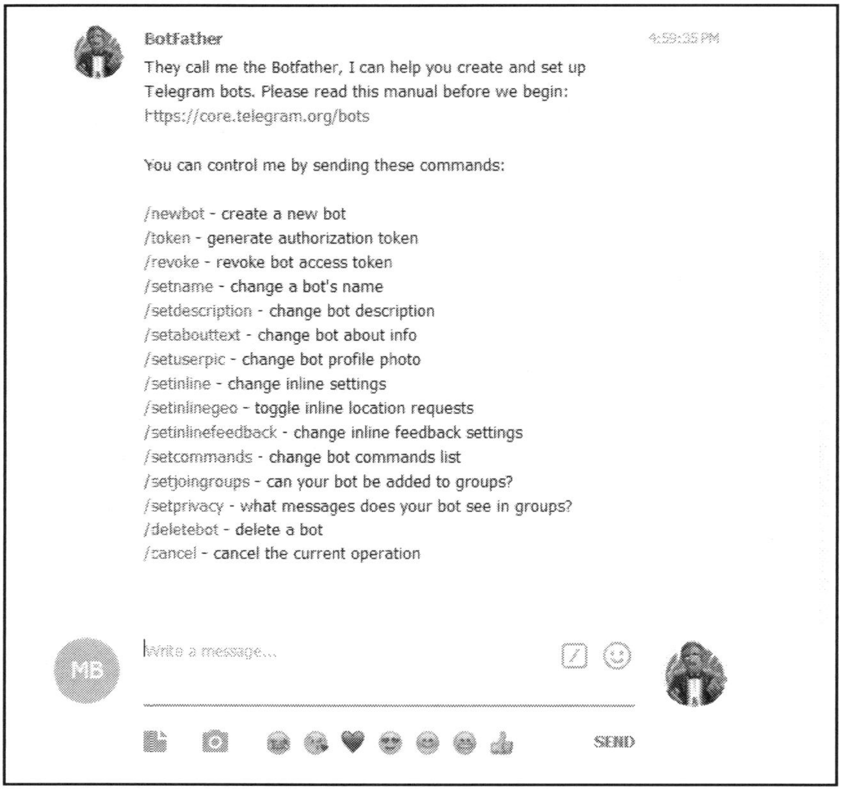

Now, let's click on link **/newbot** from our conversation with BotFather. With this command, BotFather will ask us to choose a name for our bot.

Let me choose the name `MadansNewTelegramBot`. BotFather internally validates whether the name is available. If it is available, BotFather asks for a username for the newly created bot. I have provided a username for my bot. Refer to the following conversations for the same:

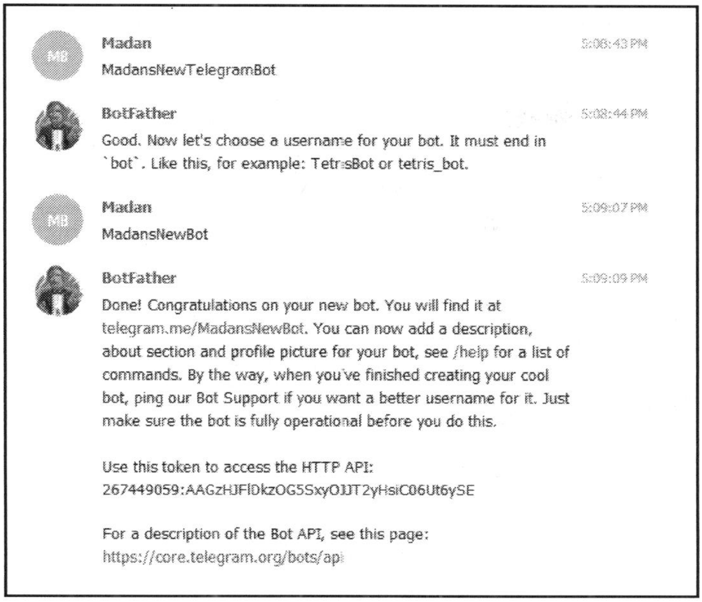

With this, BotFather has created our bot and has also provided a token for our bot. This token will be used while wiring up our bot with Telegram bot APIs.

Now we can use this bot for conversations using the URL `telegram.me/MadansNewBot` or by searching for the name of the bot in the search field, as shown in the following screenshot:

After searching once, you select the bot for further conversations.

To summarize the steps carried out so far, we've created our own account at Telegram and also created a basic Telegram bot using BotFather. Our first Telegram bot will be a no-brain bot as there is no intelligence built within it.

In the next section, we will actually build some basic intelligence with the help of Node.js We will build a bot that will tell us the sentiments of our messages. But what is sentiment analysis? Let's spend some time in understanding sentiment analysis.

What is sentiment analysis?

In simple words, sentiment analysis is simply classifying a given term or a sentence as positive, negative, or neutral. This is also known as opinion mining or deriving the attitude of the person who is writing or speaking.

In relation to Telegram, sentiment analysis can be extremely useful for media monitoring and extracting opinions on some public topics.

Sentiment analysis can be achieved with approaches such as knowledge-based techniques, statistical methods, and a combination of both. Knowledge-based techniques classify text based on words' affinity to particular emotions, such as happy, sad, and so on. Statistical methods leverage elements of machine learning.

When representing the sentiments of a term or a sentence, words having a negative, neutral or positive sentiment to them are given an associated number on a scale of -10 to +10, and the level of sentiment or the score is determined at term or at sentence level.

Considering the scope of this book, we are keeping the sentiment analysis topic quite short.

Creating a Telegram bot

Now, let's see how we can use Node.js and Telegram bot APIs in order to create our basic Telegram bot. In the previous chapter we've seen how to get Node.js installed. For our Telegram bot, we'll follow a very similar process.

Let's start by creating a folder in our local drive from the command prompt in order to store our bot:

```
mkdir telegrambot
cd telegrambot
```

Assuming we have Node.js and npm installed (if not, please refer to the steps in Chapter 1, *The Rise of Bots – Getting the Message Across*), let's create and initialize our `package.json`, which will store our bot's dependencies and definitions:

```
npm init
```

Once you have gone through the `npm init` options (which are very easy to follow), you'll see something similar to this:

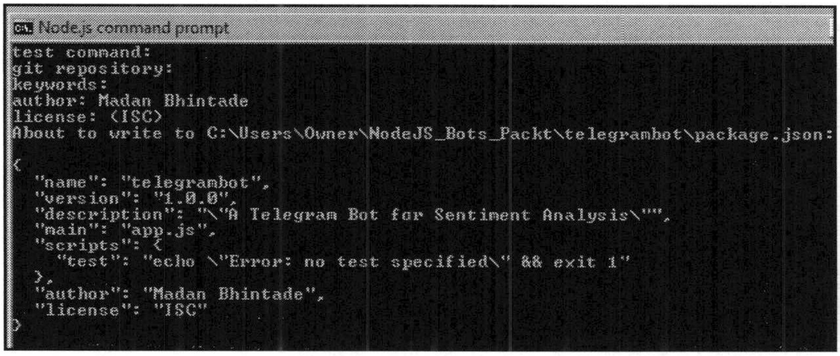

In your project folder, you'll see the result, which is your `package.json` file.

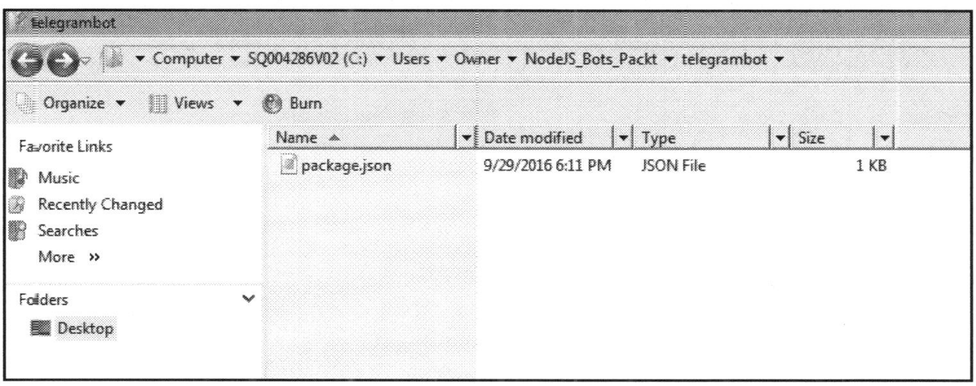

Just like we did in our previous example, we will use **Express** (`http://expressjs.com`) as our **REST** Node.js framework. We'll install it and save it to our `package.json` file as follows:

```
npm install express --save
```

Once Express has been installed, you should see something like this:

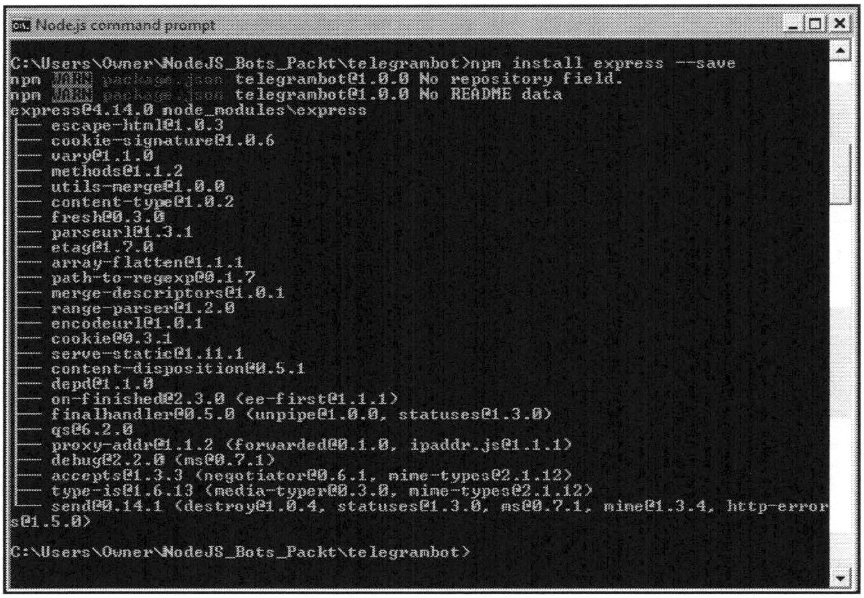

With Express setup, the next thing to do is to install the `node-telegram-bot-api` package. This can be located at `https://www.npmjs.com/package/telegram-bot-api`.

In order to install it, run this npm command:

```
npm install node-telegram-bot-api --save
```

You should then see something similar to this:

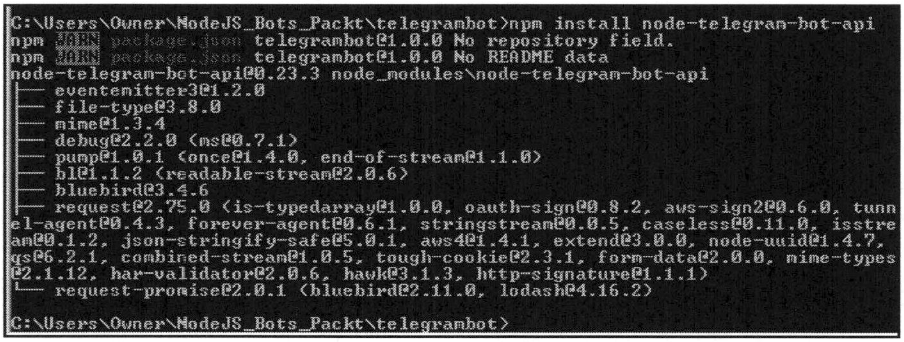

Having done this, the next thing to do is to update your `package.json` in order to include the `"engines"` attribute. Open the `package.json` file with a text editor and update it as follows:

```
"engines": {
    "node": ">=5.6.0"
}
```

Your `package.json` should then look like this:

```
{
  "name": "telegrambot",
  "version": "1.0.0",
  "description": "\"A Telegram Bot for Sentiment Analysis\"",
  "main": "app.js",
  "scripts": {
    "test": "echo \"Error: no test specified\" && exit 1"
  },
  "author": "Madan Bhintade",
  "license": "ISC",
  "dependencies": {
    "express": "^4.14.0"
  },
  "engines":{
    "node":">=5.6.0"
  }
}
```

With our bot all wired up, we can then focus on creating the core logic for our conversations with the bot. Let's create our `app.js` file, which will be the entry point to our bot.

Our `app.js` should like this:

```
var telegramBot = require('node-telegram-bot-api');

var token ='267449059:AAGzHJFlDkzOG5SxyOJJT2yHsiC06Ut6ySE';

var api = new telegramBot(token, {polling: true});

api.onText(/\/help/, function(msg, match) {
  var fromId = msg.from.id;
  api.sendMessage(fromId, "I can help you in getting the sentiments of any
text you send to me.");
});

api.onText(/\/start/, function(msg, match) {
  var fromId = msg.from.id;
  api.sendMessage(fromId, "They call me MadansFirstTelegramBot. " +
    "I can help you in getting the sentiments of any text you send to me."+
    "To help you i just have few commands.\n/help\n/start\n/sentiments");
```

```
});

console.log("MadansFirstTelegramBot has started. Start conversations in
your Telegram.");
```

Now let's look at the code snippet line by line. The first thing we do is to reference the node package we previously installed using npm.

```
var telegramBot = require('node-telegram-bot-api');
```

Once we have our reference set up, we are now connected to our bot. Remember, BotFather has provided a token to our bot for accessing Telegram bot APIs; we will be referring to the same token here, as shown in the following screenshot:

```
var token ='267449059:AAGzHJFlDkzOG5SxyOJJT2yHsiC06Ut6ySE';
var api = new telegramBot(token, {polling: true});
});
```

Now we have a handle to interact with our bot, through the token and bot APIs. Let's see how we can start the conversation with our bot. To start a bot, Telegram bots use the command `/start`. On entering the start command, my bot should introduce itself and also ask us how he can help us. This is achieved using the following code snippet:

```
api.onText(/\/start/, function(msg, match) {
  var fromId = msg.from.id;
  api.sendMessage(fromId, "They call me MadansFirstTelegramBot. " +
    "I can help you in getting the sentiments of any text you send to me."+
    "To help you i just have few commands.\n/help\n/start\n/sentiments");
});
```

This basically tells our bot that if a user sends the command `/start`, our bot will send message in response to that with the help of `api.onText()` method.

Now let's run our Node.js program to start our conversation with the bot.

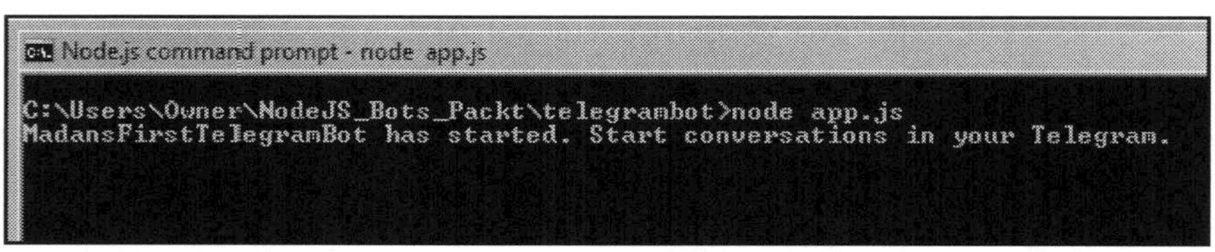

Now let's launch the Telegram web version for your own account.

Conversations with our basic Telegram bot

Search our newly created and Node.js wired bot using its name, as shown in the following screenshot:

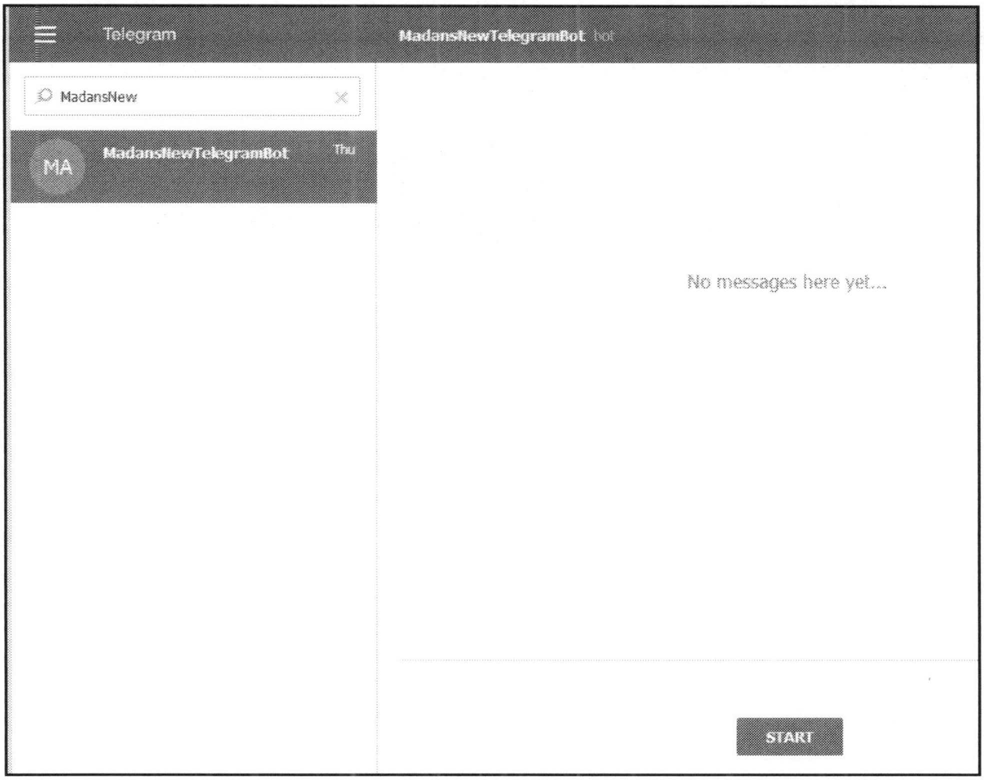

Click on the **START** button, and the `/start` command will be sent to our bot to start the conversation. Once you've done that, you'll see our bot has responded to the `/start` command. Refer to the following screen:

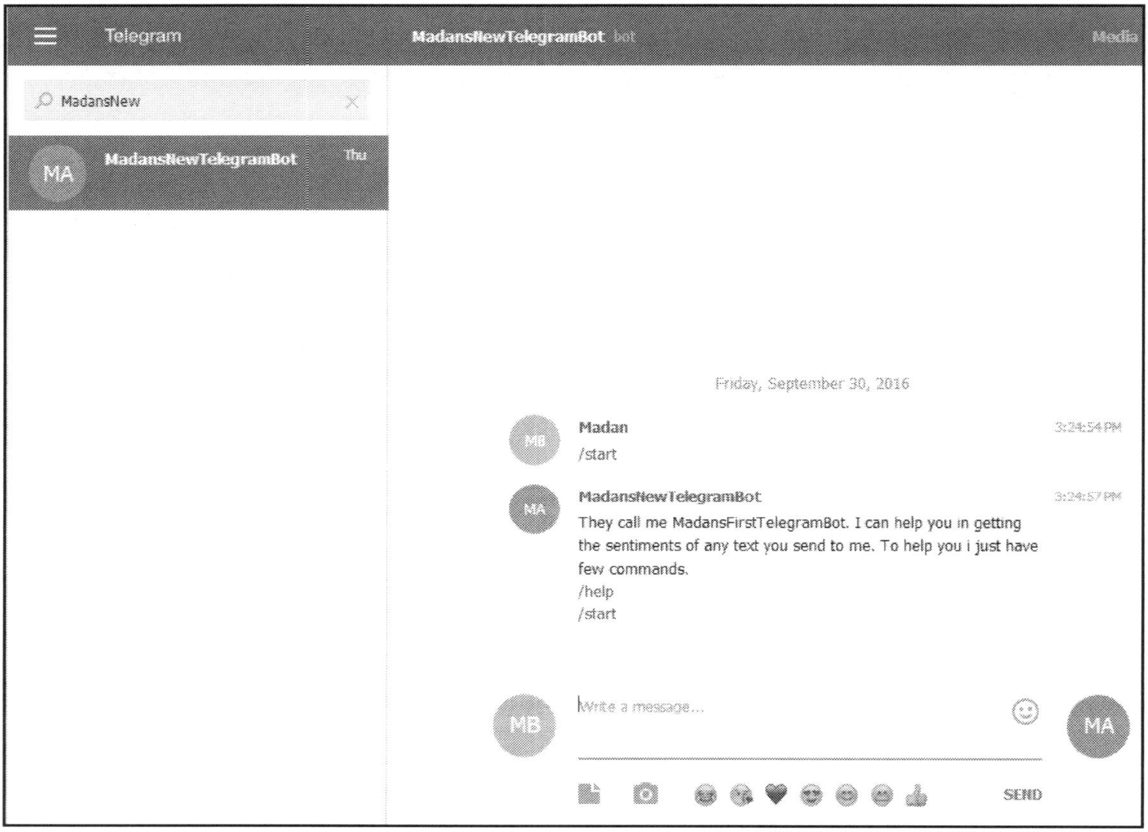

So, whatever we have written for the `/start` command in our `app.js` has executed and, through the Telegram bot APIs, the response is shown to us.

Now let's click on the **/help** command or type in `/help` for our bot. Our bot will respond to the `/help` command with following response, which we have wired into our Node.js program.

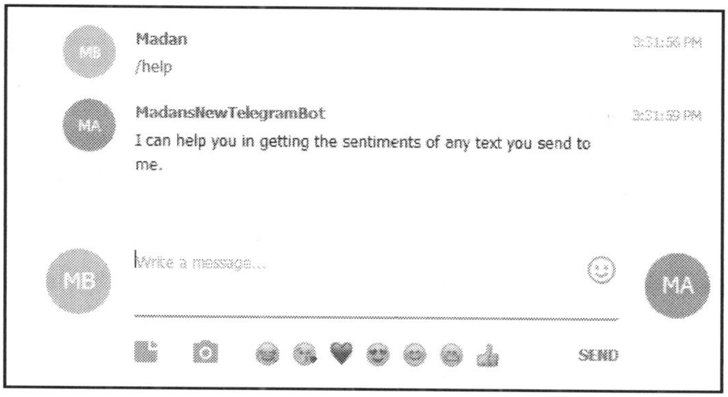

Since our Node.js program from `app.js` is running behind the scenes, our bot is responding to our commands based on what has been programmed in `app.js`.

Building a sentiment analysis bot

Having built a very basic Telegram bot, let's build a sentiment analysis bot for Telegram. Within the context of Telegram, bots would be useful for content or media monitoring. Bots can actually classify terms or sentences that Telegram users are sharing with others. Knowing this, we will build a sentiment analysis bot using Node.js.

For sentiment analysis, we will be using the sentiment package for Node.js. Sentiment is a Node.js module that uses the AFINN-111 wordlist to perform sentiment analysis on an input text. This package can be located at `https://www.npmjs.com/package/sentiment`.

In order to install it, let's determine our code location:

```
cd C:\Users\Owner\NodeJS_Bots_Packt\telegrambot
```

And then run this npm command:

```
npm install sentiment --save
```

You should then see something similar to this:

With this, we are ready to wire up our Node.js code to use the sentiment analysis package. Let's open our Node.js code and include the following code line:

```
var sentiment = require('sentiment');
```

As we know, our bot has many commands, such as `/start` and `/help`; on similar lines, we have an additional command for doing sentiment analysis. This command is `/sentiments`.

The idea here is that, once you send the command `/sentiments` to our bot, the bot will confirm your intentions and will ask you to send a term or a sentence. Upon receiving a term or a sentence, the bot will carry out sentiment analysis with the help of the sentiment package that is wired up in our Node.js program. Then bot will reply with the sentiment analysis score.

Our updated `app.js` should look like this:

```
var telegramBot = require('node-telegram-bot-api');
var sentiment = require('sentiment');

var token ='267449059:AAGzHJFlDkzOG5SxyOJJT2yHsiC06Ut6ySE';

var api = new telegramBot(token, {polling: true});

api.onText(/\/help/, function(msg, match) {
  var fromId = msg.from.id;
  api.sendMessage(fromId, "I can help you in getting the sentiments of any
text you send to me.");
});

api.onText(/\/start/, function(msg, match) {
  var fromId = msg.from.id;
  api.sendMessage(fromId, "They call me MadansFirstTelegramBot. " +
    "I can help you in getting the sentiments of any text you send to me."+
    "To help you i just have few commands.\n/help\n/start\n/sentiments");
});

var opts = {
  reply_markup: JSON.stringify(
    {
      force_reply: true
    }
  )};

//sentiment command execution is added here
api.onText(/\/sentiments/, function(msg, match) {
  var fromId = msg.from.id;
  api.sendMessage(fromId, "Alright! So you need sentiments of a text from
```

```
me. "+
      "I can help you in that. Just send me the text.", opts)
    .then(function (sended) {
      var chatId = sended.chat.id;
      var messageId = sended.message_id;
      api.onReplyToMessage(chatId, messageId, function (message) {
        //call a function to get sentiments here...
        var sentival = sentiment(message.text);
        api.sendMessage(fromId,"So sentiments for your text are, Score:" +
sentival.score +" Comparative:"+sentival.comparative);
      });
    });
});

console.log("MadansFirstTelegramBot has started. Start conversations in
your Telegram.");
```

Now let's look at the updated `app.js` code.

Firstly, we have added a reference to the sentiment package in our basic bot code as follows:

```
var sentiment = require('sentiment');
```

We also modified the `/start` command to include the new command `/sentiments`.

Then we added the actual logic of what should happen when the `/sentiments` command is sent to the bot. Upon firing up this command, the bot will confirm the intention and will ask you to send some text, a term or a sentence using the following code line:

```
api.sendMessage(fromId, "Alright! So you need sentiments of a text from me.
"+
  "I can help you in that. Just send me the text.", opts)
```

Once we send some text to a bot, the bot will reply to our message with the sentiment analysis of the text that has been sent. This particular logic is as follows:

```
api.onReplyToMessage(chatId, messageId, function (message) {
     //call a function to get sentiments here...
     var sentival = sentiment(message.text);
     api.sendMessage(fromId,"So sentiments for your text are, Score:" +
       sentival.score +" Comparative:"+sentival.comparative);
   });
```

In the preceding code, once the bot receives a text, a call to the `sentiment()` function is made and text is passed as `message.text` to get the sentiment.

Sentiments are returned in an object called `sentival`. This `sentival` object has both score and comparative values for the sentiment of the text that has been passed. These values are returned to the user using the following code lines:

```
api.sendMessage(fromId,"So sentiments for your text are, Score:" +
sentival.score +" Comparative:"+sentival.comparative);
```

Now let's run our Node.js program to start our conversation with the bot.

Now our updated code is running, let me also start my Telegram web version and start a conversation with my updated bot.

I have already searched for and added my bot. The screen should look like this:

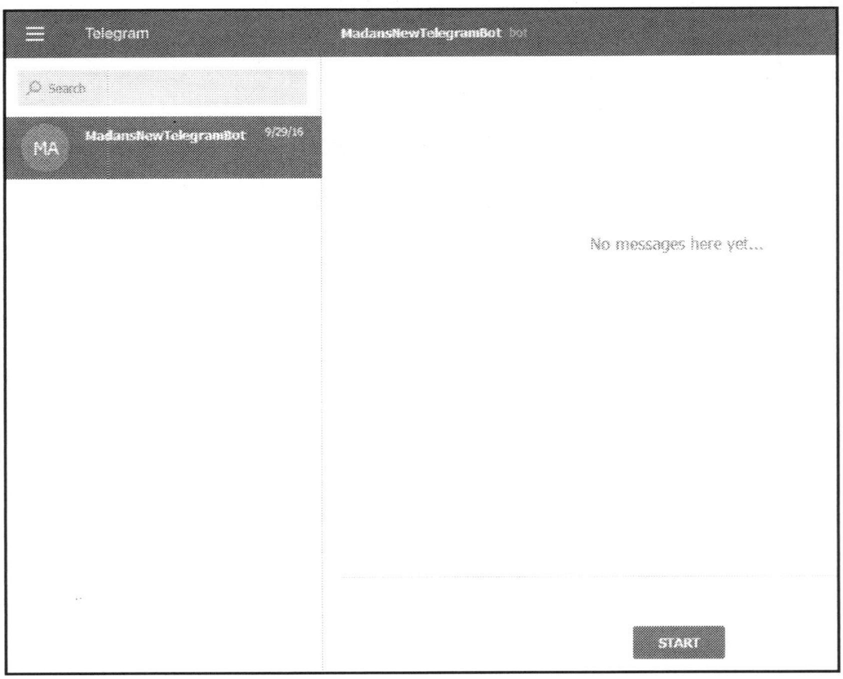

Click on the **START** button, and the `/start` command will be sent to our bot to start the conversation. Once you've done that, you'll see our bot has responded to the `/start` command. The `/start` command's response is also updated with a mention of the newly added command `/sentiments`. Refer to the following screen:

Click on the **/sentiments** link from the response from the `/start` command. This will send a `/sentiments` command to our bot and the bot will respond as follows:

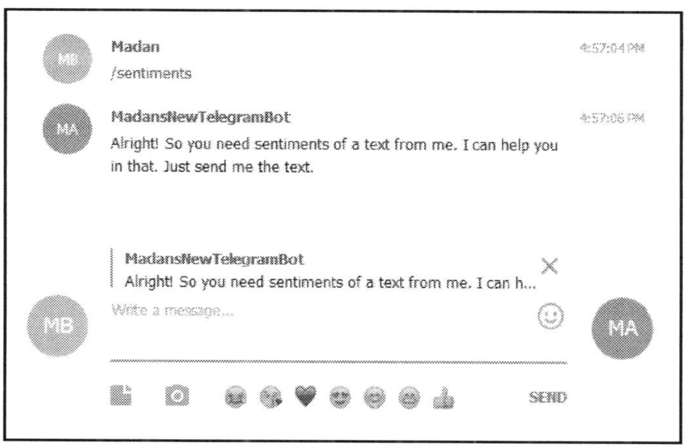

So, here, the bot is asking the user to send text as a message; in response to that, the bot will share the sentiment of the message sent by the user. Now let's write the message `Bots are awesome!` in **Write a message...**, and hit enter or click **SEND**. Do not close the message from the bot, which is shown as a small popup with a close button.

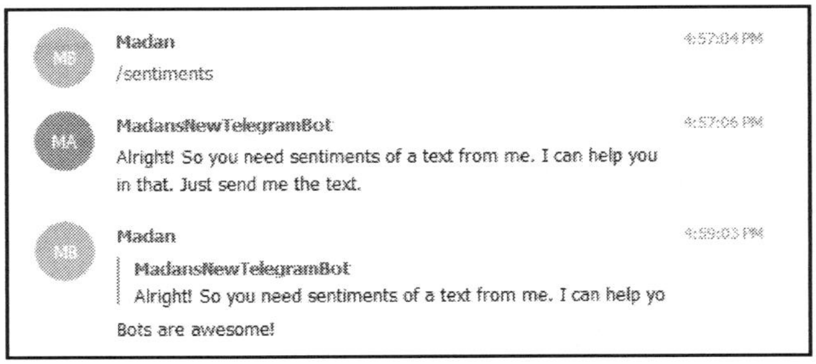

Immediately, the bot will respond with the score and the comparative value for the sentiment of your text, as follows:

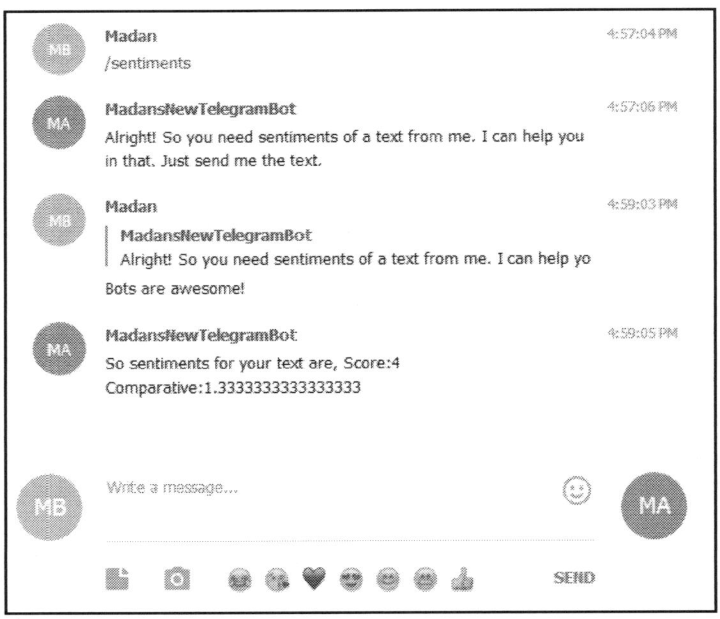

So, we entered the text `Bots are awesome!` and, in response to that, the bot sent us a sentiment **Score:4** and **Comparative:1.33**. For the text sent to the bot, with the score value coming in as positive, the bot is showing us a positive opinion.

Now to get the sentiment for a new term, again send a `/sentiments` command to our bot.

The bot will again confirm the intentions, and will ask us to share some text. Now let's send the text `The food was very bad.` and see what bot returns.

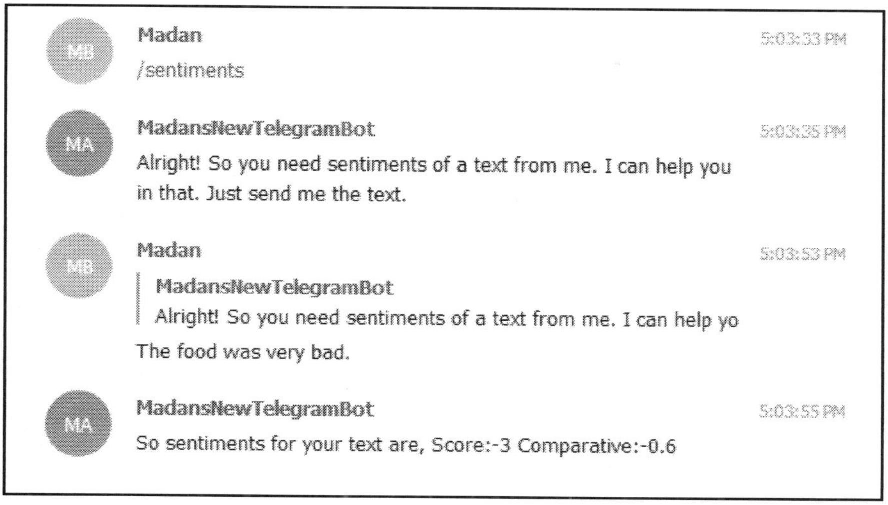

We entered the text `The food was very bad.` In response to that, the bot sent us a sentiment with **Score:-3** and **Comparative:-0.6**. This way, the bot is showing us a negative opinion here from the text.

Summary

We have had an interesting journey learning how to build a Telegram bot and how we can have a great conversational experience with the intelligence built in to it.

To summarize, we have seen how to create a Telegram account if you are new to Telegram. Further to that, we have also used an interesting way to create our own bot, using BotFather. BotFather is a Telegram bot that rules all the other Telegram bots.

After creating our bot, we wired it in to the Node.js program using the npm package and built some basic intelligence for our bot chat.

Finally, we wanted our bot to provide sentiment analysis, so we looked at the very basics of sentiment analysis. To carry out sentiment analysis, we used the npm package for sentiment analysis and enriched our basic bot to provide us with sentiment analysis. Our bot is mainly of the type that needs a chat session opening and then leverages the bot functionalities by sending it commands. There is also another Telegram bot type, which is the inline bot. Exploring Telegram inline bots further is left with the reader.

Hopefully, this chapter has given you some insight on Telegram bots, and how we can enhance them using Node.js and Telegram bot APIs to provide an enhanced conversational experience within Telegram. In the next chapter, we will explore how to build a Slack bot. For those who do not know Slack, Slack is simply a real-time messaging app specifically for team collaboration. We will actually be building a bot for Slack, which will help us to locate documents in the document repository based on the user's request.

Keep exploring further.

6

BotKit – Document Manager Agent for Slack

In `Chapter 4`, *A Slack Quote Bot*, we saw how Slack is a great collaboration platform. While collaborating, teams can get the inspirational quotes from *They Said So* services right in their Slack channels. In this chapter, we will see a use case for Slack that's a little more complex than just getting quotes. Here, we will be building a Slack bot called DocMan bot with the help of **Howdy BotKit**. DocMan bot should be able to search document(s) and also provide a link to download them, based on team members' requests.

Our Slack bot, DocMan, will be built using MongoDB for data storage and Amazon S3 for research document or file storage. Details about MongoDB and Amazon S3 storage will be detailed in the following sections of this chapter.

Awesome!! Let's Slack now.

Setting up a Slack for your team

In this section, we will start setting up Slack for a team.

Open the browser window and enter the URL–`https://slack.com`. This will launch the Slack home page as shown in the following screenshot:

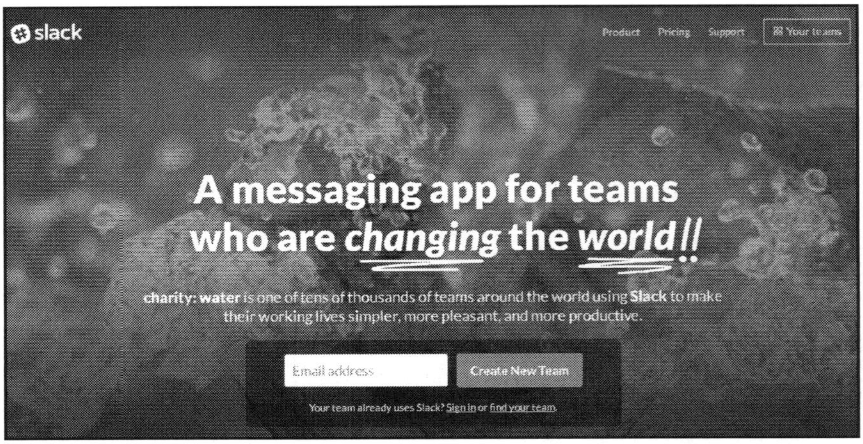

For users who are accessing Slack for the first time, you will first have to create your Slack account and then you can create your team. Users who are already on Slack can click on the **Sign in** link. Let's look at how to create our own account.

Provide your e-mail address at **Email address**. Click on the **Create New Team** link to launch the next step, as shown in the following screenshot. Slack will send a confirmation code to your e-mail id. Enter the received code.

Enter your confirmation code. The code will be verified by Slack and then the following screen will be launched:

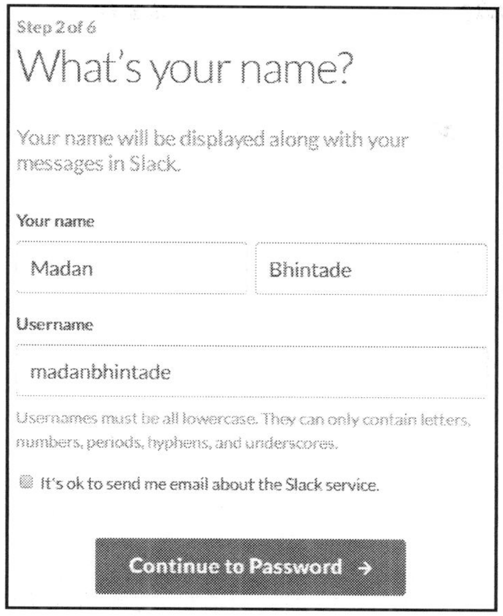

Provide your name and username in the fields **Your name** and **Username,** and click on the **Continue to Password** button to launch the following screen:

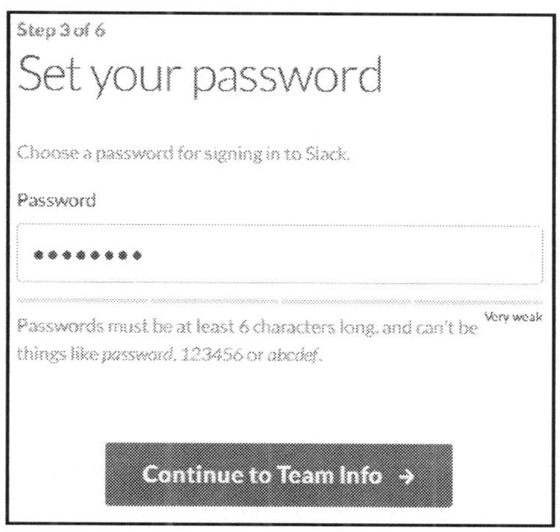

Provide your password at **Password** and click on the **Continue to Team Info** button to launch the following screen:

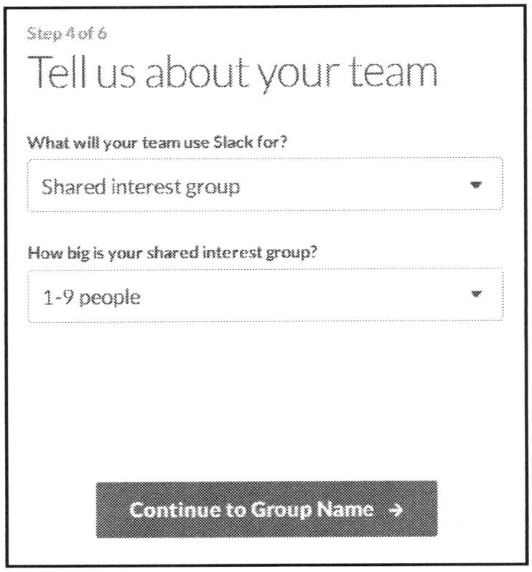

Choose the options that match your team's purposes and intentions in the **What will your team use Slack for?** and **How big is your shared interest group?** dropdowns. Click on the **Continue to Group Name** button to launch the following screen:

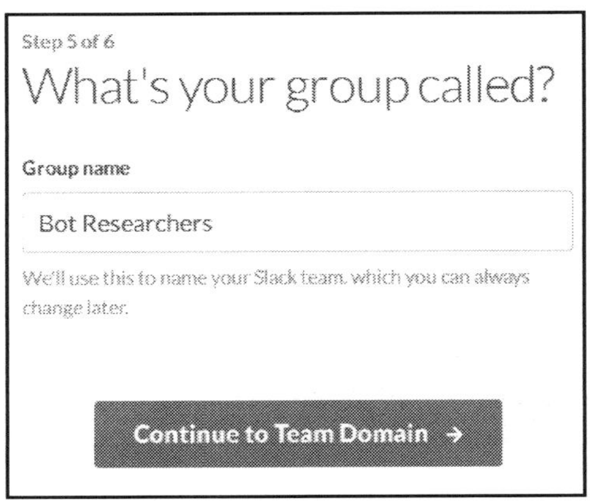

I wanted to name my team Bot Researchers, so I entered the name as **Bot Researchers** in the **Group Name** entry field and clicked on the **Continue to Team Domain** button to launch the following screen:

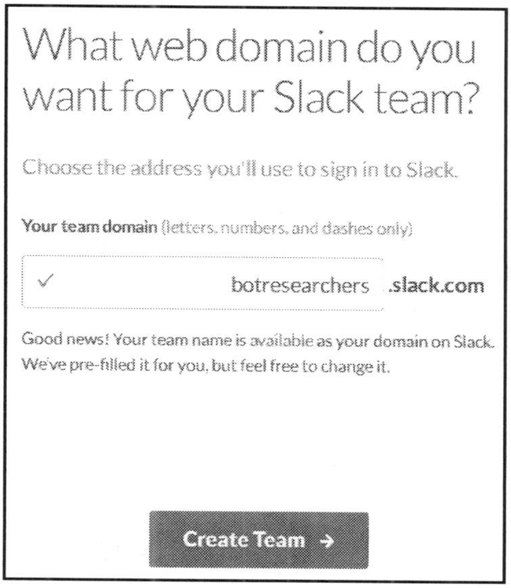

Slack verifies the domain name availability for your team. If it is available, then it shows a message saying so, as shown in the preceding screenshot. Now click on the **Create Team** button.

The next screen is **Send Invitations**, which I will be skipping for now, going straight to the welcome screen for the Bot Researchers Slack team. The screen will appear as shown in the following screenshot:

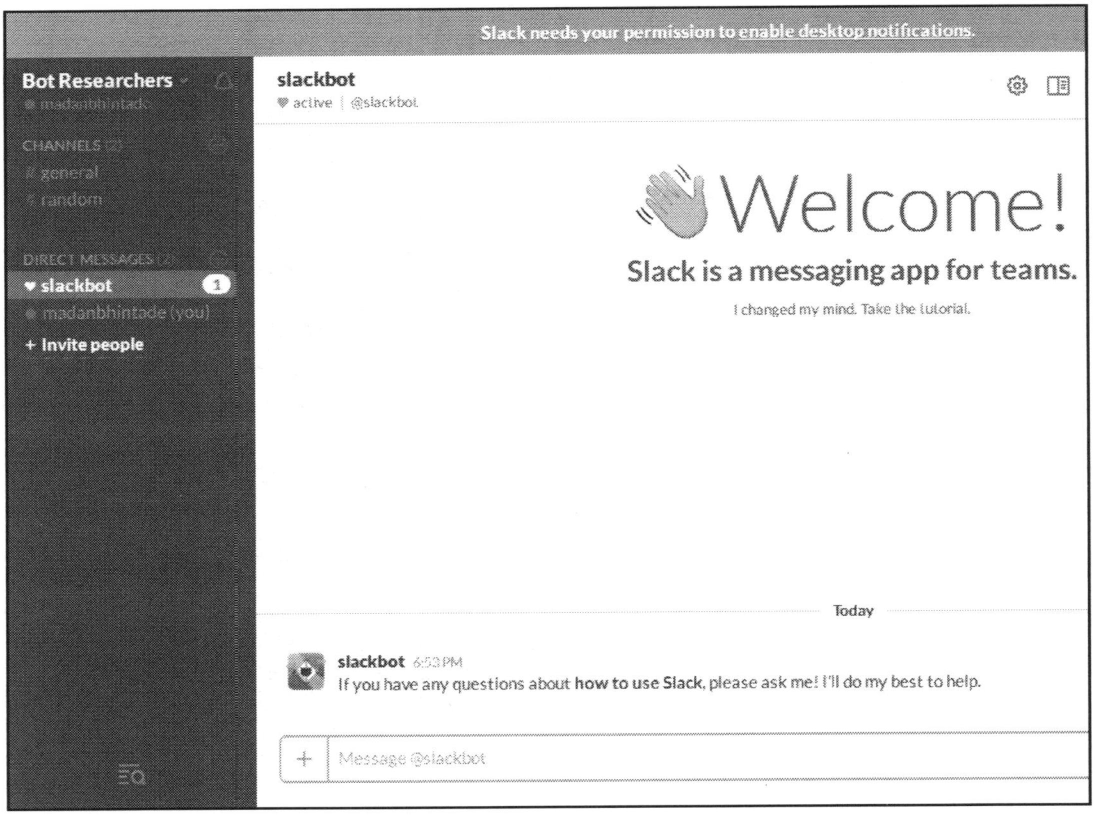

In the preceding screenshot, you might have noticed the name **slackbot**. Slack uses a bot named slackbot to greet us and help us in case of any questions. This is a wonderful use of bots to educate users in the chatting window itself.

We have now signed up with Slack and created our own team. Now we will develop our bot for this team.

Setting up a Slack bot

As a botresearcher group member, I would like my bot to provide information about all bot-related documents. This bot is called **DocMan**. Now, to create a new bot in Slack, just visit the website found at `https://botresearchers.slack.com/services/new/bot`.

Make sure you are already logged in to your Slack group. Here I have logged in to my group, `https://botresearchers.slack.com`. Since you are already logged in, this will navigate to the **Bots** | **New Configuration** screen, as shown in the following screenshot:

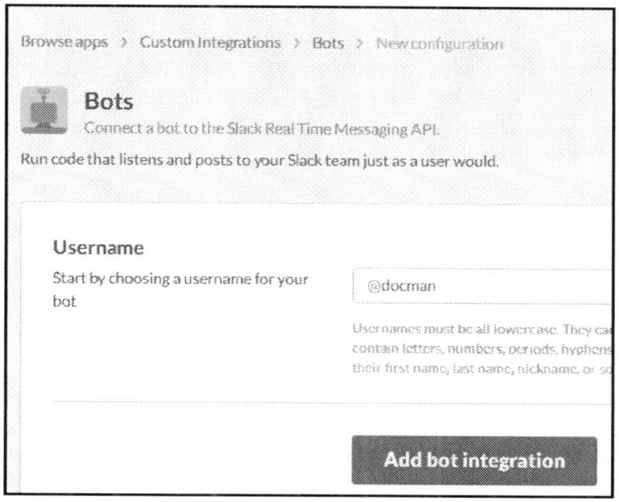

Let's enter the **Username** as `@docman` and then click on the **Add bot integration** button. Slack will ask for additional configuration information for this bot, as shown in the following screenshot:

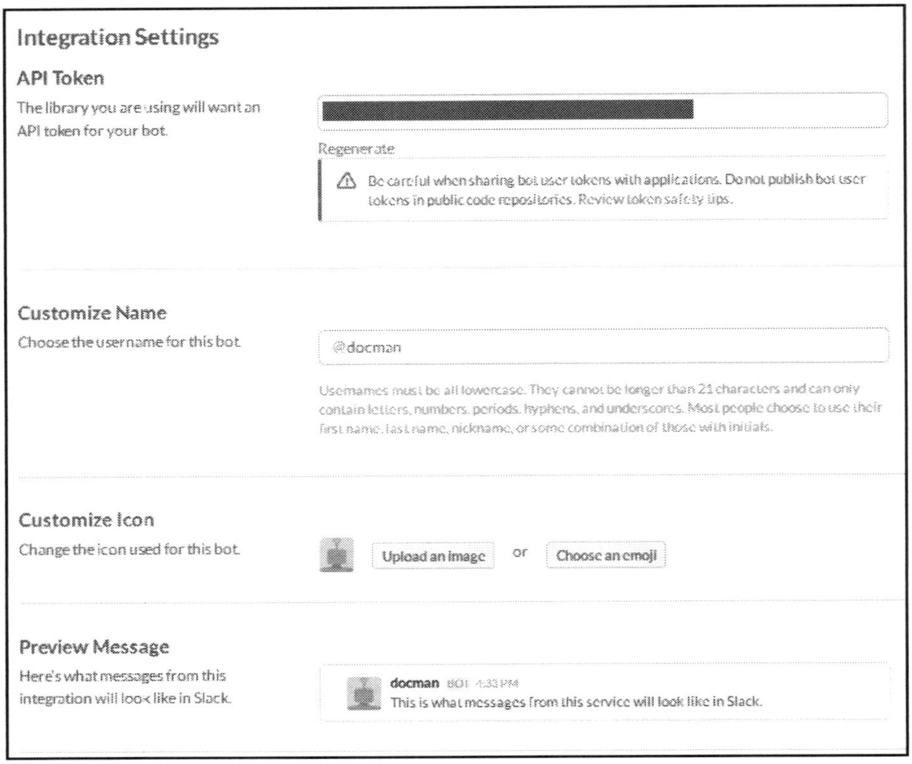

Look at the **API Token** section, under **Integration Settings**. Our bot will use this token to communicate with APIs.

The bot user token can connect to real-time streaming APIs and can perform activities, such as posting messages, so the distribution of this token should be avoided in public code repositories.

Refer to the following screenshot. You can enter the parameters of this bot's behavior within Slack channels in the **What this bot does** entry field:

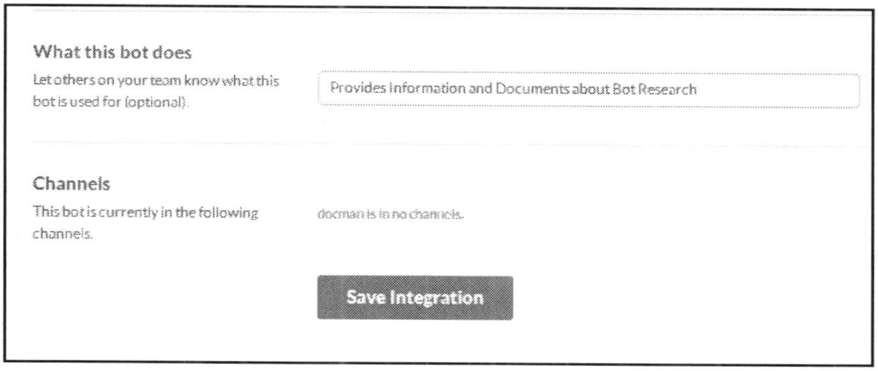

Here, I have entered **Provides Information and Documents about Bot Research**.

Now click the **Save Integration** button to save the configuration information of our bot. The information will be saved and the user will be notified at the top of the screen.

Now let's go back to our group by using the URL `https://botresearchers.slack.com/messages`. You will see **docman** under the **DIRECT MESSAGES** section. Click on the name **docman** to see a chat message screen, as shown in the following screenshot:

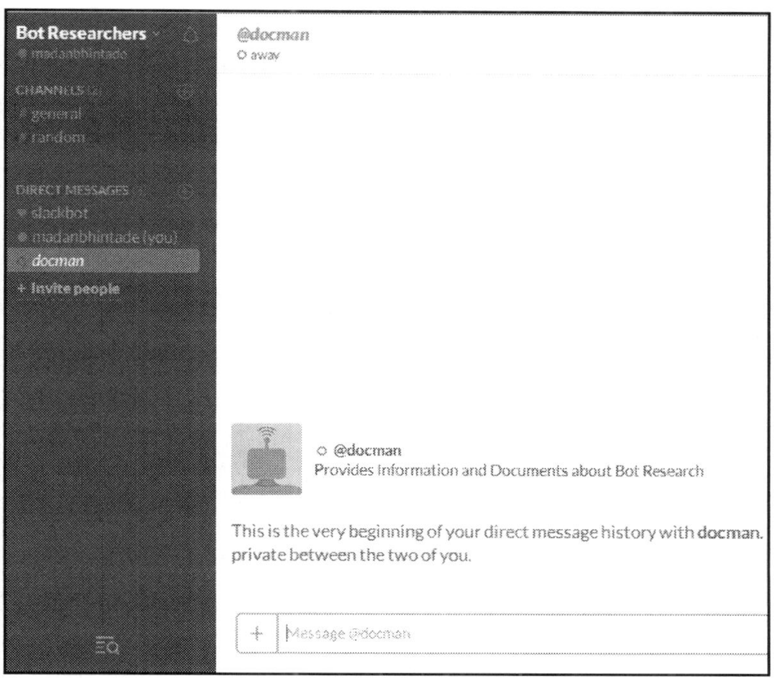

Now, our bot is showing its username as **@docman** and the description as **Provides Information and Documents about Bot Research**. We provided this information during its configuration. At the moment, this bot will not respond to any of our messages as it is not programmed yet. Also, the status of the bot is set to **away**.

To summarize so far, we have created our own Slack group and created our own Slack bot. We also looked at how to configure this bot. In the next section, we will see how we can wire up some intelligence to our bare bones bot.

Botkit and Slack

Botkit is a free to use, open source toolkit from **Howdy** (`https://howdy.ai/botkit`) for integrating bots with messaging platforms such as Slack. Botkit comes with lots of features that help developers build both types of bot integrations, for individual teams as well as for other teams using *Slack Button*.

Creating our first Slack bot using Botkit and Node.js

Let's start wiring up our bot in Node.js by first installing Botkit.

Let's start by creating a folder in our local drive in order to store our Bot from the Command Prompt:

```
mkdir slackbot
cd slackbot
```

Assuming we have Node.js and NPM installed, let's create and initialize our `package.json`, which will store our Bot's dependencies and definitions:

```
npm init
```

Once you go through the `npm init` options (which are very easy to follow), you'll see something similar to the following screenshot:

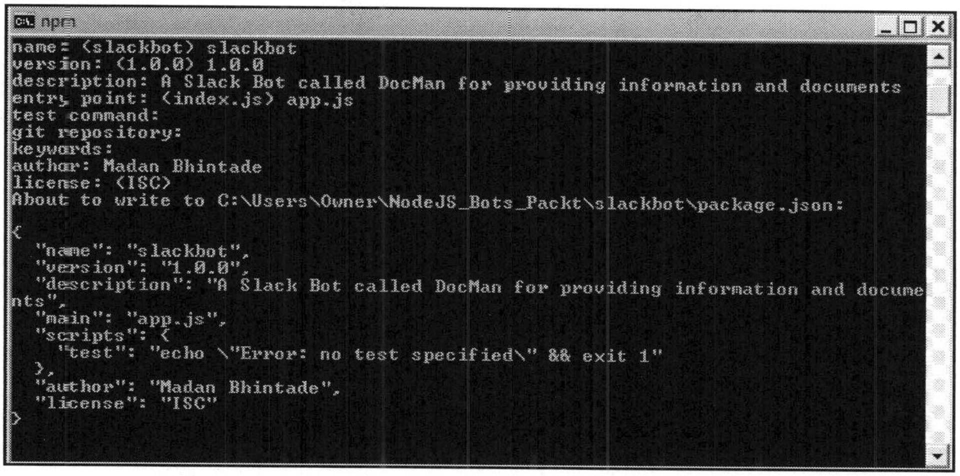

You'll see the result in your project folder; this is your `package.json` file:

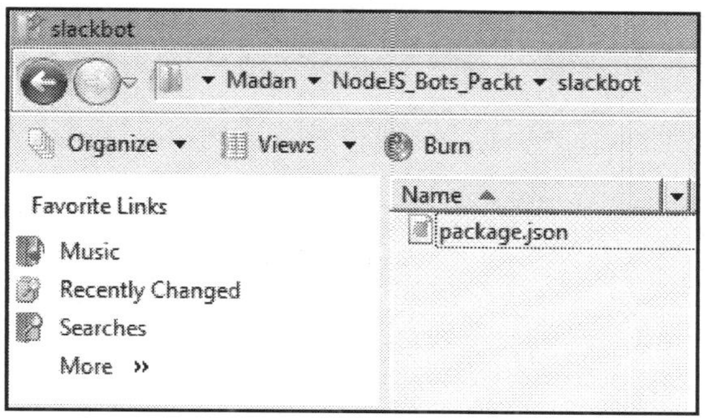

Let's install the `botkit` package from NPM. This can be located at `https://www.npmjs.com/package/botkit`.

In order to install it, run this `npm` command:

```
npm install --save botkit
```

You should then see something similar to this:

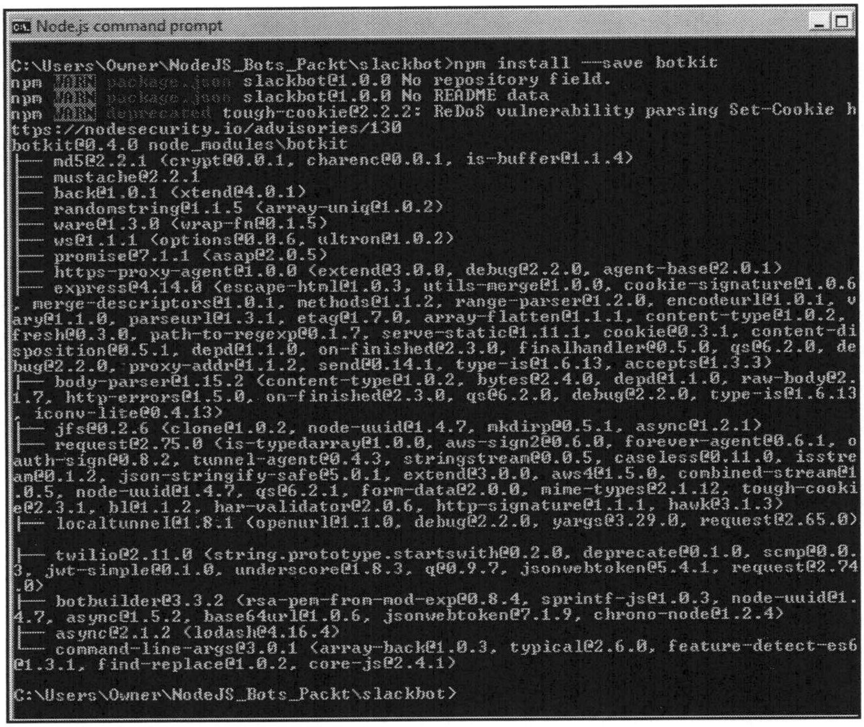

Having done this, the next thing to do is to update your `package.json` in order to include the `"engines"` attribute. Open the `package.json` file with a text editor and update it as follows:

```
"engines": {
    "node": ">=5.6.0"
}
```

Your `package.json` should then look like this:

```
package.json | app.js
{
  "name": "slackbot",
  "version": "1.0.0",
  "description": "A Slack Bot called DocMan for providing information and documents",
  "main": "app.js",
  "scripts": {
    "test": "echo \"Error: no test specified\" && exit 1"
  },
  "author": "Madan Bhintade",
  "license": "ISC",
  "dependencies": {
    "botkit": "^0.4.0"
  },
  "engines": {
    "node": ">=5.6.0"
  }
}
```

Let's create our `app.js` file, which will be the entry point for our bot, as mentioned while setting up our node package.

Our `app.js` should like the following code snippet:

```
var Botkit = require('Botkit');
var os = require('os');

var controller = Botkit.slackbot({
    debug: false,
});

var bot = controller.spawn({
    token: "<SLACK_BOT_TOKEN>"
}).startRTM();

controller.hears('hello',['direct_message','direct_mention','mention'],func
tion(bot,message) {
  bot.reply(message,'Hello there!');
});
```

Remember, our bot DocMan is still not active, and its status is away, which we have seen in our Slack group.

Now let's run our Node.js program to see how it looks in Slack, and start our basic conversations with our bot:

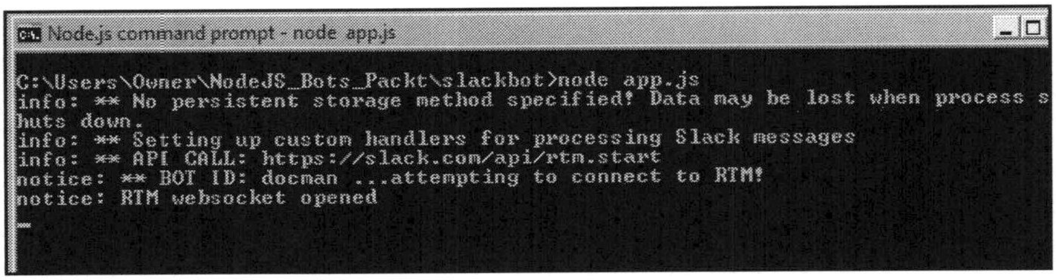

Now, if you look at the console, you will see, with the help of the token, that our bot has started communicating with Real-Time Messaging APIs through a websocket.

Let's look at our Slack group now. Our Slack group will now show our bot **@docman** under **DIRECT MESSAGES** with an active status, as shown in the following screenshot:

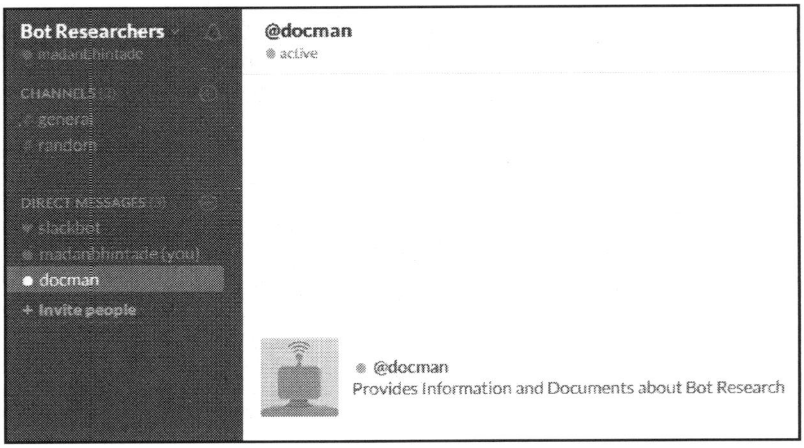

Now our bot is ready for conversation. Let's say `Hello` to our bot and see what it says:

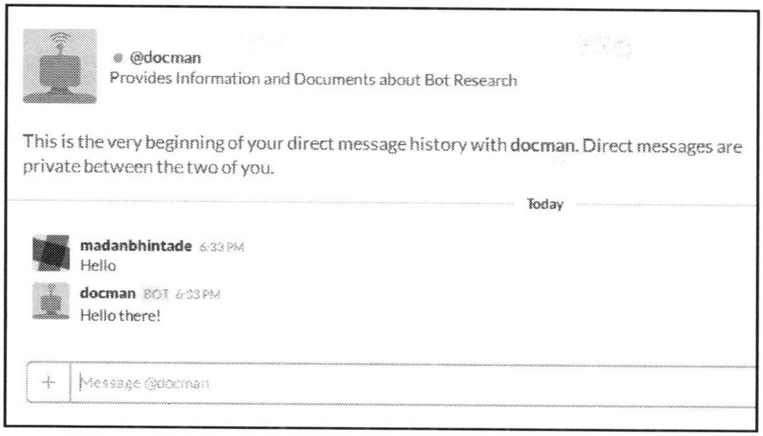

Our bot has responded to our message with **Hello there!** So the wiring up of our bot within Node.js and Botkit with Real-Time Messaging APIs has worked.

Now I want my bot to be part of the #general channel, which is the default for our group. Enter the name `@docman` in the messaging box and hit enter. Immediately **slackbot** will guide us to invite `@docman` in the #general channel, as shown in the following screenshot:

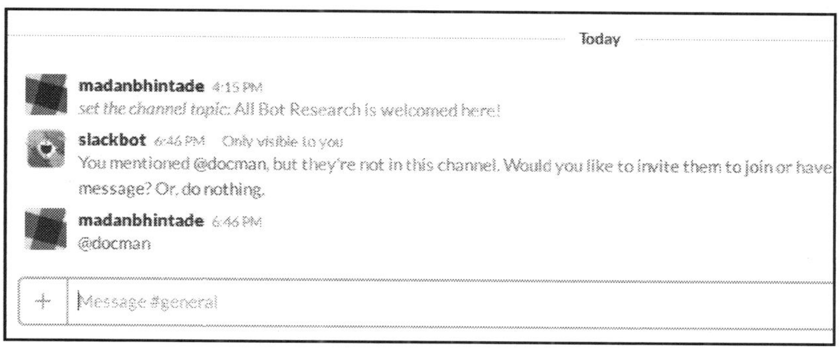

Click on the **invite them to join** link to join our bot in this channel. On the popup, just click on the **Yes, invite** them button. Refer to the following screenshot:

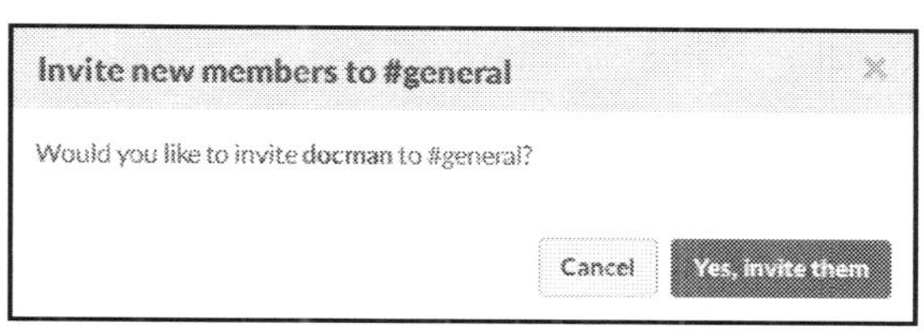

After inviting them, the Slack channel **#general** will show a notification that our bot has joined the group, as shown in the following screenshot:

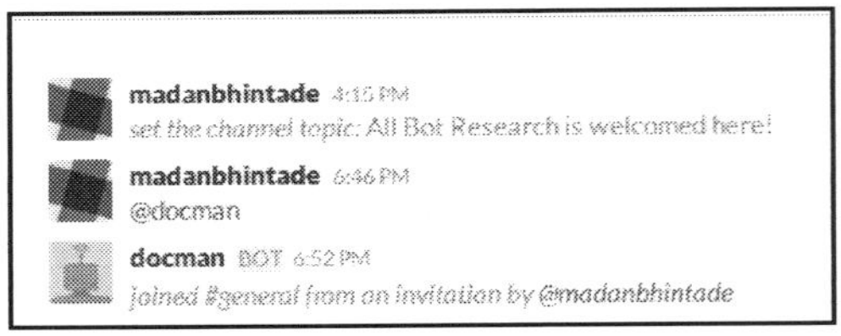

This way you can invite our bot to any of the channels, and you can also start conversations with our bot in that channel just by mentioning the name of our bot. I mentioned the name of our bot with a message reading **@docman Hello** in the **#general** channel. Our bot's reply can be seen as follows:

Enhancing our DocMan bot

Having built a very basic Slack bot, let's enhance our **DocMan** bot. Say that, following a team member's request, DocMan bot should be able to search a particular document and also be able to provide a link to download.

Let me explain how this will work. The Bot Researchers Slack team members will be communicating within their respective Slack channels. Now let's assume that one of them needs information about a research planning checklist document. The team member will enter some keywords like `Research Planning` or `Checklist` or `Template` by mentioning our bot's name. DocMan will do a keyword search within the MongoDB database and will present the searched documents. MongoDB will only have links to these documents and other metadata or attributes for the documents that will be searched. Actual documents will be stored in Amazon S3 storage.

Before going into the details, let me explain a little about MongoDB and Amazon S3 storage.

What is MongoDB?

Day by day, the use of NoSQLs is skyrocketing. MongoDB is one such NoSQL. There are various NoSQL database types, such as `Document Store`, `Key-Value Store`, `Column Store`, and `Graph Store`, to name but a few,.

MongoDB is of the Document Store type of NoSQLs, where data is stored in JSON documents. In short, MongoDB is an open source, highly scalable, high-performance NoSQL database.

The reason I am using MongoDB is because I wanted to show you how we can use a NoSQL database like MongoDB to search and store the document links using their metadata or attribute values. However, don't get confused between the documents or files that we are searching and the material that MongoDB is storing. What MongoDB is storing is just like a single record which is in JSON format. Just like our relational databases where data is stored in tables and records, MongoDB stores data in collections and JSON documents. Actual documents or files will be stored on Amazon S3, and only the link will be stored in MongoDB.

For our DocMan bot's enhancements, make sure you have installed MongoDB on your machine based on your machine's version (32 bit or 64 bit). Detailed installation steps can be obtained from `https://docs.mongodb.com/manual/administration/install-community/`.

MongoDB database for our DocMan bot

Assuming you have MongoDB up and running on your machine, let's set up a database with sample data for our bot using the following steps.

MongoDB shell

Locate the `bin` directory of your MongoDB installation using the Command Prompt and run the MongoDB shell using `mongo.exe`. If everything goes well, you will see the following screen:

Create a database

Let's create a new database called `BotDB` using the command shown in the following screenshot:

Now, to verify whether or not the database has been created, use the `show dbs` command. You will see the name `BotDB` in the list, as shown in the following screenshot:

Create a reference documents collection

To store documents, metadata, and attributes, let's create a collection called `ReferenceDocuments` using the following command:

```
db.createCollection("ReferenceDocuments")
```

You can verify a newly created collection with the help of the `show collections` command, as shown in the following screenshot:

Create data for our DocMan bot

Our `BotResearcher` group needs some documents and templates for their day to day use. These documents can be seen in the following screenshot:

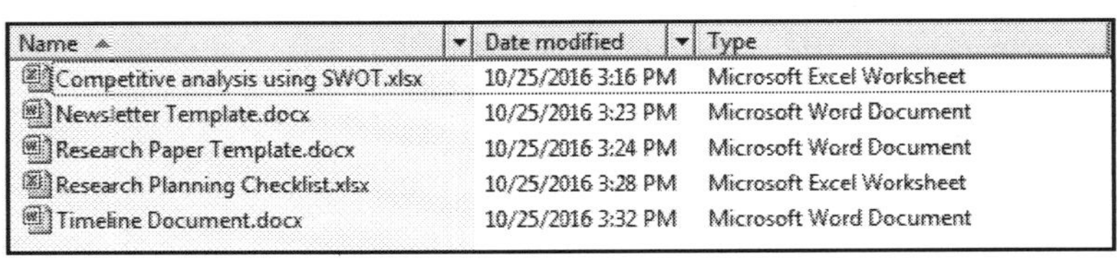

As a sample, I will use the `Research Planning Checklist` to show how we will store the metadata for this document in a MongoDB collection. Refer to the following JSON code for the metadata of this document:

```
{
   "title": "Research Planning Checklist",
   "description": "This excel sheet provides guidelines for better research
plan...",
   "version": "1.1",
   "url": "<Document URL goes here...>",
   "keywords": ["Plan","Research Plan","Checklist","SWOT"]
}
```

We will be storing the `title`, `description`, `version`, `url`, and keywords in our `ReferenceDocuments` collection using the following command:

```
>db.ReferenceDocuments.insert({ "title": "Research Planning
Checklist","description": "This excel sheet provides guidelines for better
research plan...","version": "1.1","url": "<Document URL goes
here...>","keywords": ["Plan","Research Plan","Checklist","SWOT"] })
```

After inserting the preceding record, you will see the following message as `WriteResult({"nInserted":1})`:

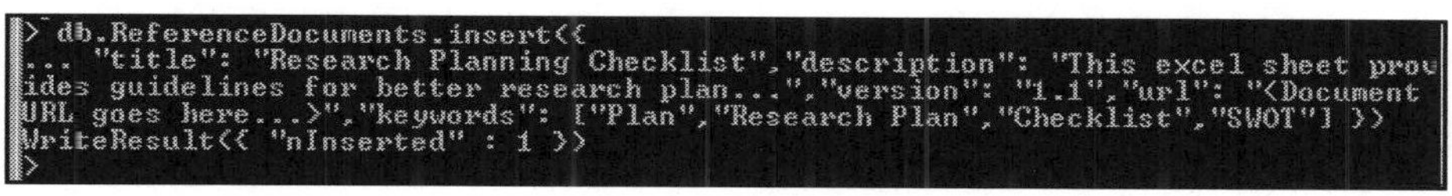

This way, we can create all the records in MongoDB for all our documents.

Indexing for search

Since a document can be searched using multiple keywords, we are storing keywords in an array for a document. When team members search documents, they will use keywords. We will apply an index to these keywords using the following command:

```
>db.ReferenceDocuments.createIndex({keywords:"text"})
```

After running a command, you will see the following output:

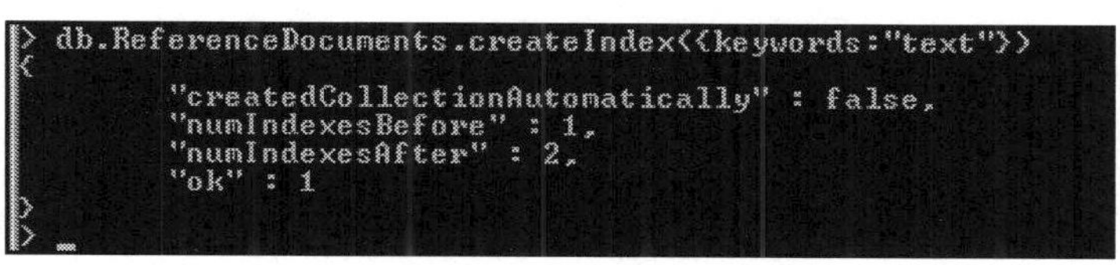

Search query

Once our index has been created, let's verify whether or not our search is working based on the keywords we enter. Let's fire the following command on the MongoDB shell:

```
db.ReferenceDocuments.find({$text:{$search:"template"}},{limit:3})
```

After executing the `search` query, you should see the following result:

```
> db.ReferenceDocuments.find({$text:{$search:"template"}},{limit:3})
{ "_id" : ObjectId("580e53552554e545d83bde37") }
{ "_id" : ObjectId("580f2bcd3cc08cc15aeb9e86") }
{ "_id" : ObjectId("580f2dad3cc08cc15aeb9e88") }
> _
```

To summarize, we created a new database for our bot to store the metadata of the documents that it searches. We added a new collection and added some sample documents. We also applied a text index to the keywords column so as to enable a search using keywords.

Now let's look at how we can wire up our database with Node.js.

What is MongoJS?

MongoJS is a Node.JS library used to connect to MongoDB APIs. Using this library, we will establish a connection with our MongoDB database and query documents based on input keywords.

Wiring up DocMan bot with MongoDB

Let's go back to our `Slackbot` directory and install the `mongojs` package from NPM. This can be located at `https://www.npmjs.com/package/mongojs`.

In order to install it, run this `npm` command:

```
npm install mongojs
```

You should then see something similar to this:

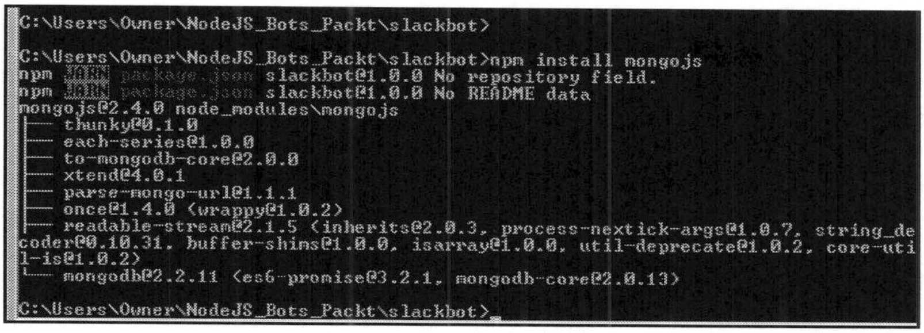

Let's modify our `app.js` file so that we can access MongoDB APIs through the `Mongojs` library.

Our `app.js` should be like this:

```
var Botkit = require('Botkit');
var os = require('os');

var mongojs = require('mongojs');
var db = mongojs('127.0.0.1:27017/BotDB',['ReferenceDocuments']);

var controller = Botkit.slackbot({
    debug: false
});

var bot = controller.spawn({
    token: "<SLACK_BOT_TOKEN>"
}).startRTM();

controller.hears('hello',['direct_message','direct_mention','mention'],func
tion(bot,message) {
  bot.reply(message,'Hello there!');

  db.ReferenceDocuments.find({title:"Newsletter Template"},function (err,
docs) {
      bot.reply(message,'I have a document with title:'+ docs[0].title);
  })
});
```

Let's look at this basic code with `mongojs` wired up as shown in the preceding code snippet. We connect to the MongoDB database through `mongojs` using the following lines:

```
var mongojs = require('mongojs');
var db = mongojs('127.0.0.1:27017/BotDB',['ReferenceDocuments']);
```

Here, MongoDB is hosted locally on my machine, so the host used is named as `127.0.0.1` and it listens to port `27017`. This IP address and port can be different for your machine, so while implementing your bots, make sure you use your machine's IP address and port for MongoDB. Within MongoDB, we connect to the `BotDB` database and a collection called `ReferenceDocuments`.

To query one of the documents from `ReferenceDocuments`, the following code is used:

```
db.ReferenceDocuments.find({title:"Newsletter Template"},function (err,
docs) {
     bot.reply(message,'I have a document with title:'+ docs[0].title);
  })
```

Let's run the modified code:

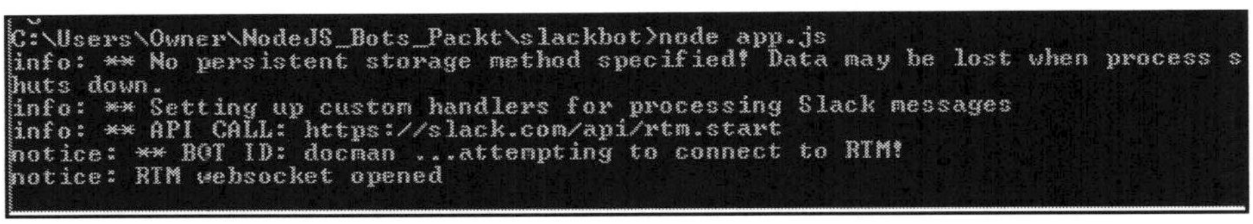

Go back to our Bot Researchers Slack group and say `hello` to our modified docman using direct messaging. You can also send mentions to docman as well, but this time I will use direct messaging.

When I messaged the `hello` directly to **docman**, docman queried the `BotDB` database and returned the title of one of the documents from the `ReferenceDocuments` collection. Refer to the following screenshot for further details:

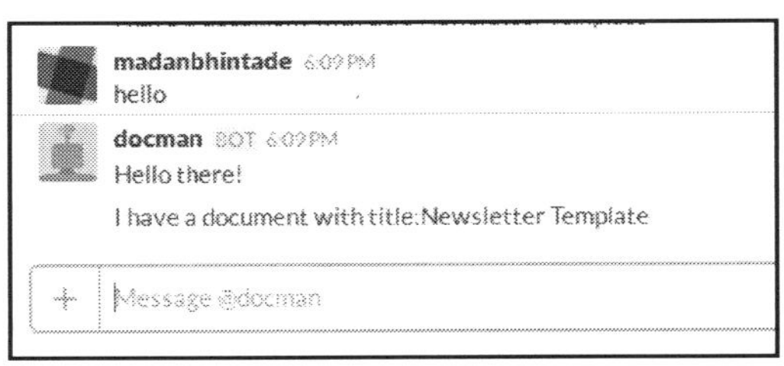

This shows how we can establish a MongoDB connectivity and query the data using `mongojs`.

Amazon S3 storage

Amazon Simple Storage Service (**Amazon S3**) is a cloud-based data storage system from **Amazon Web Services** (**AWS**). We can use Amazon S3 to store any amount of data. Amazon S3 stores data as objects within buckets. An object can be a document or a file. In our DocMan context, all the actual documents or files that are searched by Bot Researchers team members are stored in Amazon S3. In future, these files or documents can be of any types, such as media or office files of any size. Also, every bucket can have access control to decide who can access, delete, and create objects from the buckets. Given these requirements, Amazon S3 is suitable for our DocMan documents storage.

Amazon S3 console

I have my Amazon AWS account. Using that account, I have logged in to my Amazon S3 console. This console can be seen in the following screenshot:

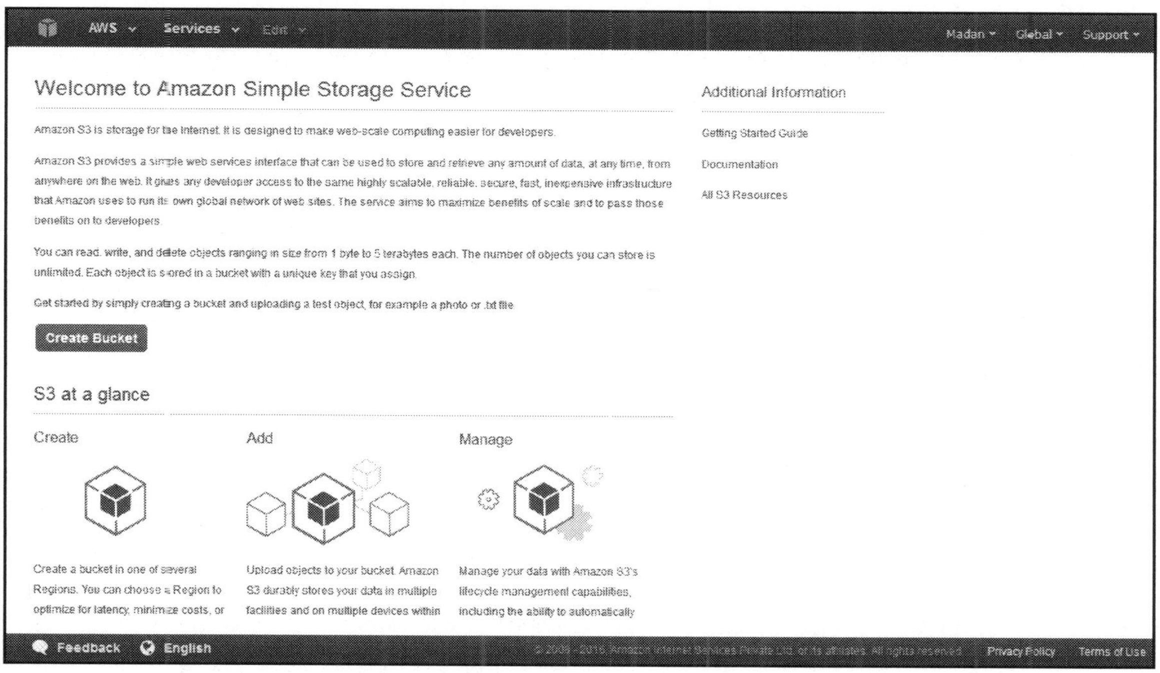

Those who are new to AWS can refer to the information at `https://aws.amazon.com/`.

Create buckets

From the preceding Amazon S3 console, click on the **Create Bucket** button to launch a **Create a Bucket** screen, as shown in the following screenshot:

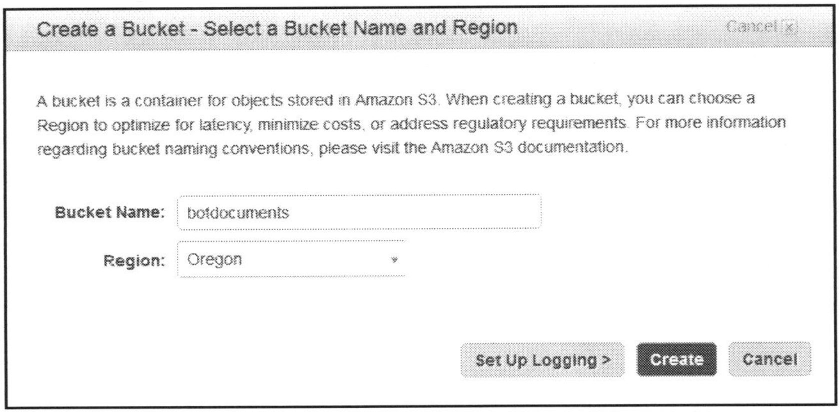

In creating my bucket, I have given the **Bucket Name** as **botdocuments** and selected the **Region** as **Oregon**. Make sure you are entering the **Bucket Name** in lowercase letters. Click on the **Create** button to create your bucket.

Your bucket will be shown under the **All Buckets** table:

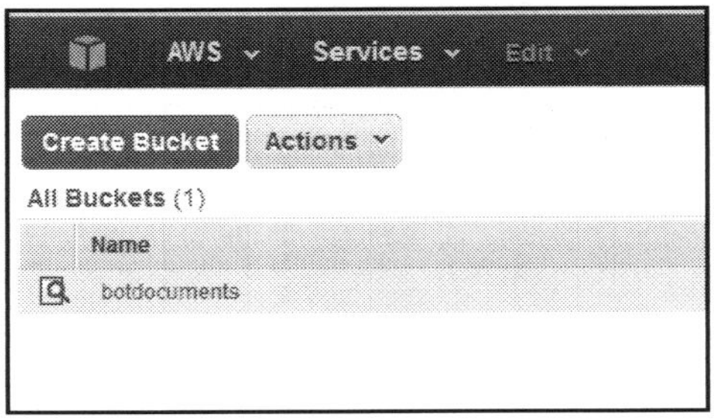

Now click on the bucket name shown under the **Name** column so that we can display a bucket view to upload and manage documents inside this bucket.

Store documents in the bucket

Once you select the bucket name from the **All Buckets** view, you will see the following screen:

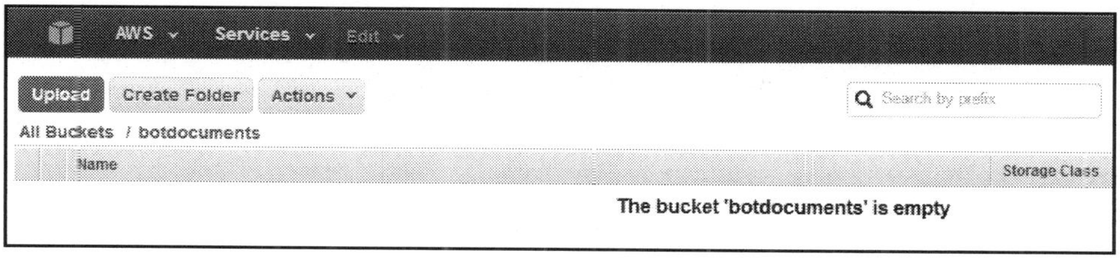

Now, to upload documents in this bucket, click on the **Upload** button and upload documents with the help of the following screenshot:

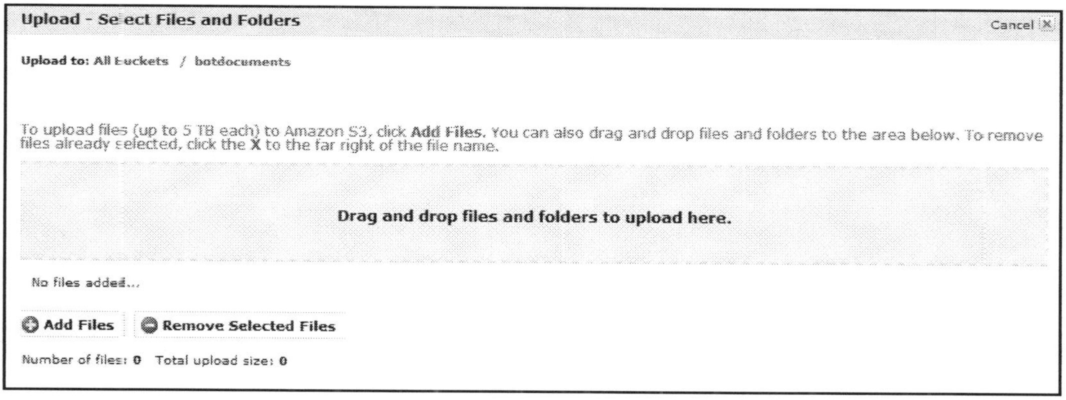

I will use the drag and drop function to upload my files. Once you have dragged and dropped all the files that you want to upload, click on **Start Upload** to upload your files. Once all the files are uploaded, the bucket will show all the files as follows:

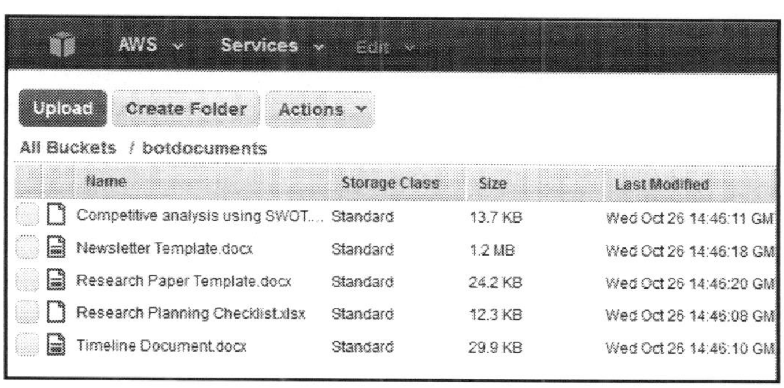

Mark documents as public

Just for demonstration purposes, we will be marking these documents as public.

This way, our `BotResearchers` group can access and download these documents from Amazon S3 storage easily. Let's go through the following steps to mark one of these documents as public. .

Select a document and, from **Actions**, select the **Make Public** option in the menu:

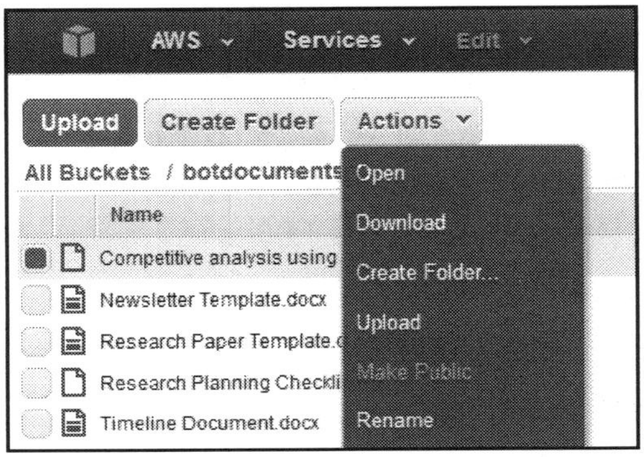

This option will mark the selected document as public. Now we need a public URL so that we can update this URL in our MongoDB database for this document. To get the public URL again, select a document and, from the **Actions** menu, select the **Properties** menu item.

This will bring up all the properties for the selected document, as shown in the following screenshot:

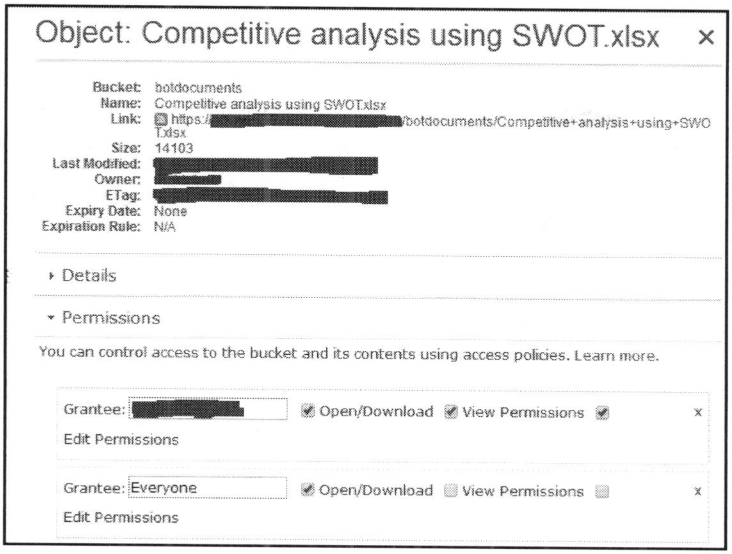

From the properties, refer to the **Link** property. This is our public URL for the document.

In this way, mark all the documents as public and copy their URLs. Update these URLs to our MongoDB database.

Update MongoDB data with Amazon S3 document links

Let's open up our Mongo shell again and select `BotDB` again using the following command:

```
Use BotDB
db.ReferenceDocuments.update(
   { title: "Competitive analysis using SWOT"},
   { $set:
      {
        url: "<YOUR AMAZON S3 URL FOR THIS DOCUMENT>"
      }
   }
)
```

Once successfully updated, you will see the number of records updated on the mongo shell. Follow the same steps to update all the rest of your documents' URL columns for their Amazon S3 public URLs. With this, we are all set with our bot docman, from a backend data perspective.

Wiring it all up together

To wire all the things up together, let's modify our earlier `app.js` as shown in the following code snippet:

```
var Botkit = require('Botkit');
var os = require('os');

var mongojs = require('mongojs');
var db = mongojs('127.0.0.1:27017/BotDB',['ReferenceDocuments']);

var controller = Botkit.slackbot({
    debug: false
});

var bot = controller.spawn({
    token: "<SLACK_BOT_TOKEN>"
}).startRTM();


controller.hears('hello',['direct_message','direct_mention','mention'],func
tion(bot,message) {
  bot.reply(message,'Hello there!');
});

controller.hears(['docs','template','research documentation','documents'],
['direct_message','direct_mention','mention'],function(bot,message) {
  bot.startConversation(message, askForKeywords);
});

askForKeywords = function(response, convo) {
  convo.ask("Pl. type the word or keywords for document search.",
function(response, convo) {
    convo.say("Awesome! Wait for a moment. Will search documents for
word(s) *" + response.text +"*");
    searchDocuments(response, convo);
    convo.next();
  });
}

searchDocuments = function(response, convo) {
var qtext ="""+response.text+""";
db.ReferenceDocuments.find({$text:{$search:qtext}},{},{limit:3},function
(err, docs) {
          var attachments = [];
          docs.forEach(function(d) {
             var attachment= {
                 "title": d.title,
```

```
                "title_link": d.url,
                "text": d.description,
                "color": '#3AA3E3',
                "footer": "From Amazon S3 | Version " +d.version
                };
              attachments.push(attachment);
            });
        convo.say({
            text: '*Document(s):*',
            attachments: attachments,
        })
    });
}
db.on('error', function (err) {
    console.log('Database error', err)
})
db.on('connect', function () {
    console.log('Database connected')
})
```

Code understanding

I have already explained how we can connect to MongoDB using `mongojs`. Now let's focus on how we have implemented the conversational experience within docman:

```
controller.hears(['docs','template','research documentation','documents'],
['direct_message','direct_mention','mention'],function(bot,message) {
  bot.startConversation(message, askForKeywords);
});
```

In the preceding code snippet, the user can start the conversations with docman using the keywords `'docs'`,`'template'`,`'research documentation'`, and `'documents'`.

Upon receiving a direct message or mention, the bot will start a conversation using `bot.startConversation()`. This function will call a related conversation sub-function `askForKeywords()`.

The bot will ask us to provide keywords based on which documents need to be searched, and will also call the sub-function to actually search the document within MongoDB. The implementation for `askForKeywords()` can be seen as shown in the following code snippet:

```
askForKeywords = function(response, convo) {
  convo.ask("Pl. type the word or keywords for document search.",
function(response, convo) {
    convo.say("Awesome! Wait for a moment. Will search documents for
```

```
word(s) *" + response.text +"*");
        searchDocuments(response, convo);
        convo.next();
    });
}
```

In the preceding code, the `convo.next()` function tells our called bot to continue the conversation. This step is required, or, our conversation will hang.

There is a final sub-function `searchDocuments()` that actually does the searching of documents within MongoDB and returns the top three documents as a part of the conversation.

Refer to the following code implementation for `searchDocuments()`:

```
searchDocuments = function(response, convo) {
var qtext ="""+response.text+""";
db.ReferenceDocuments.find({$text:{$search:qtext}},{},{limit:3},function
(err, docs) {
         var attachments = [];
         docs.forEach(function(d) {
            var attachment= {
                "title": d.title,
                "title_link": d.url,
                "text": d.description,
                "color": '#3AA3E3',
                "footer": "From Amazon S3 | Version " +d.version
                };
             attachments.push(attachment);
           });
        convo.say({
            text: '*Document(s):*',
            attachments: attachments,
        })
    });
}
```

In the preceding code, once the search query returns data, there can be single or multiple documents, so we are iterating the results and then combining them into a JSON format. Once JSON formatting is done, the bot calls the `convo.say()` function to send the message along with the searched documents.

Slack has some guidelines concerning the composing of messages and attachments. These guidelines can be referred to at `https://api.slack.com/docs/messages`.

Now let's begin our great conversation experience with our enhanced Slack bot, docman.

Firstly, start a communication in the # **general** channel by mentioning `@docman`, and type the word `docs` as shown in the following screenshot:

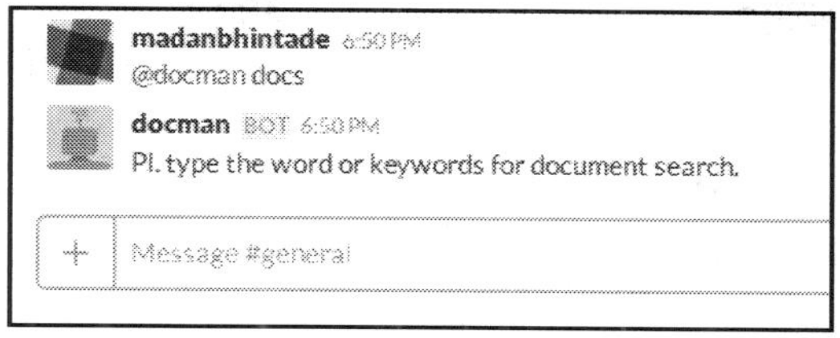

Once we entered `docs`, docman asked to type the word or keywords for the document search.

Enter the word as `template` and see what **docman** returns:

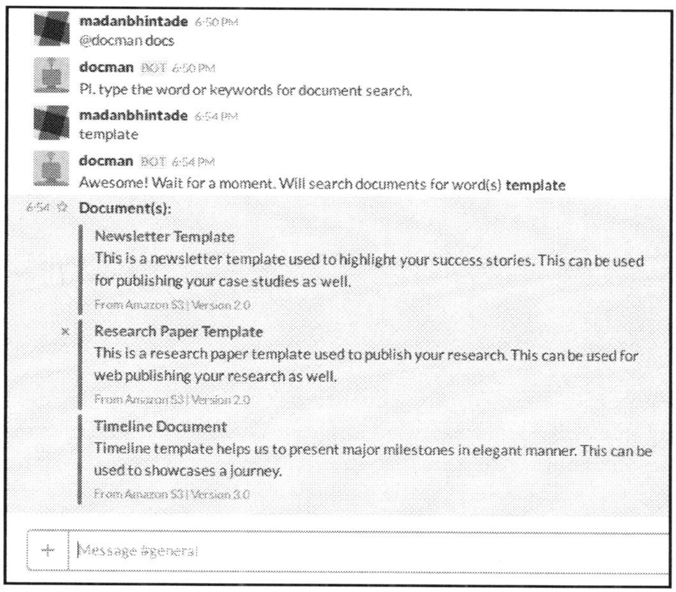

When I entered the `template` keyword, **docman** replied saying:

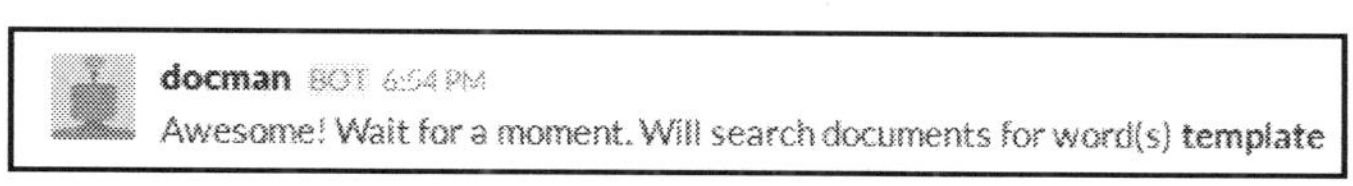

It also replied with the searched documents in a nice elegant format using the Slack messaging guidelines shown in the following screenshot:

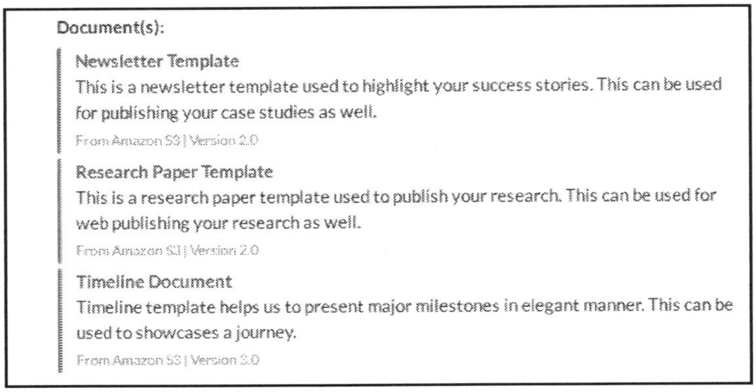

Now, select one of the documents from the search results–I selected a document titled **Timeline Document**, and `Timeline+Document.docx` was downloaded through our docman bot.

Refer to the following screenshot to see the downloaded document:

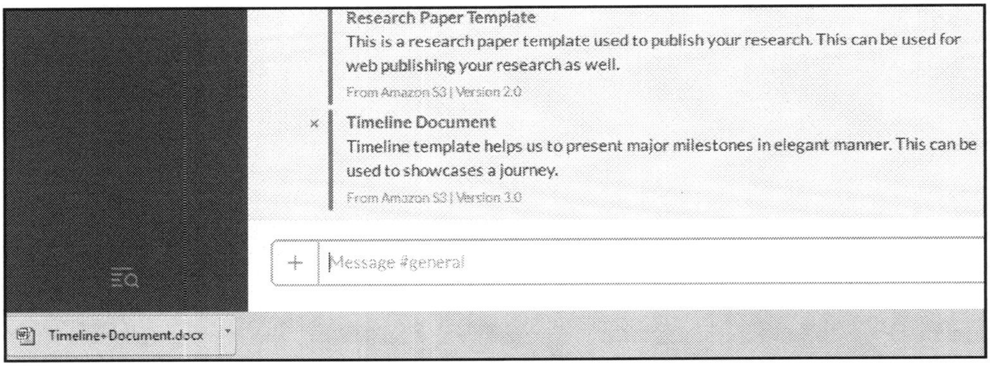

Summary

So, with Slack, we built a bot and enhanced our team's collaborative experience by building intelligence into it.

To summarize, we saw how to create a Slack group from scratch. We also created a basic bot wired up in Node.js using Botkit, and had a basic conversation as a direct message as well as within a group by inviting the bot.

Finally, we made our bot search some of the documents based on keywords, and also provided a link to download the same document.

Our DocMan bot used MongoDB to store document attributes along with keywords with which the document can be searched. Also, DocMan retrieved actual documents from Amazon S3 storage upon a user's request to download them.

Hopefully this chapter has given you an end-to-end solution overview of how your bot searches and locates documents, as well as how it downloads them from storage locations or document repositories. You should now be aware of NoSQL technologies like MongoDB and how we can utilize them for keyword searches, and how we can wire up with storage locations like Amazon S3 in Node.js. Above all, you should now be fully aware of how we can bring everything together in messaging platforms like Slack.

Amazing!

In the next chapter, we will explore how to develop IRC bots and how we can wire up within Node.js and help our developers use it for bug tracking purposes.

7

Facebook Messenger Bot, Who's Off – A Scheduler Bot for Teams

Facebook has launched its own messaging platform (`https://developers.facebook.com/docs/messenger-platform/product-overview`), which enables us to enrich our conversation experience with other users on a messengers. Companies, apart from just showing information, can now provide new ways of conversational experience using custom bots. These bots can be integrated with the company's Facebook Page. With this, customers or employees of that company can easily look for information on the page and also chat at the same time on Facebook Messenger itself.

The Facebook Messenger platform's APIs can be used not only to send messages, but also to send links, photos, videos, files, and images. Facebook Messenger has a feature called secret messages or conversations. These secret conversations are currently available only in the Messenger app, downloaded on iOS and Android devices. With these conversations, we can only send messages, pictures, and stickers. Group messages, videos, GIFs, video calling, and payments are not supported in secret conversations.

Recently, I read about Domino's pizzas getting ordered from Facebook Messenger! So just by chatting, you can now select your pizza, order it, and process the payment as well. Here, users are provided with a seamless experience during the chat itself.

In this chapter, we'll build a Facebook Messenger bot and enhance it to schedule off-hours. Our bot will also help us discover who and when a person will take off; this will all be done through an elegant calendar-based user interface.

Awesome! Let's start now.

Setting up our Facebook Messenger bot

Facebook has great documentation on how to set up a bot. You can also refer to the steps mentioned at `https://developers.facebook.com/docs/messenger-platform/guides/quick-start`.

We will be using the following steps to build a basic bot:

- Create a Facebook Page for our bot
- Create an app within Facebook
- Create a basic Facebook Messenger bot in Node.js, specifically in Microsoft Azure
- Wire up the Facebook app and the basic bot

Let's start working on these steps one by one.

The Facebook Page for our basic bot

First of all, log in to Facebook. You can use the existing pages or create a new page.

We will implement our bot in a way that it will tell users who would be off and when. Let's create a page called *Who's Off* by navigating to `https://www.facebook.com/pages/create/`.

Once you hit the URL, you will see the following screen:

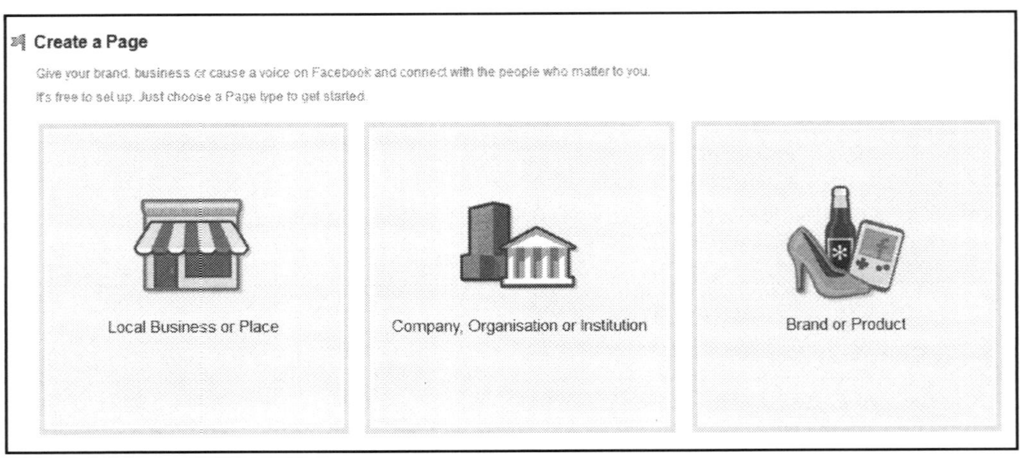

Choose the page type as **Company, Organization or Institution**. This will show the following input screen:

Provide information on this page, such as the type and name of the company.

Select **Internet Company** and set the name as `Who's Off`. Then click on the **Get Started** button. This will open up a wizard to set up all the other properties for your company, such as the profile information:

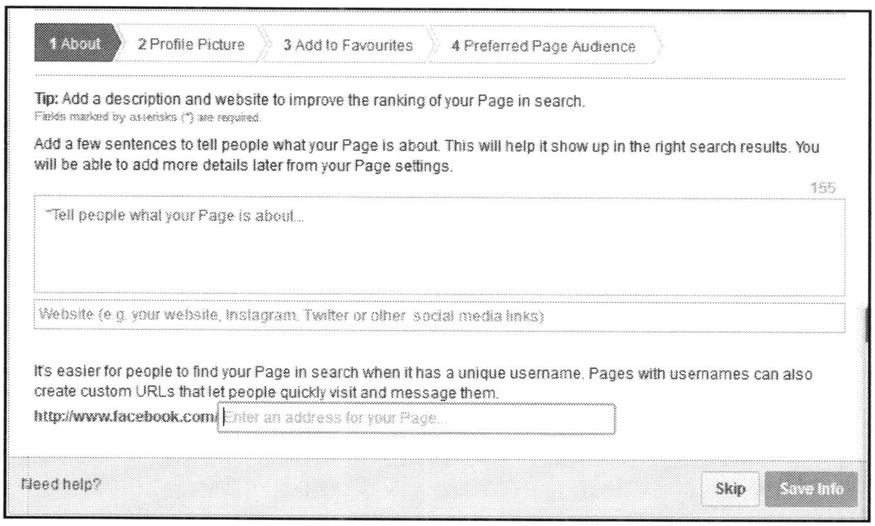

You can skip this wizard or directly go to the last tab, **4. Preferred Page Audience**, to save the information.

This creates a Facebook Page for our bot. This will appear as follows:

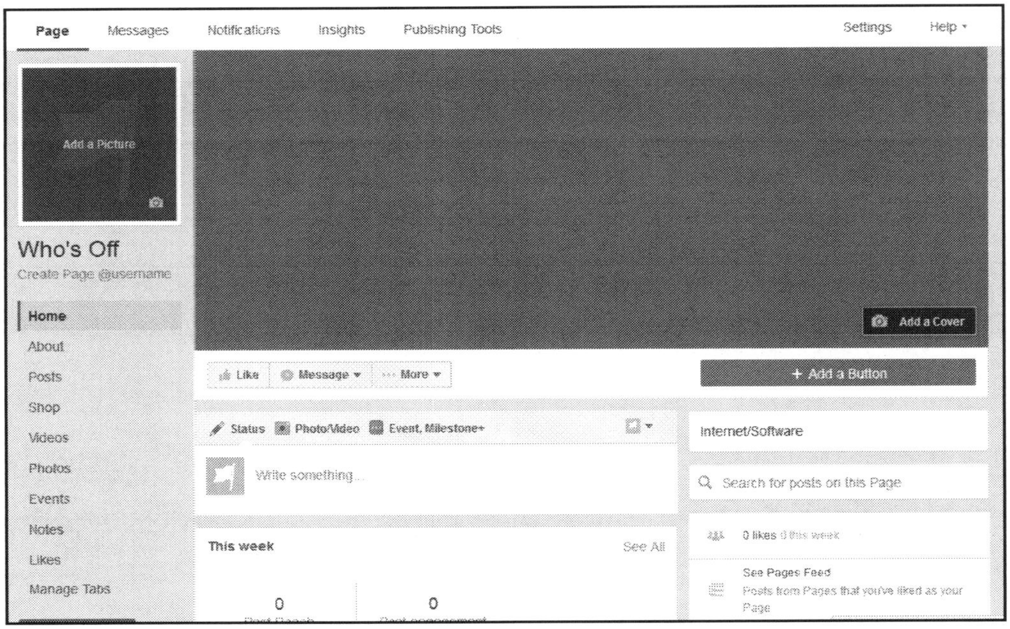

Creating a Facebook app for our basic bot

After creating a page, now let's create a Facebook app for our bot via `https://developers.facebook.com/quickstarts/`. This will lead us to a screen where we can configure our app as follows:

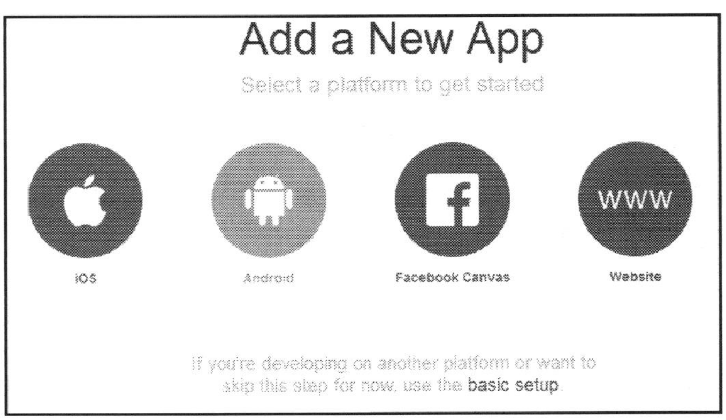

Click on **basic setup** to open a popup and enter the following information:

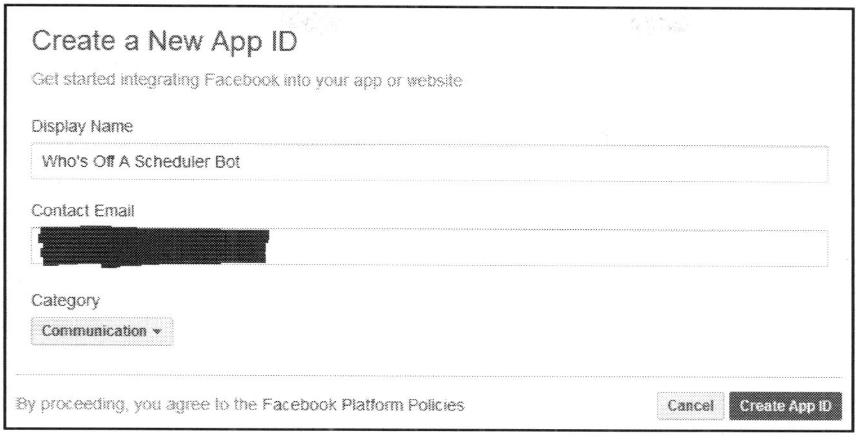

While creating the app ID, security check will be done as follows:

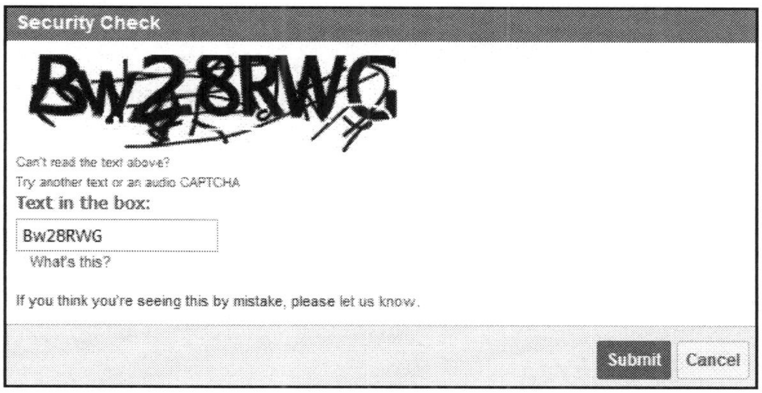

Please respond to **Security Check** and click on **Submit** to set up your Facebook app by following the instructions on this screen:

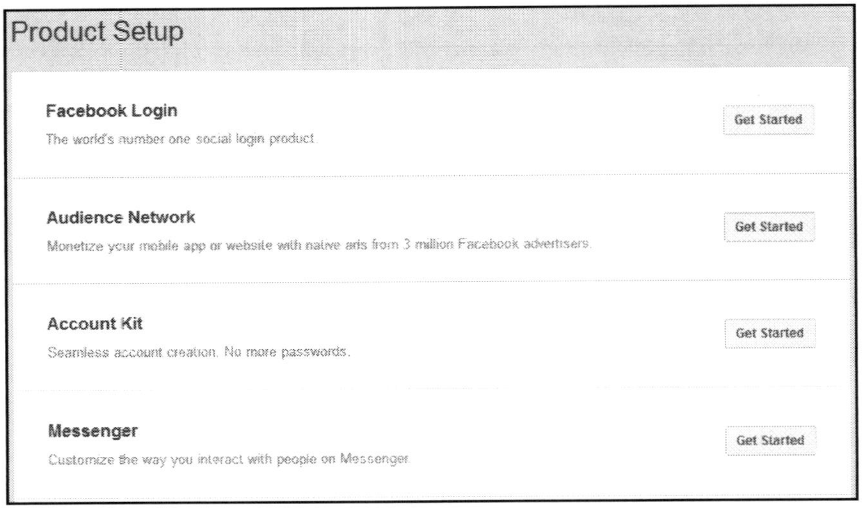

Since we want to set up a messenger, click on the **Get Started** button available in **Messenger**. This will lead you to the following screen:

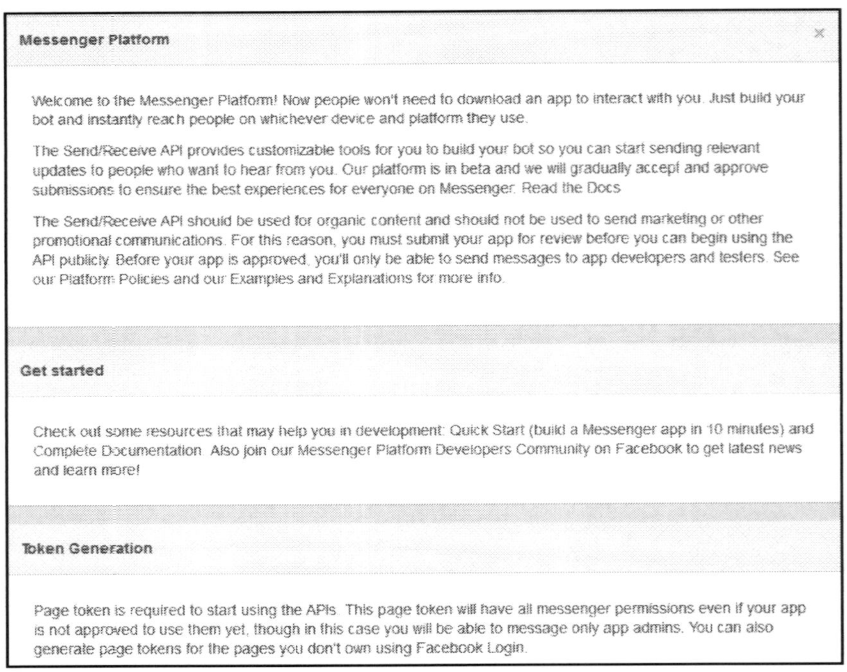

Now locate the section called **Token Generation** in the page and select the Facebook Page created earlier. This will generate a token for the selected page, as follows:

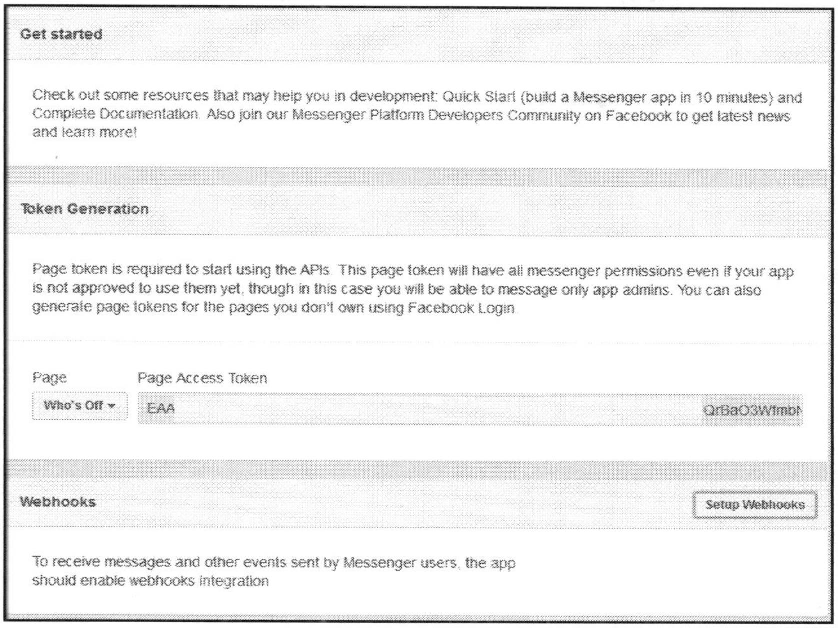

This page token will be used while communicating with the APIs.

To receive messages from users, our Facebook app needs the Webhooks integration. Before we set up Webhooks, let's create a Node.js Facebook Messenger app. The Facebook Webhook integration needs our bot app to be accessible over HTTPs. So we will need to do this using Microsoft Azure.

Setting up our bot server in Azure

As mentioned, we need an HTTPs-enabled bot server so that we can integrate it in Facebook. We will build our bot server in Microsoft Azure.

Let's log in to the Azure portal and locate **App Services** to create a Node.js-based bot server. Refer to the following screen:

Click on the **Add** link to open the following screen. Then, select the **Web + Mobile** option and search for an empty Node.js-based web app template, as follows:

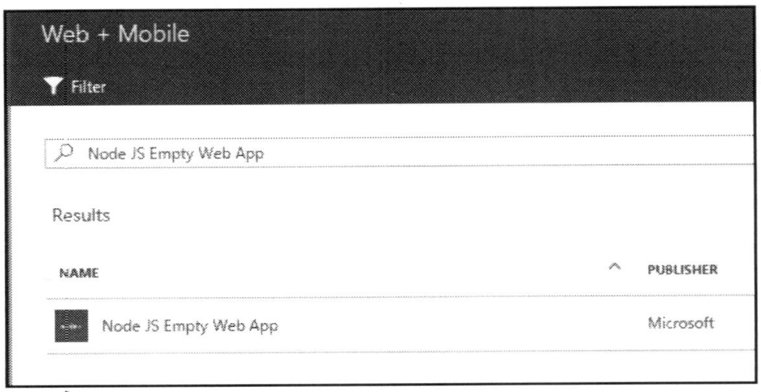

After selecting the template as **Node JS Empty Web App**, click on the **Create** button to create the Node.js-based site. The next screen will ask you to input the name of your site and resources:

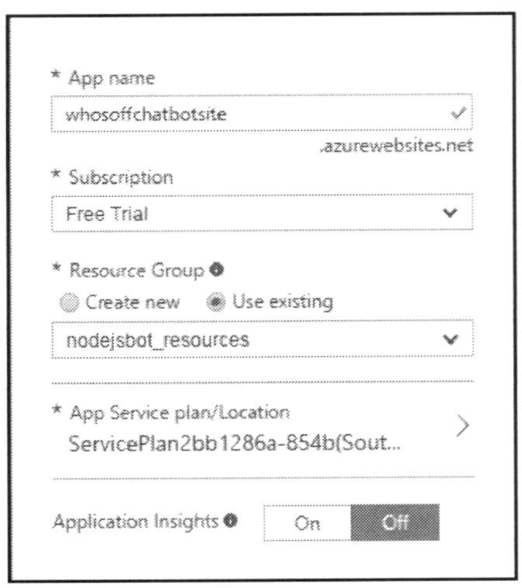

Provide the required information and click on the **Create** button at the bottom to create a site called `whosoffchatbotsite.azurewebsites.net`.

Once created, you should see the following properties of the site using the **Overview** menu option from the **App Services** selected site:

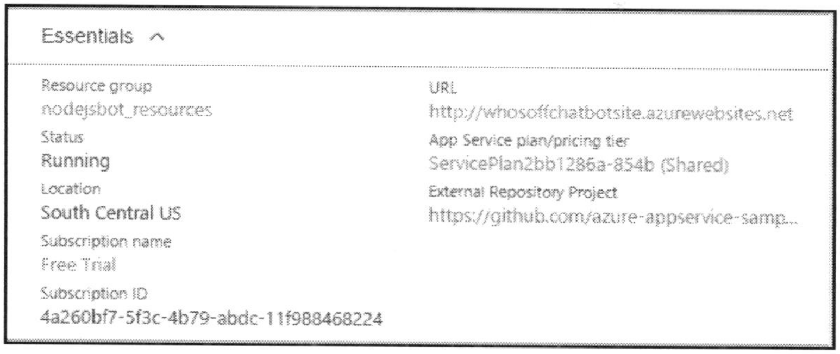

Click on `http://whosoffchatbotsite.azurewebsites.net` to check how our initial Node.js site looks or whether there are any issues:

With this, we were able to create and run Node.js from Microsoft Azure.

In `Chapter 2`, *Getting Skype to Work for You*, we looked at how to create a Node.js site using the Azure command-line interface. In this chapter, we have so far created a Node.js site in Azure itself; now, we will modify the basic Node.js site for our bot.

To modify the basic bot program, first we will clone the template on our local file system using git commands. Then, we will modify and deploy it to Microsoft Azure.

Let's start by creating a folder in our local drive in order to store our bot program from the Command Prompt:

```
mkdir whosoffchatbot
cd whosoffchatbot
```

Now go to the newly created directory and run the following command:

This command will clone our site from a remote URL to a local file system. Once the site is cloned, move to the `NodeJS-EmptySiteTemplate` directory and run `server.js` as follows:

Once the cloning is successful, you should see the bot program in Node.js running, as follows:

So far, we have used a template from a remote git repository and cloned it to a local file system. Now we'll set our own git location for the bot program. The reason is that, whenever we make a change in `server.js`, which is our bot program, we would also like the changes to be deployed to Azure; we can do this using git commands. So we will be setting up a local git repository for our bot program in Azure itself.

Setting up a local git repository for our bot server in Azure

First, disconnect the remote git library of our program using the **Disconnect** menu option:

Once disconnected, use the **Setup** option to set up a code repository for our program, as follows:

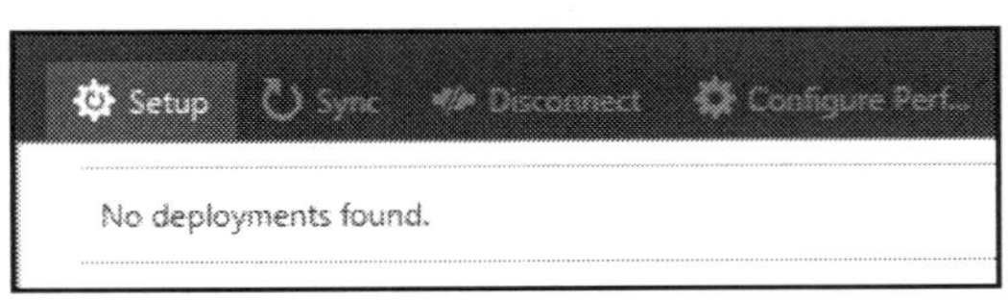

Once you click on **Setup**, the **Deployment Source** screen will be launched, as shown in the following screenshot.

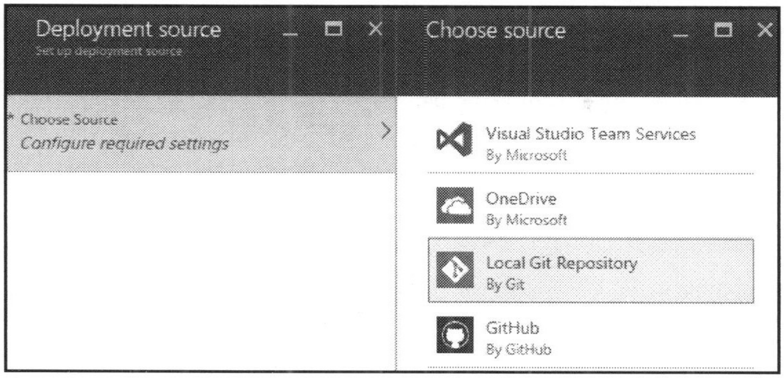

Choose the **Local Git Repository** option to set up a git-based repository for the site.

Now if you look at the website properties, you will see that a git URL as well as an FTP account has been set up. We can deploy our site to Azure using either git commands or FTP. Refer to the following screenshot for the newly updated properties:

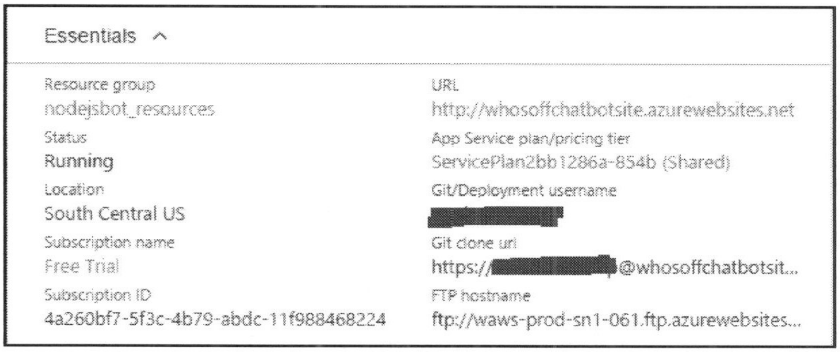

So we have set up a git repository in Azure, but the site we cloned from a local file system earlier is still pointing to a remote URL. Let's point our local git configurations to the newly created Azure clone repository using the following command:

```
C:\Packt_Book\whosoffchatbot\NodeJS-EmptySiteTemplate>git remote set-url origin
https://        p@whosoffchatbotsite.scm.azurewebsites.net:443/whosoffchatbo
tsite.git
```

Modifying our bot program for Facebook verification

When we cloned bot program code within `server.js`, the following is auto-generated:

```
var http = require('http');

http.createServer(function (req, res) {
    res.writeHead(200, { 'Content-Type': 'text/html' });
    res.end('Hello, world!');
}).listen(process.env.PORT || 8080);
```

Now let's start modifying our code. But before that, we need to install some node modules; we can do this using the following command:

```
npm install express body-parser request --save
```

The `body-parser` npm module helps in parsing the incoming requests available under `req.body`.

Now let's open our `server.js` and modify it as follows:

```
var express = require('express');
var bodyParser = require('body-parser');
var request = require('request');
var app = express();
app.use(bodyParser.urlencoded({extended: false}));
app.use(bodyParser.json());
app.get('/', function (req, res) {
    res.send('This is my Facebook Messenger Bot - Whos Off Bot Server');
});
app.get('/webhook', function (req, res) {
    if (req.query['hub.verify_token'] === 'whosoffbot_verify_token') {
        res.status(200).send(req.query['hub.challenge']);
    } else {
        res.status(403).send('Invalid verify token');
    }
});

app.listen((process.env.PORT || 8080));
```

Let's run our bot program using the following command:

Then open a browser window and hit `http://localhost:8080`:

This will show us that our Node.js program is working fine. Now let's deploy this code to Azure using git commands. This time, all our node modules, which are marked as a dependent using `--save`, will also be pushed to Azure. Sometimes, you may encounter a timeout error while pushing the code. But again, try to push the code; it should get deployed.

The git commands that we need to execute are as follows:

```
git add .
git commit -m "First Change to server.js"
git push origin master
```

Once the code is deployed to Azure, browse the site and check whether it reflects the latest changes, as follows:

Setting up a Webhook and Facebook verification of our bot program

Now let's go back to our Facebook app; we had stopped at token generation. Let's set up Webhooks in our Facebook app, as follows:

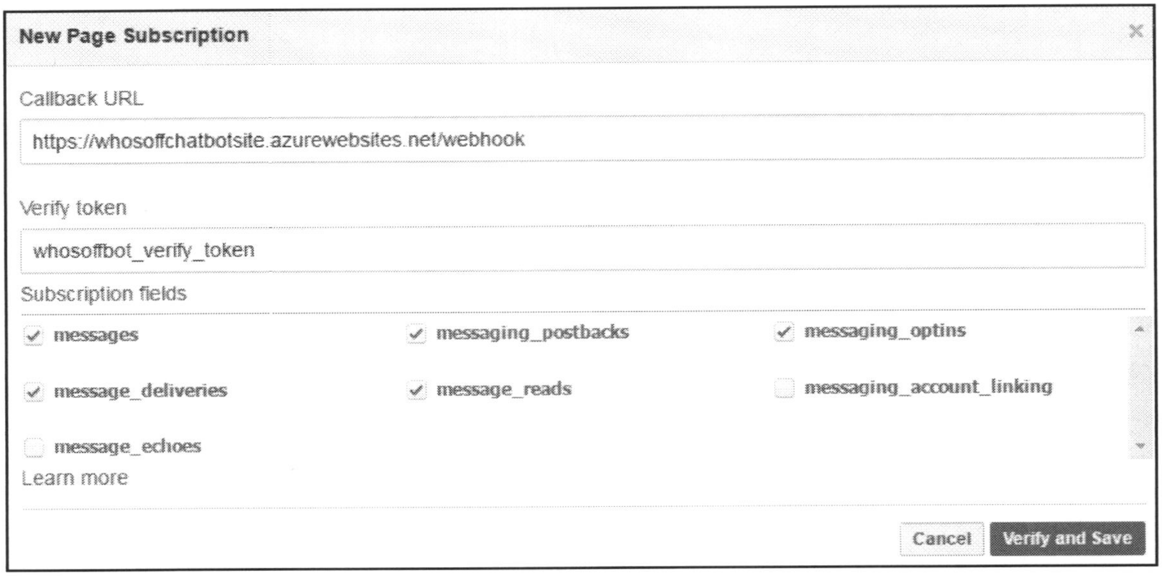

A few important things to note here:

- **Callback URL** has to be accessible from Facebook and should be on HTTPS.
- **Callback URL** with Webhook should return a token, as mentioned at **Verify token**. Verify that the token is the same as the one we referred to in `server.js`, as follows:

```
if (req.query['hub.verify_token'] === 'whosoffbot_verify_token') {
```

The token `'whosoffbot_verify_token`, provided in the code should match the token on Facebook.

Once your token is verified, you should see the following screen:

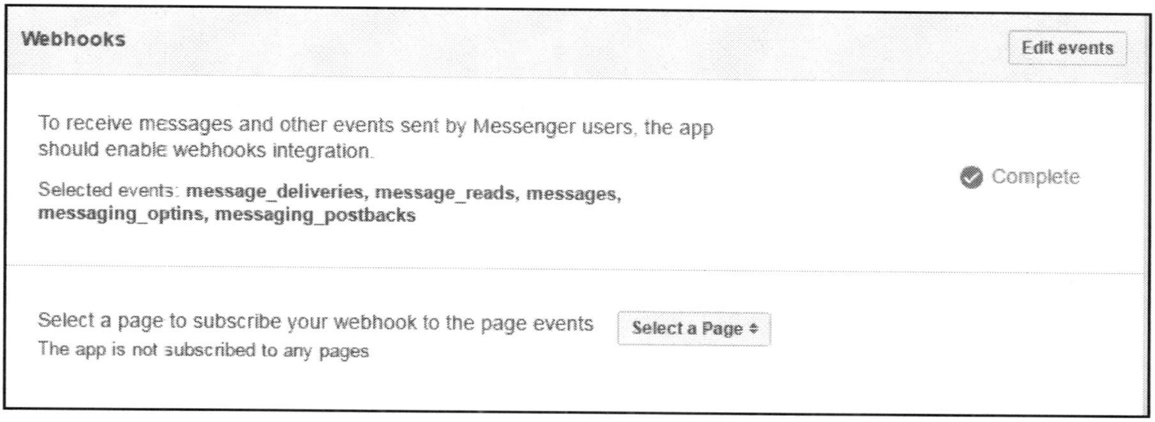

So Webhook is verified and set, but we need a page to subscribe to this Webhook. Refer to the following screen and subscribe to the **Who's Off** page, which we created at the beginning:

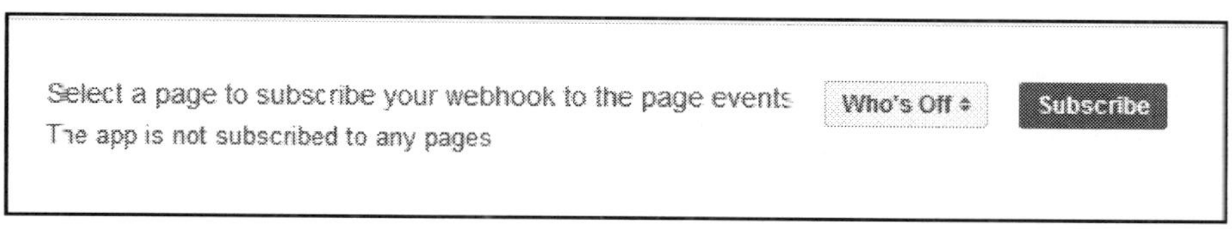

This is how we linked our basic bot to a Facebook Page. Now let's open our **Who's Off** page from Facebook and click on the **Message** button to make our bot active. You should see a green dot before the bot name indicating it is active. Refer to the following screenshot for details:

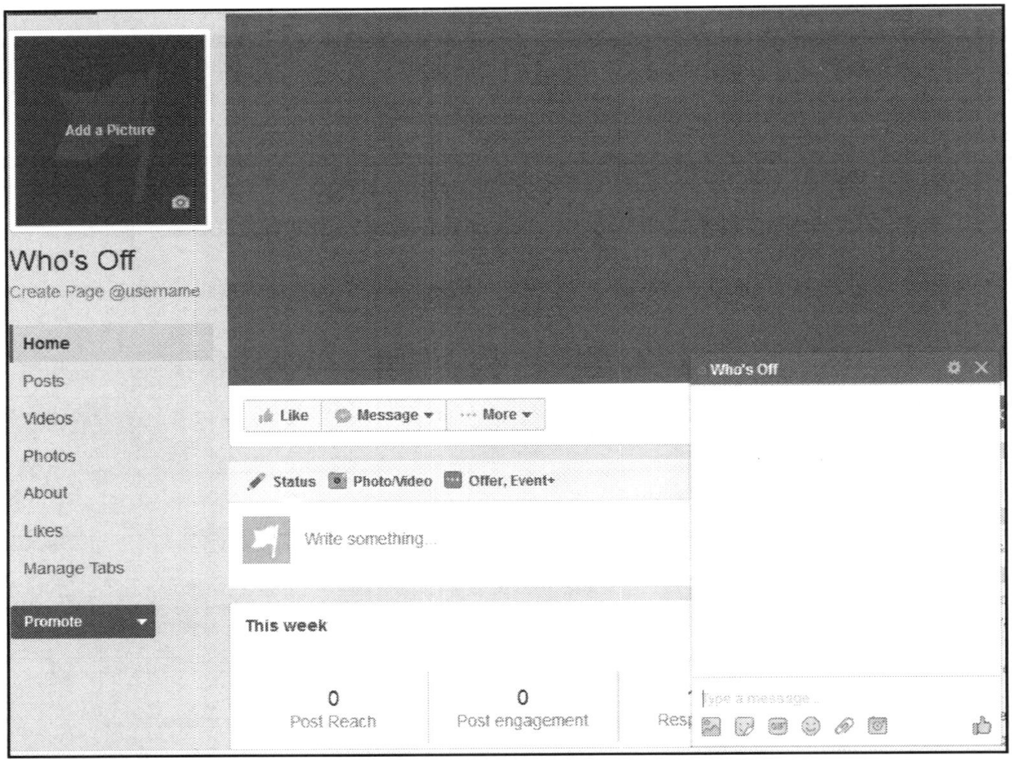

If you try to post anything to this bot, it will not do anything as we have not programmed Webhooks in relation to posting commands. Now let's ask our bot to echo what the user is saying in a chat window. To achieve this, let's include the following code snippet in our `server.js`:

```
app.post('/webhook', function (req, res) {
   var events = req.body.entry[0].messaging;
    for (i = 0; i < events.length; i++) {
        var event = events[i];
        if (event.message && event.message.text) {
            sendMessage(event.sender.id, {text: "Echo: " +
event.message.text});
        }
    }
```

```
        res.sendStatus(200);
    });
    function sendMessage(recipientId, message) {
        request({
            url: 'https://graph.facebook.com/v2.6/me/messages',
            qs: {access_token: <PAGE_ACCESS_TOKEN>},
            method: 'POST',
            json: {
                recipient: {id: recipientId},
                message: message,
            }
        }, function(error, response, body) {
            if (error) {
                console.log('Error sending message: ', error);
            } else if (response.body.error) {
                console.log('Error: ', response.body.error);
            }
        });
    };
```

Let me explain the code snippet here. When the data is posted from a page that is subscribing to the Webhook, `app.post('/webhook',function(req,res){})` will get called. This will parse the incoming messages, and bot will form an echo message and will call the `sendMessage()` function to send the message to the same recipient with the help of a page access token.

Deploying a modified bot that returns an echo

Let's use git commands to deploy the modified code and check whether the bot would echo what we say:

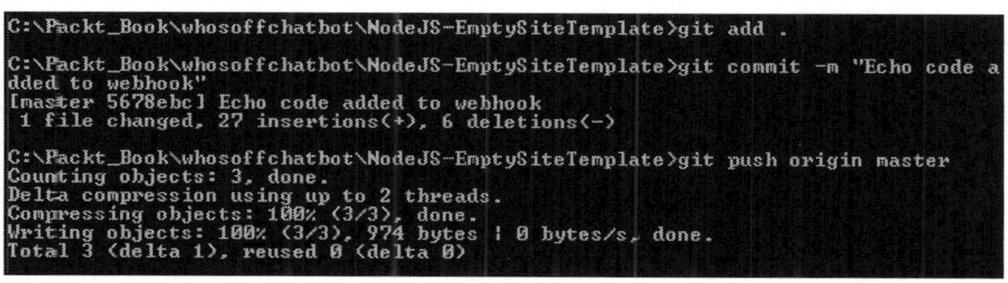

Once you deploy the updated code, hit the Facebook Page again, and the Messenger and post data as follows:

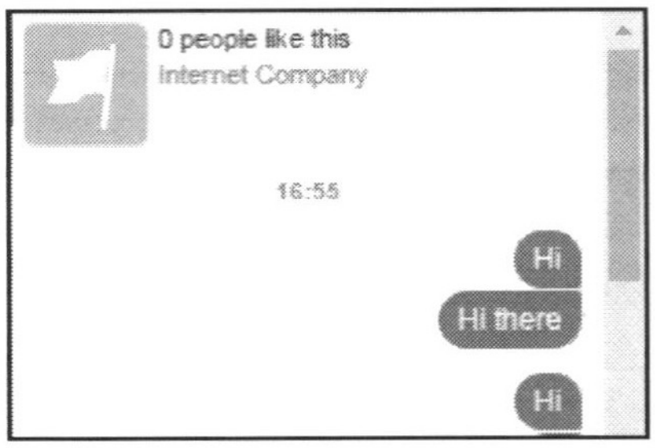

We have made multiple posts to our bot, but it is not yet doing anything. Let's see what's happening at the Azure end, that is, whether there are any errors at the application level.

Troubleshooting our bot in Azure

To troubleshoot the problem of bot not echoing anything, let's turn to **Diagnostics logs** for our site and also start **Log stream**. Log stream will show us whether there are any errors in our program:

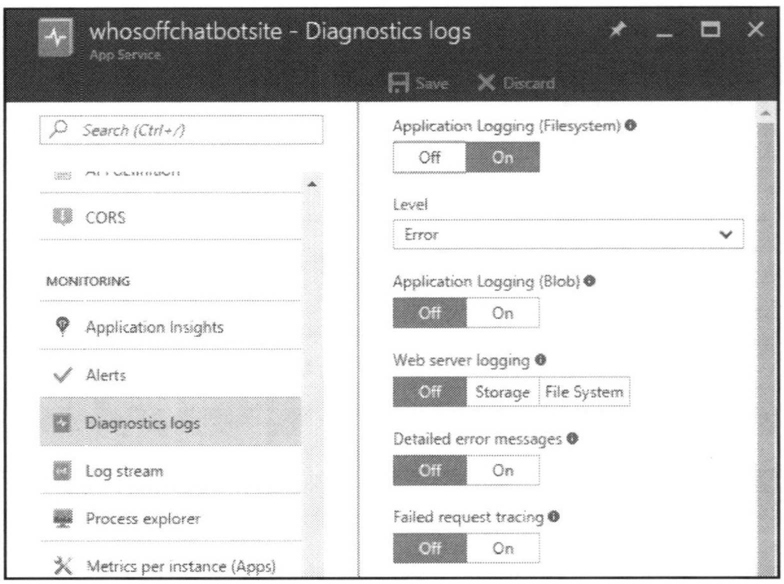

Now let's enter or post anything to our bot from the Facebook Page and refer to the log streams. You will get to see the line number and the error we will get, as follows:

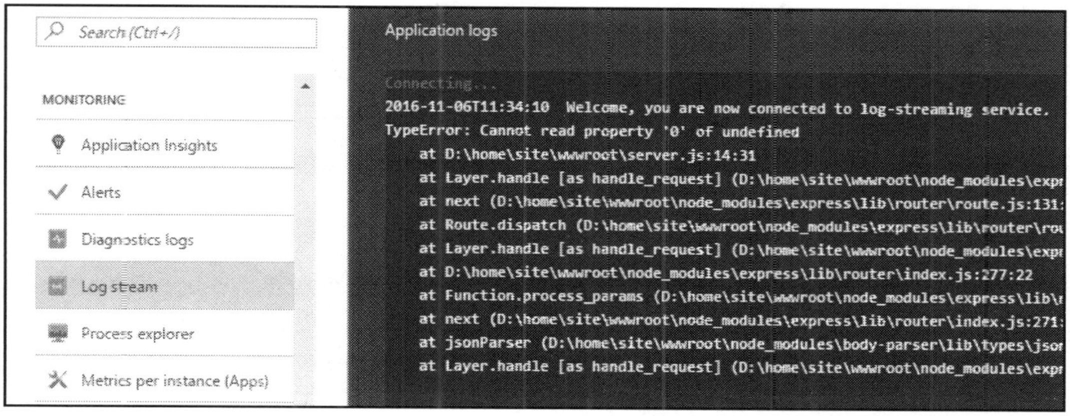

So our code is failing to parse the input, resulting into an error. To fix this, let's make a small change while parsing. Use `bodyParser` before the `urlencoded` call, as follows:

```
app.use(bodyParser.json());
app.use(bodyParser.urlencoded({extended: false}));
```

Again, deploy the modified code to Azure using git commands and try to post something to our bot. The code will run successfully and echo out what a user would post in the chat window, as follows:

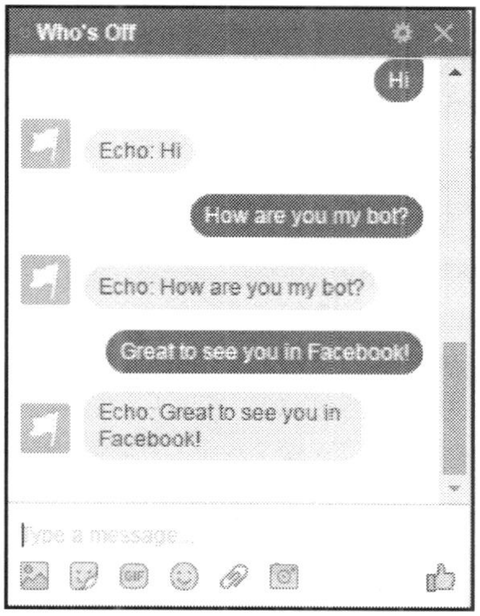

Wow! So far, we have been able to wire up our bot with the Facebook Page and Messenger as well. We have also looked at how to use Azure diagnostics for logging into our site if there are issues with our bot program; we also understood how to trace and fix the problem. Now let's look at the core functionality we are trying to build for our Who's Off bot.

Enhancing our Who's Off bot

Having built a very basic Facebook Messenger bot, let's enhance our Who's Off bot.

Assume our team members are collaborating over Facebook Messenger. Our bot should be able to help this team schedule a meeting and should also be able to show who is busy on a particular day before setting up the meeting.

Now let me show you, what we will be building in Facebook Messenger for our bot:

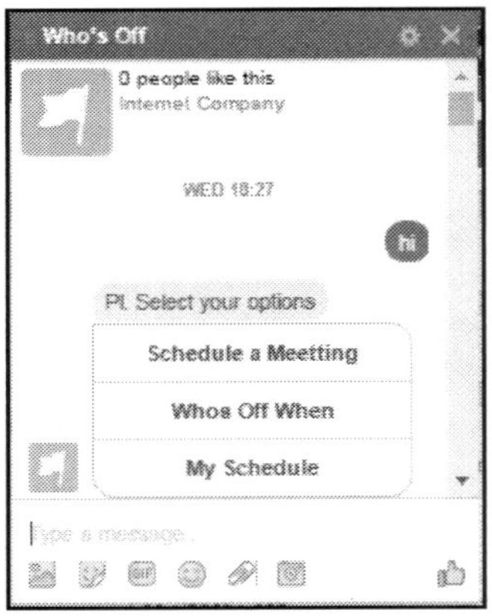

Let's dive into the flow and then look into the code implementation one by one.

When a user starts a conversation with our bot with `hi`, as shown in the preceding screenshot, then the Who's Off bot will show the first three options: **Schedule a Meeting**, **Whos Off When**, and **My Schedule**.

Depending upon the option the user chooses, the bot will prompt options for when they would like to carry out the mentioned operation, such as scheduling a meeting, seeing who is off when, or checking out their own meetings. Refer to the following screenshot for the operation's flow:

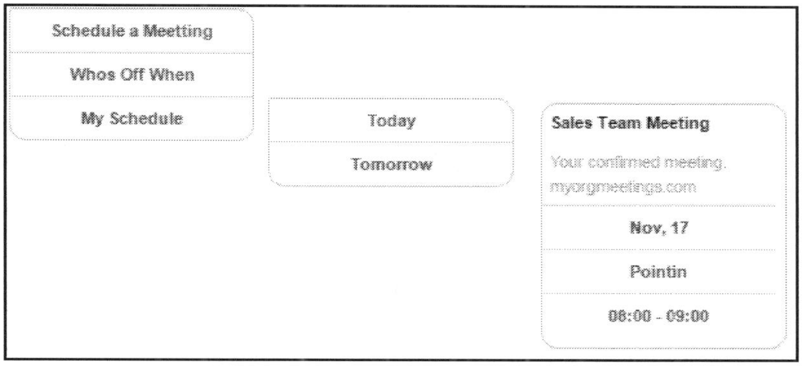

These operations will be done using options such as **Today** and **Tomorrow**. Based on what you choose, the bot will display the meeting details or will ask for it to schedule the meeting. In the preceding screenshot, it shows the meeting for the **Whos Off When** option selected in Facebook Messenger is scheduled today.

So at a higher level, we will be:

- Enhancing our basic bot program for a better conversational experience within Facebook Messenger by leveraging message templates; for more information, refer to `https://developers.facebook.com/docs/messenger-platform/send-api-reference/templates`
- Storing meeting's information in the NoSQL database-DocumentDB
- Wiring up DocumentDB APIs and Messenger platform APIs

Building a conversational experience with the Who's Off bot

We have already seen how users will arrive at our bot's Facebook Page and then start a conversation with our bot.

Setting up a Messenger greeting

Let's enhance the conversational experience of this bot now. We'll begin by adding a greeting message whenever a user starts a conversation. Follow these steps:

1. Locate your bot page on Facebook and click on the **Settings** option:

2. On the **Settings** page, locate the **Messaging** menu on the left-hand side, as follows:

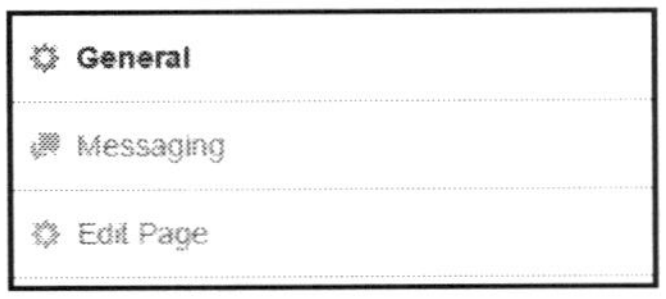

3. Choose the option **Yes** for **Show a Messenger Greeting**, as follows:

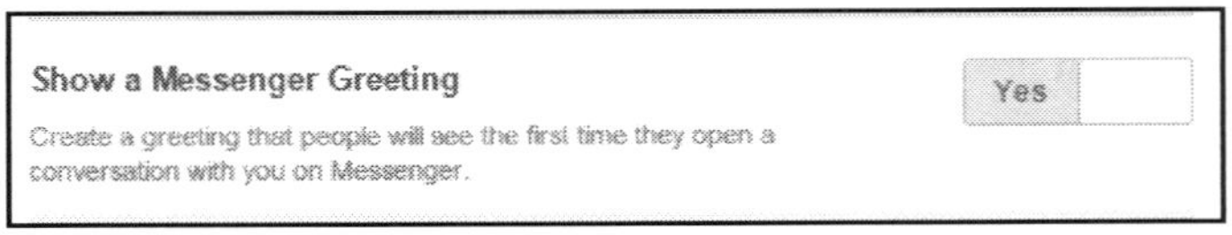

4. Provide the greeting text and click on the **Save** button to save the text:

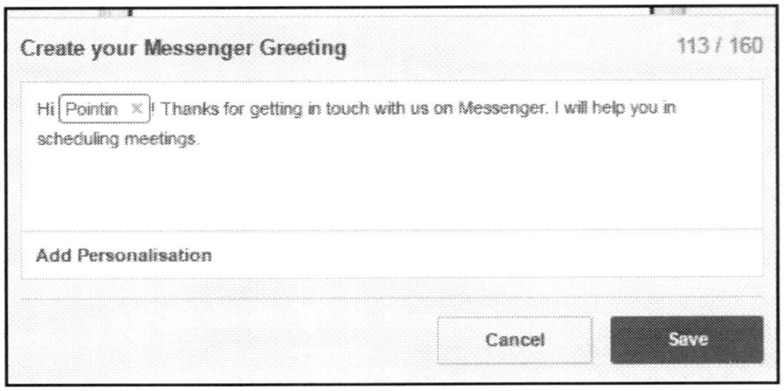

5. Go back to the bot's Facebook Page and start messaging. The first time you start a conversation, the Who's Off bot will greet you like this:

Showing the initial options of what a bot can do

At the start of a conversation, our bot will display the tasks it can perform. The user can then choose which operation he or she wants to perform. To achieve this, let's modify `server.js` as follows:

```
var express = require('express');
var bodyParser = require('body-parser');
var request = require('request');
var app = express();

app.use(bodyParser.json());
app.use(bodyParser.urlencoded({ extended: true }));

app.get('/', function (req, res) {
    res.send('This is my Facebook Messenger Bot - Whos Off Bot Server');
});

// for facebook verification
app.get('/webhook', function (req, res) {
    if (req.query['hub.verify_token'] === 'whosoffbot_verify_token') {
        res.status(200).send(req.query['hub.challenge']);
    } else {
        res.status(403).send('Invalid verify token');
    }
});
```

```
app.post('/webhook', function (req, res) {
    var events = req.body.entry[0].messaging;
    for (i = 0; i < events.length; i++) {
        var event = events[i];

        if (event.message && event.message.text) {
            if (event.message.text.indexOf('hi') > -1) {
                sendMessageWithInitialOptions(event.sender.id);
            }
        }
    }
    res.sendStatus(200);
});

function sendMessageWithInitialOptions(recipientId) {
    messageData = {
        'attachment': {
            'type': 'template',
            'payload': {
                'template_type': 'button',
                'text': 'Pl. Select your options',
                'buttons': [{
                    'type': 'postback',
                    'title': 'Schedule a Meetting',
                    'payload': 'SCHEDULE A MEETING'
                }, {
                    'type': 'postback',
                    'title': 'Whos Off When',
                    'payload': 'WHOS OFF WHEN',
                }, {
                    'type': 'postback',
                    'title': 'My Schedule',
                    'payload': 'MY SCHEDULE'
                }]
            }
        }
    };
    sendMessage(recipientId, messageData);
};

function sendMessage(recipientId, message) {
    request({
        url: 'https://graph.facebook.com/v2.6/me/messages',
        qs: { access_token: 'PAGE_ACCESS_TOKEN' },
        method: 'POST',
        json: {
            recipient: { id: recipientId },
            message: message,
```

```
            }
        }, function (error, response, body) {
            if (error) {
                console.log('Error sending message: ', error);
            } else if (response.body.error) {
                console.log('Error: ', response.body.error);
            }
        });
    };

    app.listen((process.env.PORT || 8080));
```

Use git commands to push the preceding code changes to Azure. Once deployed successfully, start a conversation with the bot by saying `hi`. The Who's Off bot will respond with what it can do for you, as follows:

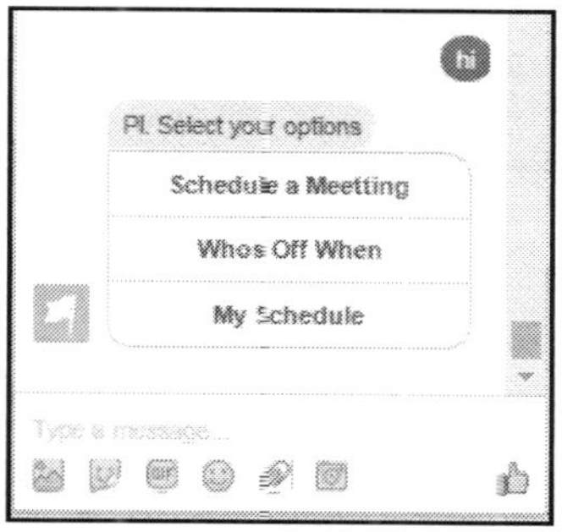

After checking out how our bot will respond, let's look at the code now.

The `app.post('/webhook')` function captures all the messages that come to our bot. So when a user says `hi`, there is a pattern-matching done and bot responds with the initial options for operations that it can perform. This is done using the following lines of code:

```
if (event.message.text.indexOf('hi') > -1) {
    sendMessageWithInitialOptions(event.sender.id);
}
```

The `sendMessageWithInitialOptions()` function actually prepares a formatted message using structured messaging templates. Since we would like to display operations that the user can choose from, we use `template_type` as `button`. Every button is of the `postback` type, and when a user clicks on one of these buttons, we can capture what the user has selected and respond to the selection.

This structured message is then returned to a sender using the `sendMessage()` function.

Based on what a user selects, the bot will respond in a button-type display. This is done to avoid wasting the end user's time in typing messages or entering keywords.

So far, we have seen how a basic conversation can happen between an end user and a bot. This same pattern will be used to further enhance our bot.

I hope you now have a little idea about how to build and enhance a conversational experience. Now let's look at how to store meeting-related information. We will use DocumentDB to store this information. Let's quickly see how we can set this up on the Azure platform.

What is DocumentDB?

In `Chapter 6`, *BotKit – Document Manager Agent for Slack,* I explained NoSQLs. DocumentDB is also a NoSQL where data is stored in JSON documents and offered by the Microsoft Azure platform.

For further details on DocumentDB, refer to `https://azure.microsoft.com/en-in/services/documentdb/`.

Setting up a DocumentDB for our Who's Off bot

Assuming you already have a Microsoft Azure subscription, follow the ensuing steps to configure a DocumentDB for your bot.

Creating an account ID for the DocumentDB

Let's create a new account called `botdb` using the following screen from the Azure portal. Select **DocumentDB** as the NoSQL API. Select the appropriate subscription and resources. Let's use existing resources for this account. You can also create a new dedicated resource. Once you enter all of the required information, hit the **Create** button at the bottom to create a new account for the DocumentDB:

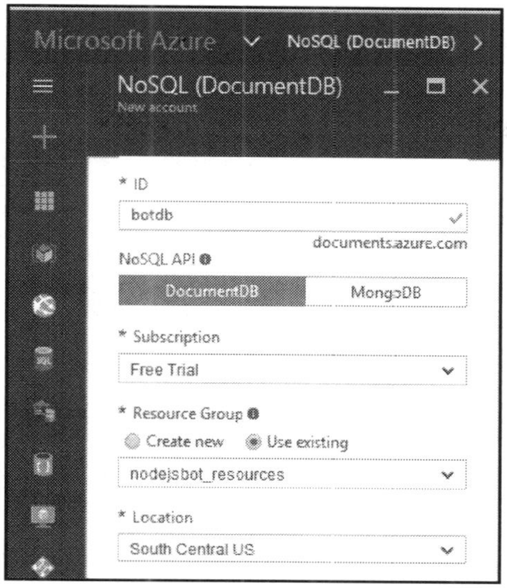

A newly created account called `botdb` will appear, as follows:

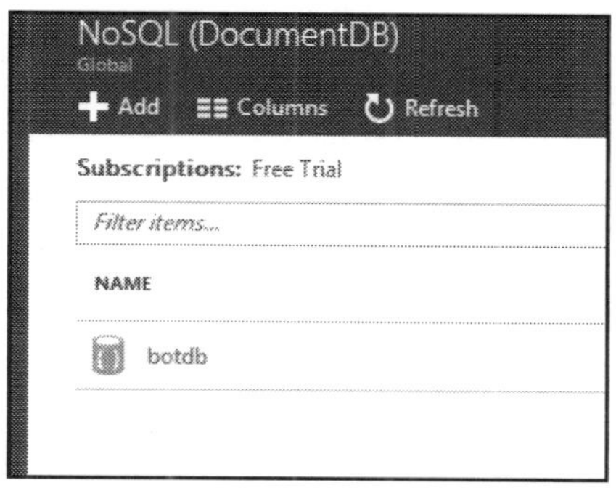

Creating a collection and database

Select a `botdb` account from the account list shown in the preceding screenshot. It will show various menu options, such as **Properties**, **Settings**, **Collections**, and so on.

Under this account, we need to create a collection to store meetings or event data. To create a new collection, click on the **Add Collection** option, as shown in the following screenshot:

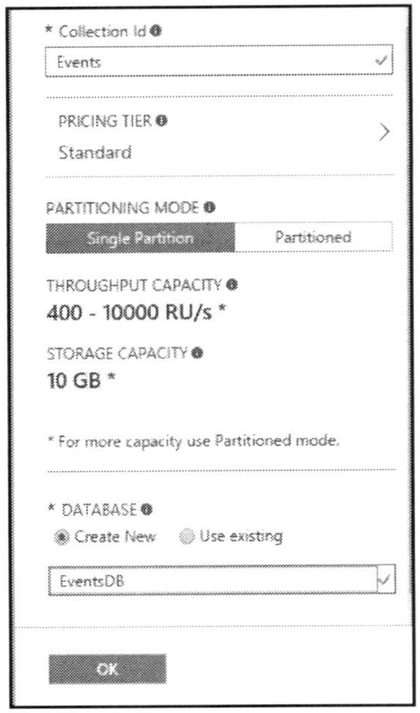

As per the preceding screenshot, we are creating a new database along with our new collection called `Events`. This new database will be named `EventsDB`. Now we can integrate this storage using the DocumentDB APIs in our Node.js program.

Wiring up DocumentDB, Moment.js, and Node.js

Let's go back to our `whosoffchatbot` directory and install the `documentdb` package from npm. This is nothing but the Node.js SDK for Microsoft Azure's DocumentDB. It can be located at `https://www.npmjs.com/package/documentdb`.

In order to install it, run this npm command:

```
npm install documentdb -save
```

While storing the meetings, we will consider the following JSON:

```
{
  "id": "8eeeb00d-5ae8-b01f-4054-cc8c3dda67f2",
  "ownerid": "<SenderId>",
  "owner": "<Facebook User Name>",
  "startdatetime": 1479376800,
  "enddatetime": 1479380400,
  "title": "<Meeting Title>"
}
```

So when the meetings get added, it'll be great if you generate a unique ID for each meeting, and the meeting information should get stored in DocumentDB. To generate these unique IDs, we will use the `guid` package. This can be located at `https://www.npmjs.com/package/guid`. Let's install the `guid` package by using the following command:

```
npm install guid -save
```

Also, all the timings for the meetings will be stored in Unix epoch or Unix time. This is done to simplify our storing process as well as query a meeting or event data with DocumentDB. So, to enable the conversion of dates to Unix epoch, we will use the npm package `moment`:

```
npm install moment -save
```

Utility functions and Node.js

Considering the functionalities to be developed for this bot, I have decided to move some of the functionalities to be helper functions. These functions can be grouped under `utils.js`. Later, these functions will be called in our main Node.js file.

Refer to the following code for `utils.js`:

```
var moment = require('moment');
var https = require('https');

function isvalidateInput(str) {
    var pattern = /^\w+[a-z A-
Z_]+?\@[0-9]{1,2}\:[0-9]{1,2}\w[to][0-9]{1,2}:[0-9]{1,2}$/;
    if (str.match(pattern) == null) {
        return false;
    } else {
        return true;
    }

};
exports.isvalidateInput = isvalidateInput;

function getFormattedTime(tsfrom, tsto) {
    var timeString = moment.unix(tsfrom).format("HH:mm") + ' - ' +
moment.unix(tsto).format("HH:mm")
    return timeString;
};
exports.getFormattedTime =getFormattedTime;

function getFormattedDay(tsfrom) {
    var dateString = moment.unix(tsfrom).format("MMM, DD");
```

```
    return dateString;
};
exports.getFormattedDay =getFormattedDay;

function
meeting(id,recipientId,ownername,strstartdatetime,strenddatetime,strtitle){
     this.id=id;
     this.ownerid=recipientId;
     this.owner=ownername;
     this.startdatetime=strstartdatetime;
     this.enddatetime=strenddatetime;
     this.title=strtitle;
};
exports.meeting =meeting;

function getUserName(uid,callback){
    https.get("https://graph.facebook.com/v2.6/" + uid +
"?fields=first_name,last_name&access_token=<PAGE_ACCESS_TOKEN> ",
function(res) {
        var d = '';
        var i;
        arr = [];
        res.on('data', function(chunk) {
            d += chunk;
        });
        res.on('end', function() {
            var e = JSON.parse(d);
            callback(e.first_name);
        });
    });
};
exports.getUserName =getUserName;
```

Looking at the preceding code, you may notice that the `isvalidateInput()` function mainly validates whether the user has entered the intended meeting information or not. If not, then the bot will help by providing sample meeting information while scheduling the meeting. This function mainly validates user input against the `Team Meeting@10:00to11:00` pattern.

The functions `getFormattedTime()` and `getFormattedDay()` convert Unix epoch to human-readable date formats.

The function `meeting()` is the constructor used during the creation of a new meeting based on the user's option.

The `getUserName()` function helps in getting the Facebook user's name, based on the recipient ID or the user ID passed to the function. When we store meetings, we will also store the recipient ID as well as the meeting owner's name with the help of this function and the `meeting()` function.

Wiring it all up together

Now that we have our utility or helper functions and the required Node.js packages in place, we are ready to finally integrate our bot in the right sense. Let's start with the breakdown of the code.

First, we will refer to all the npm modules and their instantiation for this bot implementation. This can be seen in the following code snippet:

```
var express = require('express');
var bodyParser = require('body-parser');
var request = require('request');
var moment = require('moment');
var Guid = require('guid');
var utils = require('./utils.js');

var app = express();

app.use(bodyParser.json());
app.use(bodyParser.urlencoded({ extended: true }));
```

We will also establish a connection to the DocumentDB database from Azure using the following code snippet:

```
var DocumentClient = require('documentdb').DocumentClient;
var host = "https://botdb.documents.azure.com:443/";
var masterKey = "PRIMARY KEY"
var docclient = new DocumentClient(host, { masterKey: masterKey });
```

We have a Webhook set up in Facebook, and upon receiving a call to our Webhook, our bot should capture and send us the initial options. This can be achieved using the `sendMessageWithInitialOptions()` function from the following code snippet:

```
app.post('/webhook', function (req, res) {
    var tday;
    var events = req.body.entry[0].messaging;
    for (i = 0; i < events.length; i++) {
        var event = events[i];

        if (event.message && event.message.text) {
            if (event.message.text.indexOf('hi') > -1) {
```

```
                    sendMessageWithInitialOptions(event.sender.id);
                }
```

So here, whenever a user posts `hi`, he or she will see the initial options to proceed further.

While scheduling a meeting as well, we expect the user to provide the meeting details in a specific format. Based on what the user has sent, we will validate the input and process it further with the help of the `processMeetingDetails()` function. This is achieved using the following code snippet:

```
else if (event.message.text.indexOf('@') > -1) {
                if (utils.isvalidateInput(event.message.text)) {
                    sendMessage(event.sender.id, { 'text': 'Sure! Let me
set up your meeting for '+payloadm });
                    if (payloadm=='Today'){
                        tday = moment().format("MM/DD/YYYY");
                    }
                    else if (payloadm=='Tomorrow'){
                        tday = moment().add(1, 'day').format("MM/DD/YYYY");
                    }
                    processMeetingDetails(event.message.text, tday + ' ',
event.sender.id);
                }
                else {
                    console.log('Invalid format!');
                    sendMessage(event.sender.id, { 'text': 'Pl. input
meeting details e.g. Team Meeting@10:00to11:00' });
                }
            }
```

Based on the options shown to the user, when they respond, the response is captured in `event.postback.payload`. Based on what the user has selected to proceed further, we'll execute the next options. This is done using the following code snippet:

```
else if (event.postback && event.postback.payload) {
            payload = event.postback.payload;
            // Handle a payload from this sender
            console.log(JSON.stringify(payload));
            if (payload == 'SCHEDULE A MEETING') {
                sendMessageWithScheduleOptions(event.sender.id);
            }
            else if (payload == 'SCHEDULETODAY') {
                payloadm='Today';
                sendMessage(event.sender.id, { 'text': 'Pl. provide meeting
details e.g. Team Meeting@10:00to11:00' });
            }
            else if (payload == 'SCHEDULETOMORROW') {
```

```
                payloadm='Tomorrow';
                sendMessage(event.sender.id, { 'text': 'Pl. provide
meeting details e.g. Team Meeting@10:00to11:00' });
            }
            else if (payload=='WHOS OFF WHEN'){
                sendMessageWithAllScheduleOptions(event.sender.id);
            }
            else if (payload == 'ALLSCHEDULETODAY') {
                sendMessage(event.sender.id, 'Meeting(s) Scheduled for
Today as..');
                var tilltonight = moment().add(1,
'day').startOf('day').unix();
                var startnow = moment().unix();
                showWhosIsBusyWhen(event.sender.id, startnow, tilltonight);
            }
            else if (payload == 'ALLSCHEDULETOMORROW') {
                sendMessage(event.sender.id, 'Meeting(s) Scheduled for
tomorrow as..');
                var tilltomnight = moment().add(2,
'day').startOf('day').unix();
                var starttonight = moment().endOf('day').unix();
                showWhosIsBusyWhen(event.sender.id, starttonight,
tilltomnight);
            }
        }
```

If you look at the preceding code lines, you will see payloads captured as `SCHEDULE A MEETING`, `SCHEDULETODAY`, and so on. So when a user selects these options from the Messenger screen, a post back or a call goes to our Webhook and we get what the user has selected. The function `sendMessageWithScheduleOptions()` shows options to the user for scheduling a meeting either today or tomorrow.

When a user responds to an option, Whos Off When, the Webhook is called and the function `sendMessageWithAllScheduleOptions()` gets executed to show the options to choose the day for which you would like to see who is busy and when. This again shows the options `Today` or `Tomorrow` to the end user on the screen. Based on the option selected by the user, the function `showWhosIsBusyWhen()` gets called with appropriate parameters to get the details of who is busy and when, meaning whose meetings are scheduled when.

While building this bot, we are not asking the user to key in or type in options; instead, we are showing options to choose from the screen. These options are nothing but structured message templates. We are using a button template and list template while showing the options and data to the end user.

One of the templates we are using in the function `sendMessageWithInitialOptions()` is as follows:

```
function sendMessageWithInitialOptions(recipientId) {
    messageData = {
        'attachment': {
            'type': 'template',
            'payload': {
                'template_type': 'button',
                'text': 'Pl. Select your options',
                'buttons': [{
                    'type': 'postback',
                    'title': 'Schedule a Meetting',
                    'payload': 'SCHEDULE A MEETING'
                }, {
                    'type': 'postback',
                    'title': 'Whos Off When',
                    'payload': 'WHOS OFF WHEN',
                }, {
                    'type': 'postback',
                    'title': 'My Schedule',
                    'payload': 'MY SCHEDULE'
                }]
            }
        }
    };
    sendMessage(recipientId, messageData);
};
```

The preceding function generates a structured message with the help of a button template and using function `sendMessage()`, message with initial options are shown to end user.

On similar lines, we have the function `sendMessageWithScheduleOptions()`. This generates a structured message to show the options `Today` and `Tomorrow` so as to select when to schedule a meeting:

```
function sendMessageWithScheduleOptions(recipientId) {
    messageData = {
        'attachment': {
            'type': 'template',
            'payload': {
                'template_type': 'button',
                'text': 'Select day to schedule a meeting',
                'buttons': [{
                    'type': 'postback',
                    'title': 'Today',
                    'payload': 'SCHEDULETODAY'
```

```
                }, {
                    'type': 'postback',
                    'title': 'Tomorrow',
                    'payload': 'SCHEDULETOMORROW',
                }]
            }
        }
    };
    sendMessage(recipientId, messageData);
};
```

To process meeting data and check whether there are any conflicts, the following function is used:

```
function processMeetingDetails(str, todaysdate, recipientId) {
    var title, stime, etime, starttime, endtime, ownername

    //parsing input provided for extracting meeting information
    title = str.substring(0, str.indexOf('@'));
    stime = str.substring(title.length + 1, str.indexOf('to')) + ':00';
    etime = str.substring(str.indexOf('to') + 2, str.length) + ':00';

    starttime = moment(todaysdate + stime).unix();
    endtime = moment(todaysdate + etime).unix();

    console.log(starttime + ' to ' + endtime + ' title' + title);
    //function to get Fb User Name
    utils.getUserName(recipientId, function (d) {
        ownername = d;
        var objMeeting = new utils.meeting(Guid.raw(), recipientId,
ownername, starttime, endtime, title)
        CheckMeetingsIfExistsOrInsert(objMeeting);
    });
}
```

The preceding function extracts the meeting details and passes them to check whether there are any conflicts. This function uses the utility function from `Utils.js` to get the username of the current user and check whether there are any meeting conflicts in relation to the current user. If there are no conflicts, then the meeting is scheduled with the help of the `CheckMeetingsIfExistsOrInsert()` function:

```
function CheckMeetingsIfExistsOrInsert(objMeeting) {
    var querySpec = {
        query: 'SELECT * FROM Events b WHERE  (b.ownerid= @id) and (@start
between b.startdatetime and b.enddatetime)',
        parameters: [
            {
```

```
                    name: '@id',
                    value: objMeeting.ownerid
                },
                {
                    name: '@start',
                    value: objMeeting.startdatetime
                }
            ]
        };

        docclient.queryDocuments('dbs/EventsDB/colls/Events',
    querySpec).toArray(function (err, results) {
            console.log(objMeeting.title);
            if (results.length === 0) {
                console.log('No data found' + objMeeting.title);
                var documentDefinition = {
                    'id': objMeeting.id,
                    'ownerid': objMeeting.ownerid,
                    'owner': objMeeting.owner,
                    'startdatetime': objMeeting.startdatetime,
                    'enddatetime': objMeeting.enddatetime,
                    'title': objMeeting.title
                };
                docclient.createDocument('dbs/EventsDB/colls/Events',
    documentDefinition, function (err, document) {
                    if (err) return console.log(err);
                    console.log('Created A Meeting with id : ', document.id);
                    sendMessage(objMeeting.ownerid, { 'text': 'Meeting has been
    scheduled.' });
                });
            } else {
                console.log('Data found');
                sendMessage(objMeeting.ownerid, { 'text': 'Meeting exists for
    this schedule. Pl. schedule another time.' });
            }
        });
    }
```

This function queries our DocumentDB-based database and checks whether any meeting is scheduled for that duration with the help of the `docclient.queryDocuments()` function.

If there are no meetings for the said duration, a new meeting is created using the `docclient.createDocument()` function. For a newly created meeting, the user who is scheduling a meeting is made the meeting owner by default.

When a user selects an option for **Whos Off When**, the `showWhosIsBusyWhen()` function gets invoked and displays the information of all the meetings scheduled along with their owners and time slots:

```
function showWhosIsBusyWhen(recipientId,start, end) {
    var querySpec = {
        query: 'SELECT * FROM Events b WHERE  b.startdatetime<= @end and
b.startdatetime>= @start ORDER BY b.startdatetime',
        parameters: [
            {
                name: '@end',
                value: end
            },
            {
                name: '@start',
                value: start
            }
        ]
    };
    docclient.queryDocuments('dbs/EventsDB/colls/Events',
querySpec).toArray(function (err, results) {
        if (results.length > 0) {
            sendMessageWithMeetingsOwnerInList(recipientId, results)
        }
    });
}
```

Based on the passed dates, the scheduled meeting's details are shown in a list along with their owners using the `sendMessageWithMeetingsOwnerInList()` function:

```
function sendMessageWithMeetingsOwnerInList(recipientId, results) {
    var card;
    var cards = [];
    var messageData;

    messageData = {
        attachment: {
            type: 'template',
            payload: {
                template_type: 'generic',
                elements: []
            }
        }
    };

    for (i = 0; i < results.length; i++) {
        card = {
            title: results[i].title,
```

```
                item_url: 'https://myorgmeetings.com/' + results[i].id,
                image_url: '',
                subtitle: 'Your confirmed meeting.',
                buttons: [
                    {
                        type: 'web_url',
                        url: 'https://myorgmeetings.com/' + results[i].id,
                        title: utils.getFormattedDay(results[i].startdatetime)
                    },
                     {
                        type: 'web_url',
                        url: 'https://myorgmeetings.com/' + results[i].id,
                        title: results[i].owner
                    },
                    {
                        type: 'web_url',
                        url: 'https://myorgmeetings.com/' + results[i].id,
                        title: utils.getFormattedTime(results[i].startdatetime,
results[i].enddatetime)
                    }
                ]
            };
            cards.push(card);
        }

    messageData.attachment.payload.elements = cards;
    sendMessage(recipientId, messageData);
};
```

The preceding function generates a list of meetings using a generic template and displays them as cards.

I hope you now have an overall understanding of the code implementations we have done for this bot. Our final `server.js` should look as follows:

```
var express = require('express');
var bodyParser = require('body-parser');
var request = require('request');
var moment = require('moment');
var Guid = require('guid');
var utils = require('./utils.js');

var app = express();

app.use(bodyParser.json());
app.use(bodyParser.urlencoded({ extended: true }));

var DocumentClient = require('documentdb').DocumentClient;
```

```
var host = "https://botdb.documents.azure.com:443/";
var masterKey = "PRIMARY KEY"
var docclient = new DocumentClient(host, { masterKey: masterKey });

var payloadm;

app.get('/', function (req, res) {
    res.send('This is my Facebook Messenger Bot - Whos Off Bot Server');
});

// for facebook verification
app.get('/webhook', function (req, res) {
    if (req.query['hub.verify_token'] === 'whosoffbot_verify_token') {
        res.status(200).send(req.query['hub.challenge']);
    } else {
        res.status(403).send('Invalid verify token');
    }
});

app.post('/webhook', function (req, res) {
    var tday;
    var events = req.body.entry[0].messaging;
    for (i = 0; i < events.length; i++) {
        var event = events[i];

        if (event.message && event.message.text) {
             if (event.message.text.indexOf('hi') > -1) {
                sendMessageWithInitialOptions(event.sender.id);
            }
            else if (event.message.text.indexOf('@') > -1) {
                if (utils.isvalidateInput(event.message.text)) {
                    sendMessage(event.sender.id, { 'text': 'Sure! Let me
set up your meeting for '+payloadm });
                    if (payloadm=='Today'){
                        tday = moment().format("MM/DD/YYYY");
                    }
                    else if (payloadm=='Tomorrow'){
                        tday = moment().add(1, 'day').format("MM/DD/YYYY");
                    }
                    processMeetingDetails(event.message.text, tday + ' ',
event.sender.id);
                }
                else {
                    console.log('Invalid format!');
                    sendMessage(event.sender.id, { 'text': 'Pl. input
meeting details e.g. Team Meeting@10:00to11:00' });
                }
            }
```

```
        }
          else if (event.postback && event.postback.payload) {
            payload = event.postback.payload;
            // Handle a payload from this sender
            console.log(JSON.stringify(payload));
            if (payload == 'SCHEDULE A MEETING') {
                sendMessageWithScheduleOptions(event.sender.id);
            }
            else if (payload == 'SCHEDULETODAY') {
                payloadm='Today';
                sendMessage(event.sender.id, { 'text': 'Pl. provide meeting
details e.g. Team Meeting@10:00to11:00' });
            }
            else if (payload == 'SCHEDULETOMORROW') {
                 payloadm='Tomorrow';
                 sendMessage(event.sender.id, { 'text': 'Pl. provide
meeting details e.g. Team Meeting@10:00to11:00' });
            }
            else if (payload=='WHOS OFF WHEN'){
                sendMessageWithAllScheduleOptions(event.sender.id);
            }
            else if (payload == 'ALLSCHEDULETODAY') {
                sendMessage(event.sender.id, 'Meeting(s) Scheduled for
Today as..');
                var tilltonight = moment().add(1,
'day').startOf('day').unix();
                var startnow = moment().unix();
                showWhosIsBusyWhen(event.sender.id, startnow, tilltonight);
            }
            else if (payload == 'ALLSCHEDULETOMORROW') {
                sendMessage(event.sender.id, 'Meeting(s) Scheduled for
tomorrow as..');
                var tilltomnight = moment().add(2,
'day').startOf('day').unix();
                var starttonight = moment().endOf('day').unix();
                showWhosIsBusyWhen(event.sender.id, starttonight,
tilltomnight);
            }
        }

    }
    res.sendStatus(200);
});

function sendMessageWithInitialOptions(recipientId) {
    messageData = {
        'attachment': {
            'type': 'template',
```

```
            'payload': {
                'template_type': 'button',
                'text': 'Pl. Select your options',
                'buttons': [{
                    'type': 'postback',
                    'title': 'Schedule a Meetting',
                    'payload': 'SCHEDULE A MEETING'
                }, {
                    'type': 'postback',
                    'title': 'Whos Off When',
                    'payload': 'WHOS OFF WHEN',
                }, {
                    'type': 'postback',
                    'title': 'My Schedule',
                    'payload': 'MY SCHEDULE'
                }]
            }
        }
    };
    sendMessage(recipientId, messageData);
};

function sendMessageWithScheduleOptions(recipientId) {
    messageData = {
        'attachment': {
            'type': 'template',
            'payload': {
                'template_type': 'button',
                'text': 'Select day to schedule a meeting',
                'buttons': [{
                    'type': 'postback',
                    'title': 'Today',
                    'payload': 'SCHEDULETODAY'
                }, {
                    'type': 'postback',
                    'title': 'Tomorrow',
                    'payload': 'SCHEDULETOMORROW',
                }]
            }
        }
    };
    sendMessage(recipientId, messageData);
};

function processMeetingDetails(str, todaysdate, recipientId) {
    var title, stime, etime, starttime, endtime, ownername

    //parsing input provided for extracting meeting information
```

```
    title = str.substring(0, str.indexOf('@'));
    stime = str.substring(title.length + 1, str.indexOf('to')) + ':00';
    etime = str.substring(str.indexOf('to') + 2, str.length) + ':00';

    starttime = moment(todaysdate + stime).unix();
    endtime = moment(todaysdate + etime).unix();

    console.log(starttime + ' to ' + endtime + ' title' + title);
    //function to get Fb User Name
    utils.getUserName(recipientId, function (d) {
        ownername = d;
        var objMeeting = new utils.meeting(Guid.raw(), recipientId,
ownername, starttime, endtime, title)
        CheckMeetingsIfExistsOrInsert(objMeeting);
    });
}

function CheckMeetingsIfExistsOrInsert(objMeeting) {
    var querySpec = {
        query: 'SELECT * FROM Events b WHERE  (b.ownerid= @id) and (@start
between b.startdatetime and b.enddatetime)',
        parameters: [
            {
                name: '@id',
                value: objMeeting.ownerid
            },
            {
                name: '@start',
                value: objMeeting.startdatetime
            }
        ]
    };

    docclient.queryDocuments('dbs/EventsDB/colls/Events',
querySpec).toArray(function (err, results) {
        console.log(objMeeting.title);
        if (results.length === 0) {
            console.log('No data found' + objMeeting.title);
            var documentDefinition = {
                'id': objMeeting.id,
                'ownerid': objMeeting.ownerid,
                'owner': objMeeting.owner,
                'startdatetime': objMeeting.startdatetime,
                'enddatetime': objMeeting.enddatetime,
                'title': objMeeting.title
            };
            docclient.createDocument('dbs/EventsDB/colls/Events',
documentDefinition, function (err, document) {
```

```
                if (err) return console.log(err);
                console.log('Created A Meeting with id : ', document.id);
                sendMessage(objMeeting.ownerid, { 'text': 'Meeting has been
scheduled.' });
                });
        } else {
            console.log('Data found');
            sendMessage(objMeeting.ownerid, { 'text': 'Meeting exists for
this schedule. Pl. schedule another time.' });
        }
    });
}

function sendMessageWithAllScheduleOptions(recipientId) {
    messageData = {
        'attachment': {
            'type': 'template',
            'payload': {
                'template_type': 'button',
                'text': 'Select your schedule for',
                'buttons': [{
                    'type': 'postback',
                    'title': 'Today',
                    'payload': 'ALLSCHEDULETODAY'
                }, {
                    'type': 'postback',
                    'title': 'Tomorrow',
                    'payload': 'ALLSCHEDULETOMORROW',
                }]
            }
        }
    };
    sendMessage(recipientId, messageData);
};

function showWhosIsBusyWhen(recipientId,start, end) {
    var querySpec = {
        query: 'SELECT * FROM Events b WHERE  b.startdatetime<= @end and
b.startdatetime>= @start ORDER BY b.startdatetime',
        parameters: [
            {
                name: '@end',
                value: end
            },
            {
                name: '@start',
                value: start
            }
```

```
        ]
    };
    docclient.queryDocuments('dbs/EventsDB/colls/Events',
querySpec).toArray(function (err, results) {
        if (results.length > 0) {
            sendMessageWithMeetingsOwnerInList(recipientId, results)
        }
    });
}

function sendMessageWithMeetingsOwnerInList(recipientId, results) {
    var card;
    var cards = [];
    var messageData;

    messageData = {
        attachment: {
            type: 'template',
            payload: {
                template_type: 'generic',
                elements: []
            }
        }
    };

    for (i = 0; i < results.length; i++) {
        card = {
            title: results[i].title,
            item_url: 'https://myorgmeetings.com/' + results[i].id,
            image_url: '',
            subtitle: 'Your confirmed meeting.',
            buttons: [
                {
                    type: 'web_url',
                    url: 'https://myorgmeetings.com/' + results[i].id,
                    title: utils.getFormattedDay(results[i].startdatetime)
                },
                 {
                    type: 'web_url',
                    url: 'https://myorgmeetings.com/' + results[i].id,
                    title: results[i].owner
                },
                {
                    type: 'web_url',
                    url: 'https://myorgmeetings.com/' + results[i].id,
                    title: utils.getFormattedTime(results[i].startdatetime,
results[i].enddatetime)
                }
```

```
            ]
        };
        cards.push(card);
    }

    messageData.attachment.payload.elements = cards;
    sendMessage(recipientId, messageData);
};

function sendMessage(recipientId, message) {
    request({
        url: 'https://graph.facebook.com/v2.6/me/messages',
        qs: { access_token: 'PAGE_ACCESS_TOEKN' },
        method: 'POST',
        json: {
            recipient: { id: recipientId },
            message: message,
        }
    }, function (error, response, body) {
        if (error) {
            console.log('Error sending message: ', error);
        } else if (response.body.error) {
            console.log('Error: ', response.body.error);
        }
    });
};

app.listen((process.env.PORT || 8080));
```

Running our bot – the Who's Off bot

Having understood the code implementation and assuming our final code is up and running on Microsoft Azure, let's look at how our bot is executed from the end user's perspective.

Initial options

Here are some initial options as in the following screenshot:

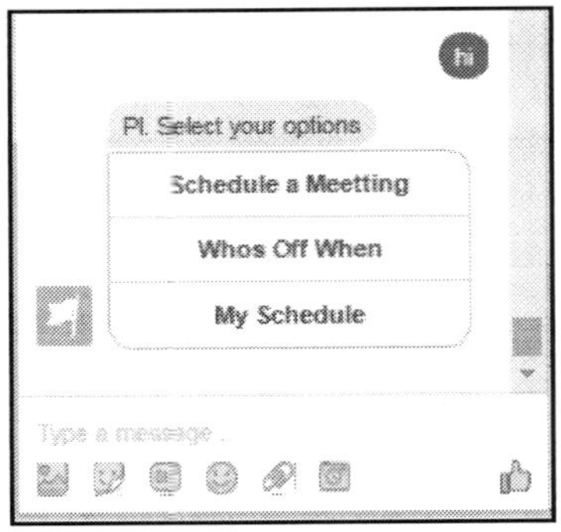

Scheduling a meeting

When a user clicks on **Schedule a Meeting**, two options are sent by our bot, as follows:

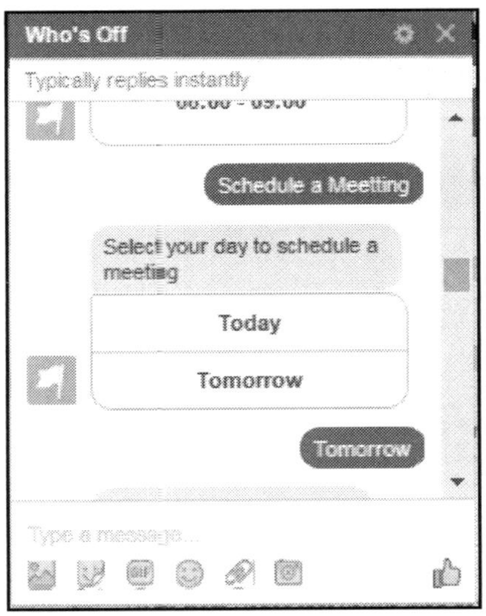

Now when the user clicks on **Tomorrow**, our bot will respond with some guiding text to the end user as **Pl. provide meeting details e.g. Team Meeting@10:00to11:00**:

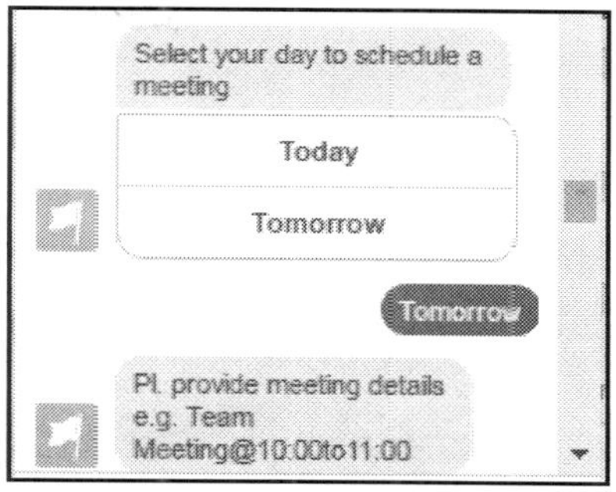

After receiving the guiding text, the user would enter the meeting details as `Team Meeting@10:00to11:00`:

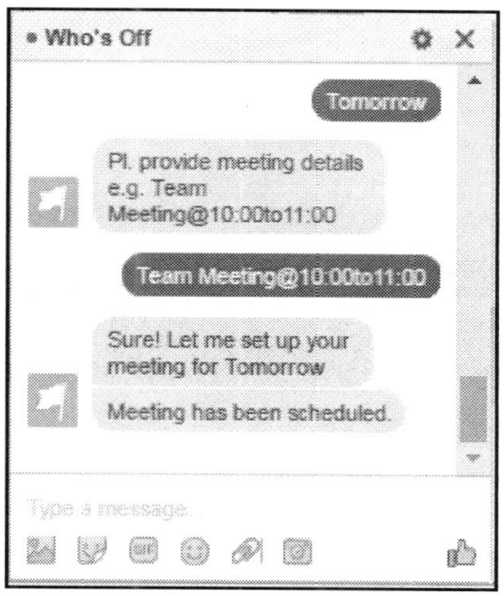

The bot checks for conflicts, and if no conflicts are found, the meeting is scheduled and the bot responds with the message **Meeting has been scheduled.**, as shown in the preceding screenshot.

Whos Off When

When the user selects an option for **Whos Off When**, the following screen shows the options from which days, **Today** or **Tomorrow,** you would like to see who is off when.

If the user selects the option **Today**, the meetings for that day are shown as follows:

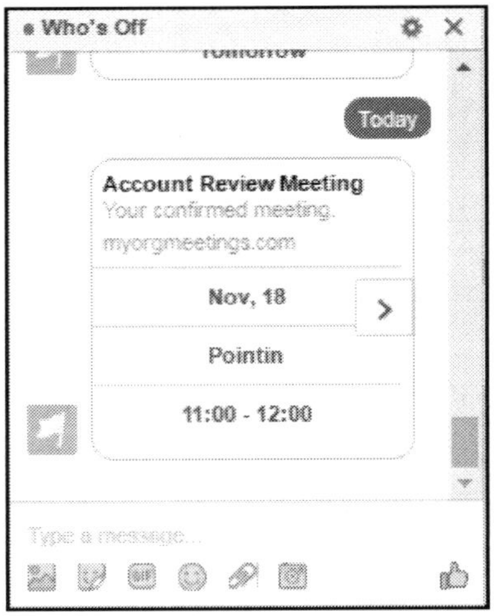

The arrow on the right-hand side shows there are multiple meetings. Just scroll to the left to see the meetings, as follows:

This way, we are showing who is busy when, based on the meetings scheduled by individual members.

So we have implemented our bot in a way that it can schedule our meetings and also show all our scheduled meetings in an elegant way within the Facebook Messenger interface. There is one more operation left: **My Schedule**. I will leave the implementation of this operation to you now.

Summary

So with Facebook, we built a bot and enhanced our team's collaborative experience. With this bot, our team can just send the meeting details on a chat window to our bot, such as the name and start and end date, and the bot will take care of rest.

To summarize, we learned how to create a Facebook Page and app. We also created a basic bot wired up in Node.js and deployed this basic bot to Microsoft Azure. We did this as Facebook Messenger needs an HTTPS-based Webhooks integration. Then, we subscribed to a page within Webhooks so that the messages that come from our bot pages could be accepted by our Node.js bot.

Finally, we enhanced our bot to display information, such as who is off when, and displayed it within a Facebook Messenger interface.

We saw that the Who's Off bot with its little intelligence can check for a conflict and then scheduled a meeting accordingly. It can also present us with a team's schedule in a Facebook-compatible Messenger template format.

Further, if you would really like to develop intelligent bots, then it's worth taking a look at `https://wit.ai/` and `https://api.ai/`. These platforms enable us to develop chat bots that can understand humans in a better way.

Hopefully, this chapter has given you an amazing experience of building Facebook Messenger bots!

In the next chapter, we will explore how to develop IRC bots and how we can wire them up within Node.js and help our developers use it for bug-tracking purposes.

8 A Bug-Tracking Agent for Teams

InternetRelayChat (**IRC**) enables us to communicate in real time in the form of text. This chat runs on a TCP protocol in a client-server model. IRC supports group messaging, which is called as channels, and also supports private messaging.

IRC is organized into many networks with different audiences. IRC being a client server, users need IRC clients to connect to IRC servers. IRC client software comes as packaged software, as well as web-based clients. Some browsers are also providing IRC clients as add-ons. Users can either install them on their systems, and then they can be used to connect to IRC servers or networks. While connecting to these IRC servers, users will have to provide a unique nickname and choose an existing channel for communication, or users can start a new channel while connecting to these servers.

In this chapter, we are going to develop one such IRC bot for bug-tracking purposes. This bug-tracking bot will provide information about bugs as well as details about a particular bug. All this will be done seamlessly within the IRC channel itself. It's going to be one window operation for a team, when it comes to knowing about their bugs or defects.

Great!!

IRC client and server

As mentioned in the introduction, to initiate an IRC communication, we need an IRC client, and a server or a network to which our client will be connected. We will be using a freenode network for our client to connect to. Freenode is the largest free, open source, software-focused IRC network.

IRC web-based client

We will be using the IRC web-based client through a URL (`https://webchat.freenode.net/`). After opening the URL, you will see the following screen:

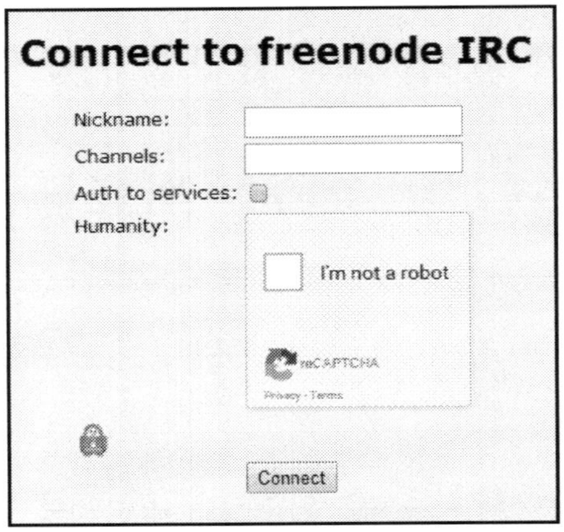

As mentioned earlier, while connecting, we need to provide **Nickname:** and **Channels:**.

I have provided **Nickname:** as `Madan` and at **Channels:** as `#BugsChannel`. In IRC, channels are always identified by a #, so I used # to begin the name of my bugs channel. This is the new channel that we will be starting for communication. All the developers or team members can similarly provide their nicknames and this channel name to join the communication. Now let's prove **Humanity:** by selecting **I'm not a robot** and clicking the **Connect** button.

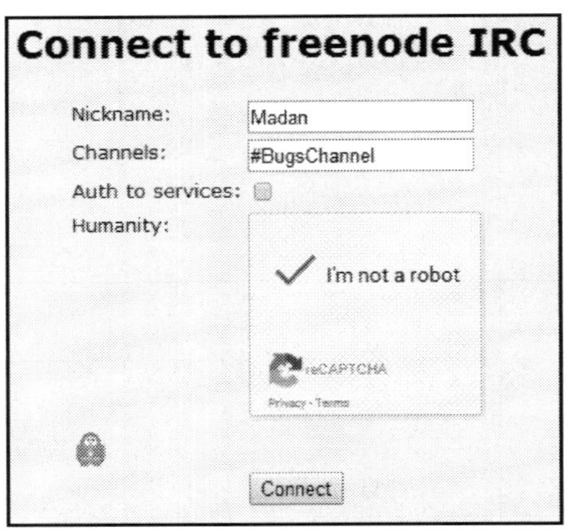

Once connected, you will see the following screen:

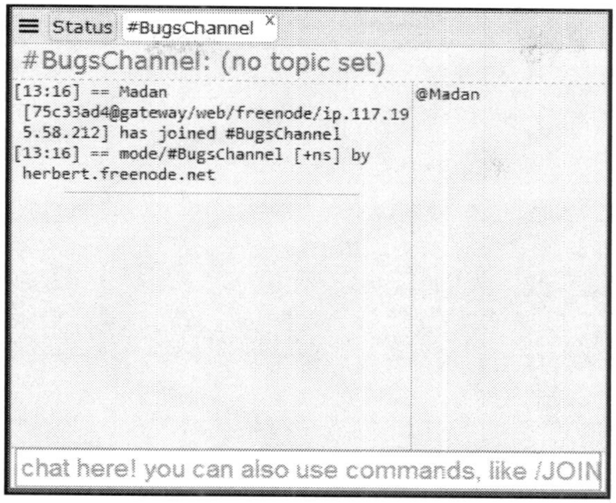

With this, our IRC client is connected to the freenode network. You can also see the username on the right-hand side is `@Madan`, and within this **#BugsChannel**. Whoever joins this channel, using this channel name and a network, will be shown on the right-hand side.

In the next section, we will ask our bot to join this channel and the same network, and will see how it appears within the channel.

IRC bots

IRC bot is a program that connects to IRC as one of the clients and appears as one of the users in the IRC channels. These IRC bots are used to provide IRC services or to host chat-based custom implementations that will help teams to efficiently collaborate.

Creating our first IRC bot using IRC and Node.js

Let's start by creating a folder on our local drive, in order to store our bot program, from the Command Prompt:

```
mkdir ircbot
cd ircbot
```

Assuming we have Node.js and npm installed, let's create and initialize our `package.json`, which will store our bot's dependencies and definitions:

```
npm init
```

Once you have gone through the `npm init` options (which are very easy to follow), you'll see something similar to this:

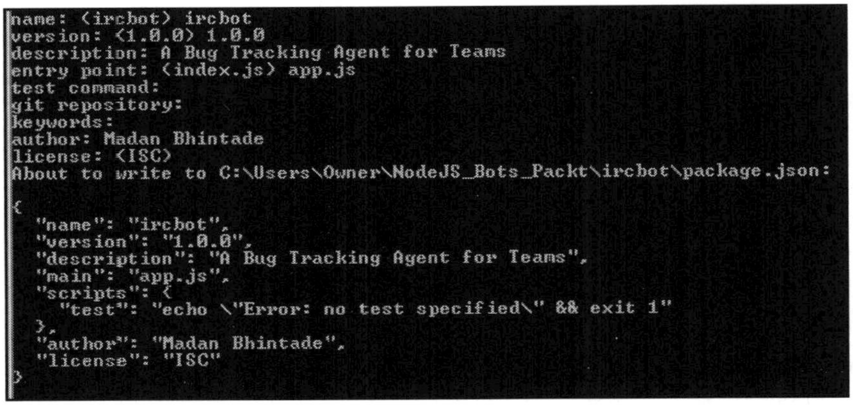

In your project folder, you'll see the result, which is your `package.json` file:

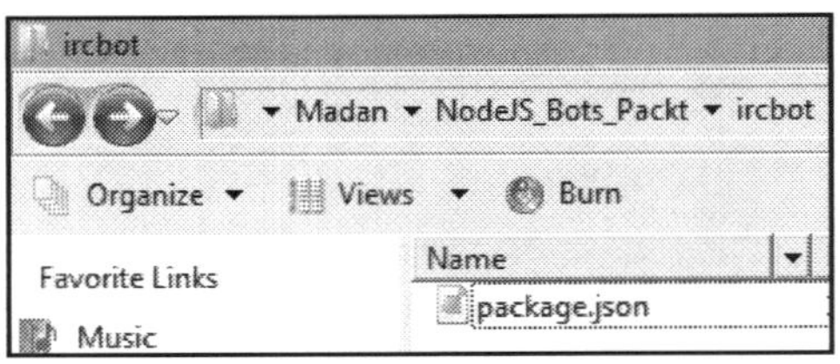

Let's install the `irc` package from npm. This can be located at `https://www.npmjs.com/package/irc`.

In order to install it, run this npm command.

```
npm install --save irc
```

You should then see something similar to this:

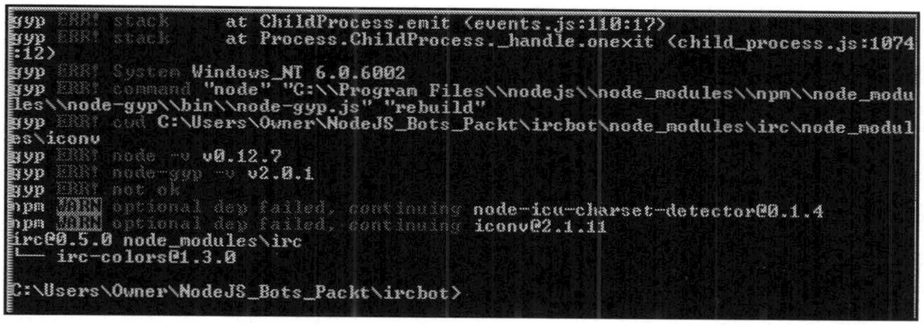

Having done this, the next thing to do is to update your `package.json` in order to include the `"engines"` attribute. Open the `package.json` file with a text editor and update it as follows:

```
"engines": {
    "node": ">=5.6.0"
}
```

Your `package.json` should then look like this:

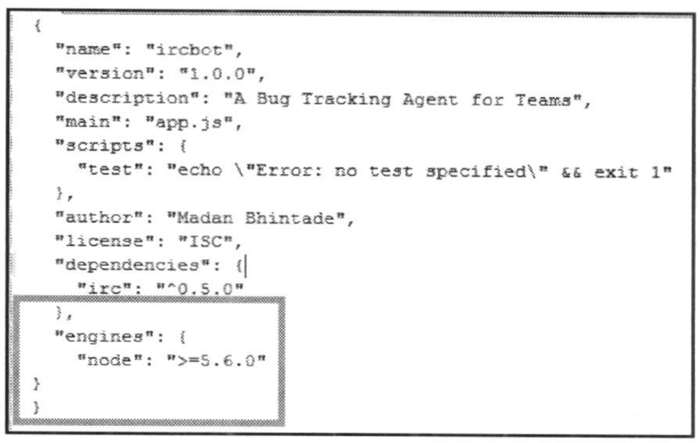

Let's create our `app.js` file, which will be the entry point to our bot, as mentioned while setting up our node package.

Our `app.js` should look like this:

```
var irc = require('irc');
var client = new irc.Client('irc.freenode.net', 'BugTrackerIRCBot', {
  autoConnect: false
});
client.connect(5, function(serverReply) {
  console.log("Connected!\n", serverReply);
```

```
    client.join('#BugsChannel', function(input) {
      console.log("Joined #BugsChannel");
      client.say('#BugsChannel', "Hi, there. I am an IRC Bot which track bugs
  or defects for your team.\n I can help you using following commands.\n
  BUGREPORT \n BUG # <BUG. NO>");
    });
  });
```

Now let's run our Node.js program and see how our console looks. If everything works well, our console should show our bot as being connected to the required network and also joined to a channel. The console can be seen to be the following:

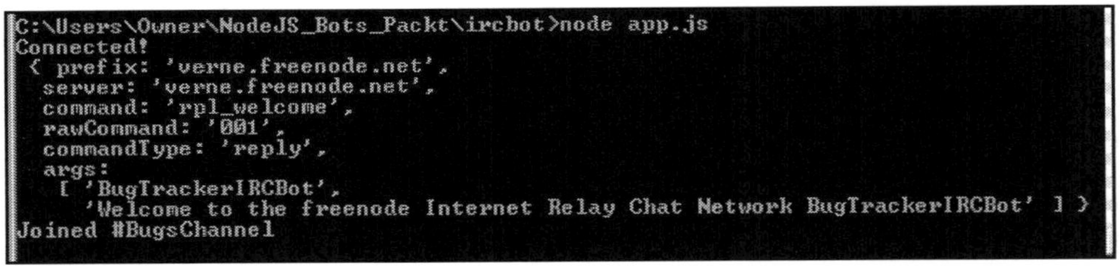

Now, if you look at our channel **#BugsChannel** in our web client, you should see our bot has joined it and also sent a welcome message as well. Refer to the following screen:

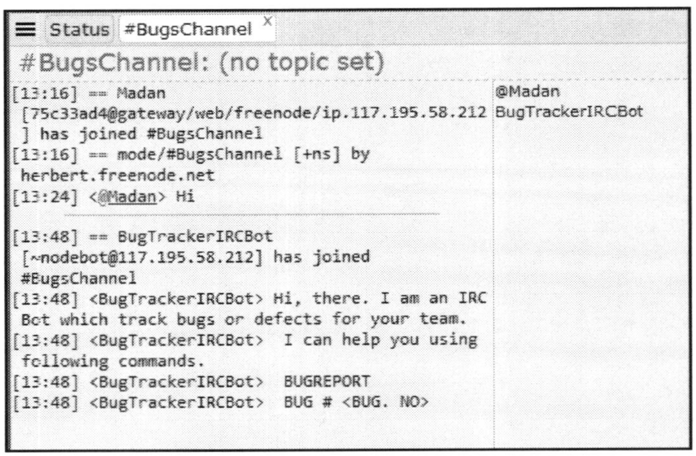

If you look at the the preceding screen, our bot program has executed successfully. Our bot `BugTrackerIRCBot` has joined the channel **#BugsChannel**, and also the bot has sent an introduction message to all who are on the channel. If you look at the right side of the screen under usernames, we see `BugTrackerIRCBot` below `@Madan`.

Code understanding of our basic bot

After seeing how our bot looks in IRC client, let's look at the basic code implementation from `app.js`.

We used `irc` library with the following line:

```
var irc = require('irc');
```

Using `irc` library, we instantiated the client to connect to one of the IRC networks using the following code snippet:

```
var client = new irc.Client('irc.freenode.net', 'BugTrackerIRCBot', {
  autoConnect: false
});
```

Here, we connected to network `irc.freenode.net` and provided a nickname of `BugTrackerIRCBot`. This name has been given because I would like my bot to track and report any bugs found in the future. Now, we ask the client to connect and join a specific channel using the following code snippet:

```
client.connect(5, function(serverReply) {
  console.log("Connected!\n", serverReply);
  client.join('#BugsChannel', function(input) {
    console.log("Joined #BugsChannel");
    client.say('#BugsChannel', "Hi, there. I am an IRC Bot which track bugs
or defects for your team.\n I can help you using following commands.\n
BUGREPORT \n BUG # <BUG. NO>");
  });
});
```

In the preceding code snippet, once the client is connected, we get a reply from the server. This reply is shown on a console. Once successfully connected, we ask the bot to join a channel using the following code line:

```
client.join('#BugsChannel', function(input) {
```

Remember, `#BugsChannel` is what we have joined to from the web client at the start. Now, using `client.join()`, I am asking my bot to join the same channel. Once the bot has joined, the bot gives a welcome message in the same channel using the function `client.say()`.

Hopefully, this has given you some basic understanding of our bot and it's code implementations.

In the next section, we will enhance our bot so that our teams can have an effective communication experience while chatting.

Enhancing our BugTrackerIRCBot

Having built a very basic IRC bot, let's enhance our BugTrackerIRCBot.

As developers, we would always like to know how our programs or a system is functioning. To do this, typically, our testing teams carry out testing of a system or a program, and log the bugs or defects in a bug-tracking software package or system. We developers can later take a look at those bugs and address them as part of our development life cycle. During this journey, developers will collaborate and communicate over messaging platforms such as IRC. We would like to provide a unique experience during their development by leveraging IRC bots.

So, this is exactly what we are doing. We are creating a channel for communication; all the team members will be joined to it and our bot will also be there. In this channel, bugs will be reported and communicated based on developers' requests. Also, if developers need some additional information about a bug, the chat bot can help them by providing a URL from the bug-tracking system.

Awesome!!

But, before going into detail, let me summarize how we are going to do this using the following steps:

- Enhance our basic bot program for a more conversational experience
- Create a bug-tracking system or bug storage where bugs will be stored and tracked for developers

Here we mention a bug storage system. In this chapter, I would like to explain **DocumentDB**, which is a NoSQL JSON-based cloud storage system. In earlier chapters we looked at MongoDB. Now we will look at DocumentDB for our bug system.

What is DocumentDB?

In an earlier chapter, I have already explained NoSQLs. DocumentDB is one such NoSQL, in which data is stored in JSON documents, and is offered on the Microsoft Azure platform.

Details of DocumentDB can be referred to at `https://azure.microsoft.com/en-in/services/documentdb/`.

Setting up a DocumentDB for our BugTrackerIRCBot

Assuming you already have a Microsoft Azure subscription, follow these steps to configure DocumentDB for your bot.

Create account ID for DocumentDB

Let's create a new account called `botdb` using the following screenshot from the Azure portal. Select NoSQL API as **DocumentDB**. Select an appropriate subscription and resources. I am using the existing resources for this account. You can also create a new dedicated resource for this account. Once you enter all the required information, hit the **Create** button at the bottom to create the new account for DocumentDB.

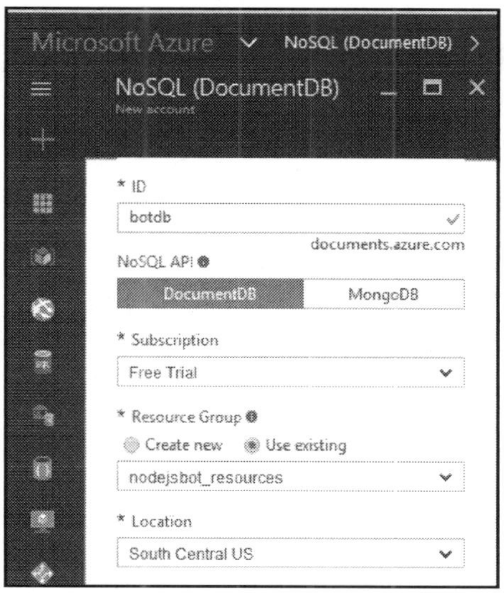

The newly created account, `botdb`, can be seen as follows:

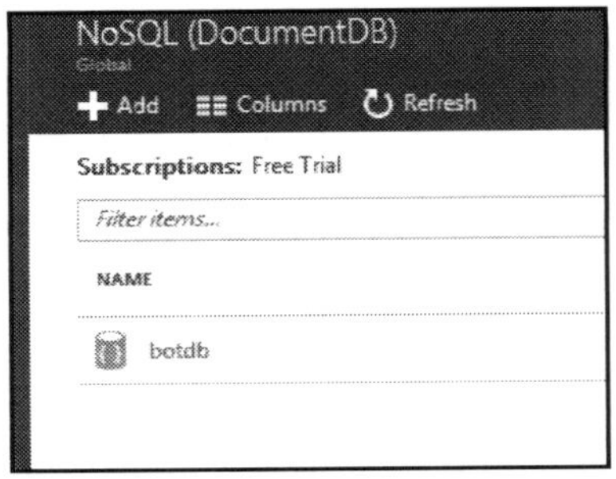

Create a collection and database

Select a `botdb` account from the account lists shown previously. This will show various menu options such as **Properties**, **Settings**, **Collections**, etc.

Under this account, we need to create a collection to store the bug data. To create a new collection, click on the **Add Collection** option, as shown in the following screenshot:

On clicking on the **Add Collection** option, the following screen will be shown on the right side of the screen. Please enter the details as shown in the following screenshot:

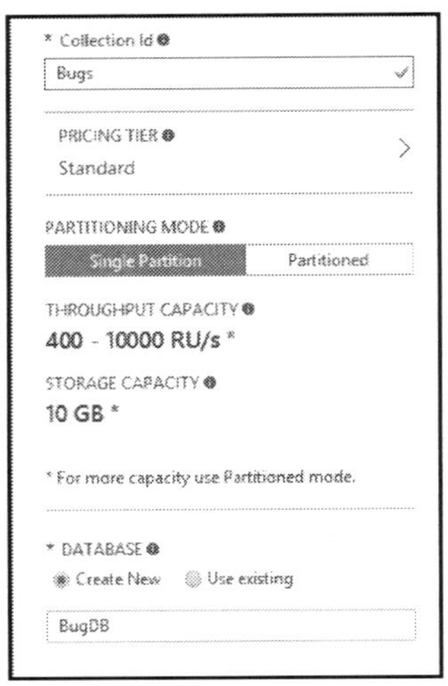

In the preceding screen, we are creating a new database along with our new collection, **Bugs**. This new database will be named `BugDB`. Once this database has been created, we can add other bug-related collections in future to the same database. This can be done using the option **Use** existing from the preceding screen. Once you have entered all the relevant data, click **OK** to create the database as well as the collection. Refer to the following screenshot:

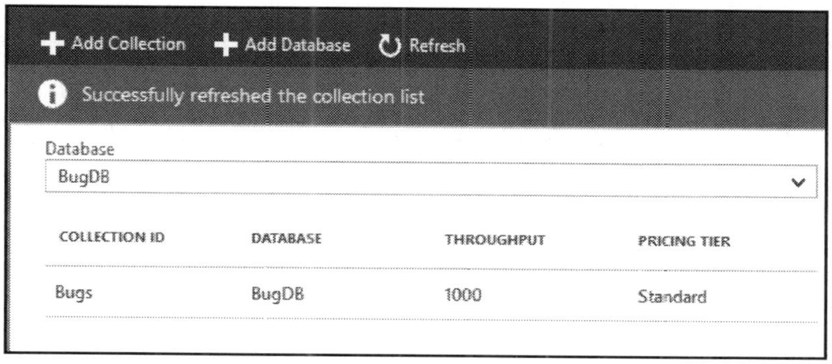

From the preceding screen, the **COLLECTION ID** and **DATABASE** shown will be used while enhancing our bot.

Create data for our BugTrackerIRCBot

Now we have the `BugsDB` with the bugs collection, which will hold all the data for bugs. Let's add some data into our collection. To add a data item, let's use the menu option **Document Explorer** shown in the following screenshot:

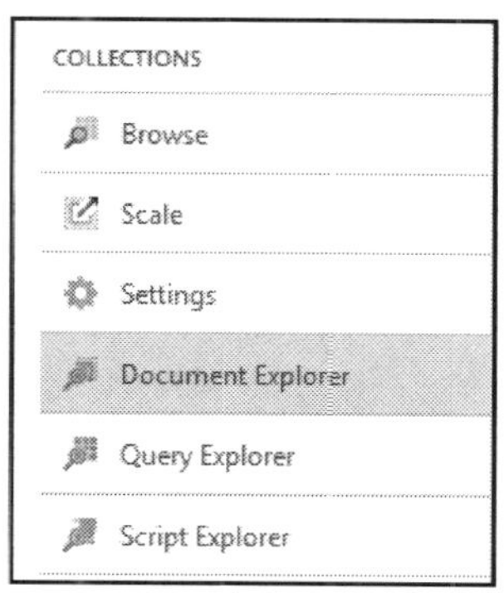

This will open up a screen showing the list of **Databases** and **Collections** created so far. Select our database of `BugDB` and the collection of `Bugs` from the available list. Refer to the following screenshot:

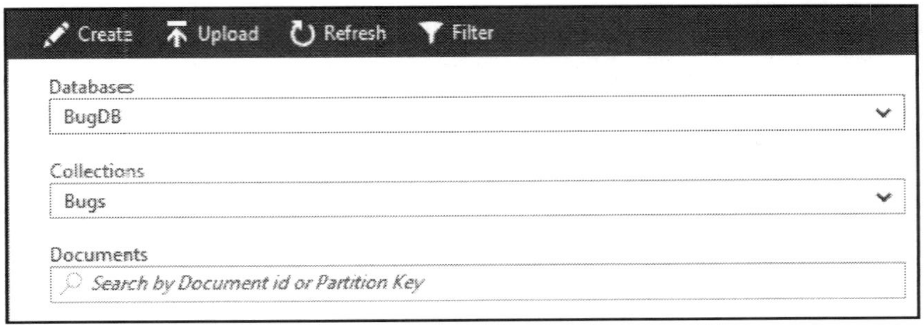

To create a JSON document for our bugs collection, click on the **Create** option. This will open up a **New Document** screen to enter the JSON-based data. Please enter a data item as per the following screenshot:

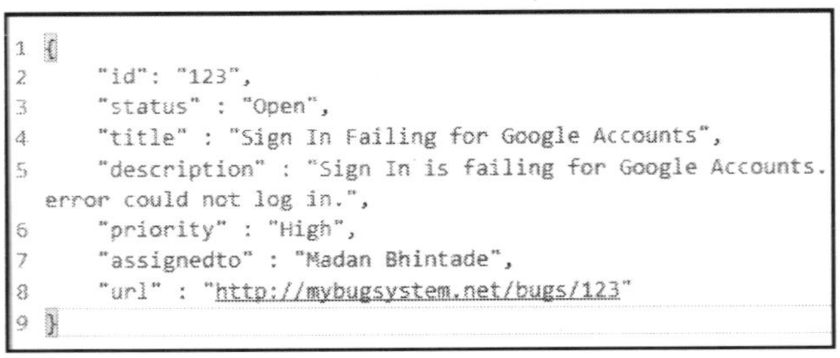

We will be storing `id`, `status`, `title`, `description`, `priority`,`assignedto`, and `url` attributes for our single bug document, which will be stored in the bugs collection. To save the JSON document in our collection, click the **Save** button. Refer to the following screenshot:

This way we can create sample records in the bugs collection, which will later be wired up in a Node.js program. A sample list of bugs can be seen in the following screenshot:

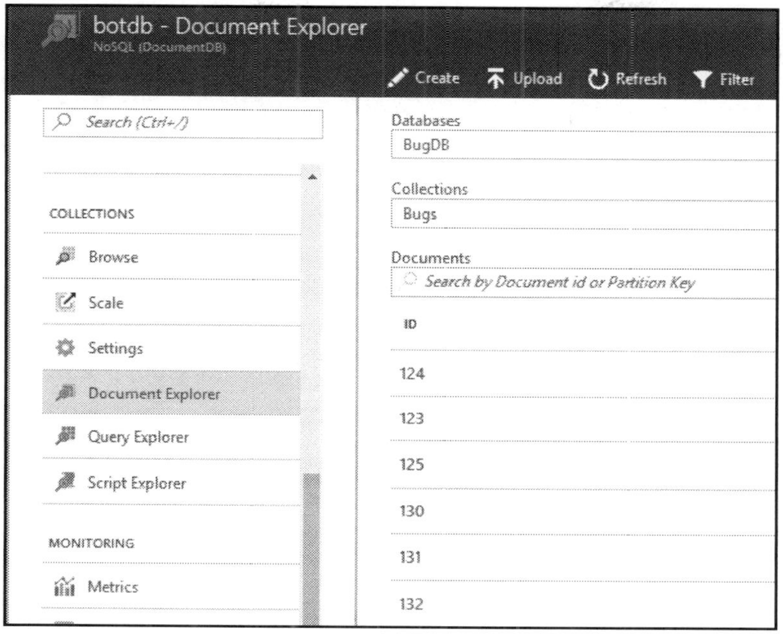

To summarize the section so far, we have determined how to use DocumentDB from Microsoft Azure. Using DocumentDB, we created a new collection along with new database to store bug data. We also added some sample JSON documents in the bugs collection.

Now let's lock at how we can wire up our DocumentDB with Node.js.

Wiring up DocumentDB and Node.js

Let's go back to our `ircbot` directory and install the `documentdb` package from npm. This is simply Node.js SDK for Microsoft Azure DocumentDB. This is located at URL `https://www.npmjs.com/package/documentdb`.

In order to install it, run this npm command:

```
npm install documentdb --save
```

You should then see something similar to this:

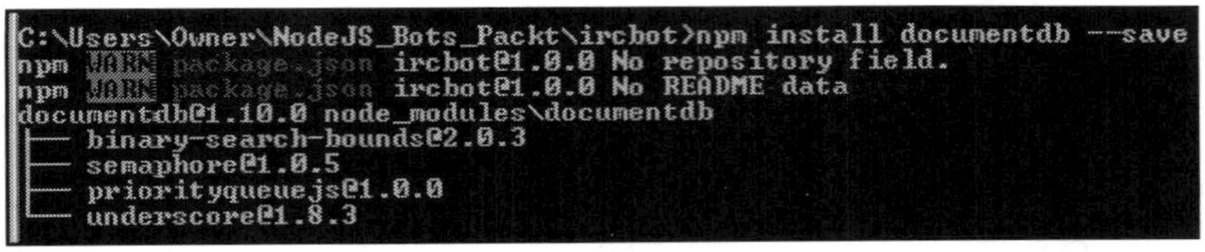

Let's modify our `app.js` file so that we can access DocumentDB-based data using DocumentDB APIs.

To wire up DocumentDB with Node.js, we will use the following code:

```
var DocumentClient = require('documentdb').DocumentClient;
var host = "https://botdb.documents.azure.com:443/";
var masterKey = "<YOUR PRIMARY KEY>";
var docclient = new DocumentClient(host, {masterKey: masterKey});

docclient.readDocuments('dbs/BugDB/colls/Bugs').toArray(function (err,
docs) {
    console.log(docs.length + ' Documents found');
});
```

In the the preceding code, we are trying to read documents from our DocumentDB. Now, to instantiate `DocumentClient`, we need the `host` and `masterkey` of our DocumentDB account. Refer to the following screenshot to locate `host`, which is only a **URl** and `masterkey` is only a **PRIMARY KEY**.

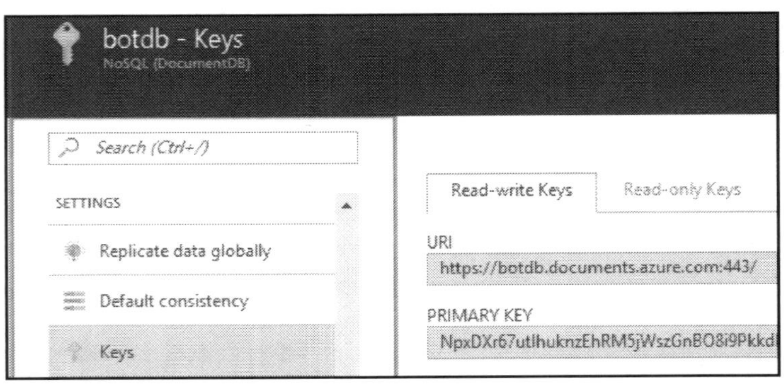

To read all the documents from our collection, we use the following code lines:

```
docclient.readDocuments('dbs/BugDB/colls/Bugs').toArray(function (err,
docs) {
    console.log(docs.length + ' Documents found');
});
```

`readDocuments()` needs an argument of collection link. This collection link is simply the path to our collection. This is given as the following:

```
dbs/<Your Database>/colls/<Your Collection ID>
```

Our `app.js` now should look like this:

```
var irc = require('irc');
var client = new irc.Client('irc.freenode.net', 'BugTrackerIRCBot', {
  autoConnect: false
});
client.connect(5, function(serverReply) {
  console.log("Connected!\n", serverReply);
  client.join('#BugsChannel', function(input) {
    console.log("Joined #BugsChannel");
    client.say('#BugsChannel', "Hi, there. I am an IRC bot which track bugs
or defects for your team.\n I can help you using following commands.\n
BUGREPORT \n BUG # <BUG. NO>");
  });
});

var DocumentClient = require('documentdb').DocumentClient;
var host = "https://botdb.documents.azure.com:443/";
var masterKey = "<YOUR PRIMARY KEY>";
var docclient = new DocumentClient(host, {masterKey: masterKey});

docclient.readDocuments('dbs/BugDB/colls/Bugs').toArray(function (err,
docs) {
    console.log(docs.length + ' Documents found');
});
```

Let's go back to our `ircbot` directory with a Command Prompt and run our node program. Once you run this, the program will connect to our collection using Microsoft Azure DocumentDB Node.js SDK. After reading the documents, on the Command Prompt we will see the number of documents read. For details, please refer the following screenshot:

Since our IRC client is connecting asynchronously, we will see a reply from IRC Server once received. In this case, we got the response from DocumentDB early, so we see `6 Documents found` on the console.

So far, we are able to connect to DocumentDB and able to retrieve documents from the same. Now, in the next and final section, we will wire up all of this together and we will also enhance the conversational experience of our bot.

Wiring up all of this together

To wire up all the things together, let's modify our earlier `app.js` to be the following:

```
var irc = require('irc');

var client = new irc.Client('irc.freenode.net', 'BugTrackerIRCBot', {
    autoConnect: false
});

client.connect(5, function(serverReply) {
    console.log("Connected!\n", serverReply);
    client.join('#BugsChannel', function(input) {
        console.log("Joined #BugsChannel");
        client.say('#BugsChannel', "Hi, there. I am an IRC Bot which track
bugs or defects for your team.\n I can help you using following commands.\n
BUGREPORT \n BUG # <BUG. NO>");
    });
});

var DocumentClient = require('documentdb').DocumentClient;
var host = "https://botdb.documents.azure.com:443/";
var masterKey = "<PRIMARY KEY>";
var docclient = new DocumentClient(host, {masterKey: masterKey});

client.addListener('message', function (from, to, text) {
    var str = text;
    if (str.indexOf('BUGREPORT') === -1){
        if (str.indexOf('BUG #') === -1){
            client.say('#BugsChannel', "I could not get that!\n Send me
commands like,\n BUGREPORT \n BUG # <BUG. NO>");
        }
        else {
            client.say('#BugsChannel', "So you need info about "+text);
            client.say('#BugsChannel', "Wait for a moment!");
            var t= text.substring(6,text.length);
            var temp = t.trim();
            var querySpec = {
```

```
                query: 'SELECT * FROM Bugs b WHERE b.id= @id',
                parameters: [
                {
                    name: '@id',
                    value: temp
                }
                ]
            };
            docclient.queryDocuments('dbs/BugDB/colls/Bugs',
querySpec).toArray(function (err, results) {
                if (results.length>0){
                    client.say('#BugsChannel', "["+ results[0].url+"]
[Status]: "+results[0].status+" [Title]:"+results[0].title);
                }
                else{
                    client.say('#BugsChannel', 'No bugs found.');
                }
            });
        }
    }
    else{
        client.say('#BugsChannel', "So you need a Bug Report!");
        client.say('#BugsChannel', "Wait for a moment!");
        var querySpec = {
            query: 'SELECT * FROM Bugs b WHERE b.status= @status',
            parameters: [
            {
                name: '@status',
                value: 'Open'
            }
            ]
        };
        docclient.queryDocuments('dbs/BugDB/colls/Bugs',
querySpec).toArray(function (err, results) {
            client.say('#BugsChannel','Total Open Bugs:'+results.length);
        });
        var querySpec = {
            query: 'SELECT * FROM Bugs b WHERE b.status= @status',
            parameters: [
            {
                name: '@status',
                value: 'Closed'
            }
            ]
        };

        docclient.queryDocuments('dbs/BugDB/colls/Bugs',
querySpec).toArray(function (err, results) {
```

```
            client.say('#BugsChannel','Total Closed Bugs:'+results.length);
        });
    }
});
```

Code understanding

I have already explained how we can connect to DocumentDB using **URI** and **PRIMARY KEY**. Now let's focus on how we have implemented the conversational experience and how we are getting bug information based on that within our BugTrackerIRCBot.

```
client.addListener('message', function (from, to, text) {
    var str = text;
    if (str.indexOf('BUGREPORT') === -1){
     if (str.indexOf('BUG #') === -1){
        client.say('#BugsChannel', "I could not get that!\n Send me
commands like,\n BUGREPORT \n BUG # <BUG. NO>");
     }
```

In the the preceding code, our IRC client has been added with a listener that listens to all the messages within the channel. So, as our bot joins channel, the bot mentions which commands can be used. These commands are `BUGREPORT` and `BUG # <BUG NO.>`.

Knowing this, when our incoming message contains words like `BUGREPORT` and `BUG #` then our bot BugTrackerIRCBot gathers information based on those commands. If the message does not match, then the bot replies with a proper message and also provides usable commands.

Let's assume one of the developers is looking for the total number of defects and so the developer enters the command `BUGREPORT`, then our bot will query the DocumentDB database and will get the report for open and closed bugs from our bugs collection. This code is as follows:

```
client.say('#BugsChannel', "So you need a Bug Report!");
client.say('#BugsChannel', "Wait for a moment!");
var querySpec = {
    query: 'SELECT * FROM Bugs b WHERE  b.status= @status',
    parameters: [
        {
            name: '@status',
            value: 'Open'
        }
    ]
};
docclient.queryDocuments('dbs/BugDB/colls/Bugs',
```

```
querySpec).toArray(function (err, results) {
    client.say('#BugsChannel','Total Open Bugs:'+results.length);
});
```

In the the preceding code, once the developer's intention of getting a report is clear, our bot replies with confirmation using the `client.say()` function. The bot interactively asks the developer to wait for a moment and in the mean time queries DocumentDB using the function `docclient.queryDocuments()`. Once the data is received, again the bot uses the `client.say()` function and returns the information in a chat window. In the preceding code, the bot first returns `Total Open Bugs` and then `Total Closed Bugs`.

Now you may ask why two different calls are made for `Open` and `Closed` bugs; the reason is that, currently, there is no native support for AGGREGATE functions in DocumentDB. We need to know only the `Open` and `Closed` numbers of bugs, so we use the `docclient.queryDocuments()` function twice to get the data.

BugTrackerIRCBot can also give us information about individual bugs using the command `BUG #`. The implementation for the same can be seen in the following code snippet:

```
client.say('#BugsChannel', "So you need info about "+text);
client.say('#BugsChannel', "Wait for a moment!");
var t= text.substring(6,text.length);
var temp = t.trim();
var querySpec = {
    query: 'SELECT * FROM Bugs b WHERE  b.id= @id',
    parameters: [
    {
        name: '@id',
        value: temp
    }
    ]
};
docclient.queryDocuments('dbs/BugDB/colls/Bugs',
querySpec).toArray(function (err, results) {
    if (results.length>0){
        client.say('#BugsChannel', "["+ results[0].url+"] [Status]:
"+results[0].status+" [Title]:"+results[0].title);
    }
    else{
        client.say('#BugsChannel', 'No bugs found.');
    }
});
```

In the the preceding code, when the developer gives the `BUG #` command while chatting, our code will extract only the bug number after the symbol `#`.Then our bot will reply with which bug details will be retrieved from the database. If the records are not found, our bot will reply with an appropriate message as well.

The variable `querySpec` will formulate a query with the parameter of the bug number entered by the developer in a chat window and then will be processed using the function `docclient.queryDocuments()`. Once the function retrieves the data for a specified bug number, our bot will formulate the following response:

```
client.say('#BugsChannel', '[http://mybugsystem.net/'+ results[0].id +"]
[Status]: "+results[0].status+" [Title]:"+results[0].title);
```

To the end user or a developer, we show the URL of a bug from the bug-tracking system, as well as status of the bug and a title.

Lots of code to understand so far!!

Let's run our bot now, and see how it interacts and provides us with a great conversational experience.

Running our enhanced BugTrackerIRCBot

Let's go back to our `ircbot` directory, on a Command Prompt, and run our modified `app.js`. Once the code has run successfully, you should see the following at the Command Prompt:

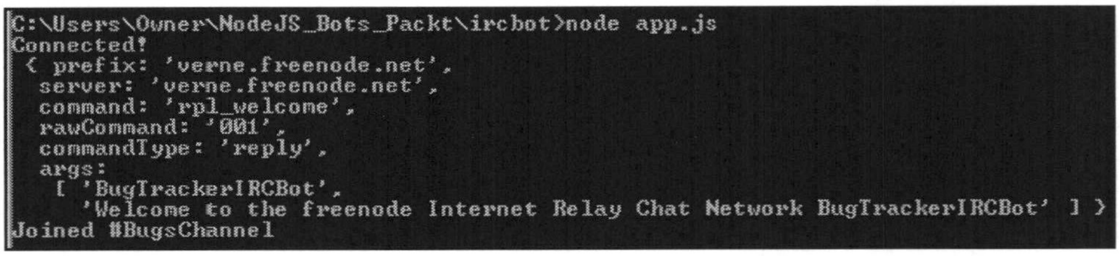

This is assuming that you have already connected to the IRC client, as stated earlier. Now let's look at our channel #BugsChannel from an IRC client. We should see our bot as the following:

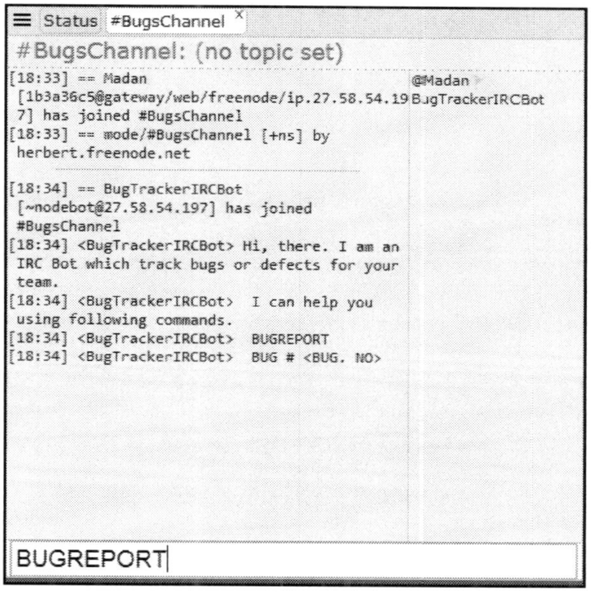

In the the preceding screenshot, you can see the bot has joined the channel and has also introduced itself to us with usable commands.

Let's enter the command `BUGREPORT` and see what the bot replies to us. Here, the bot is getting the bug report, as explained earlier in the code description. The reply seen is as follows:

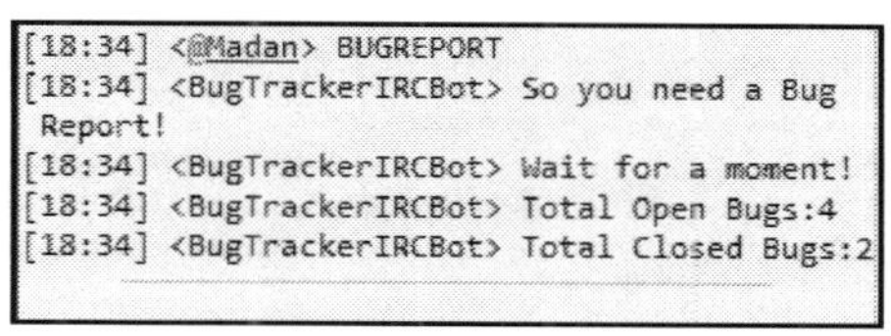

Now let's ensure our other command also works. So, now we are interested in information about an individual bug, enter the command `BUG # 125` and see what our bot replies:

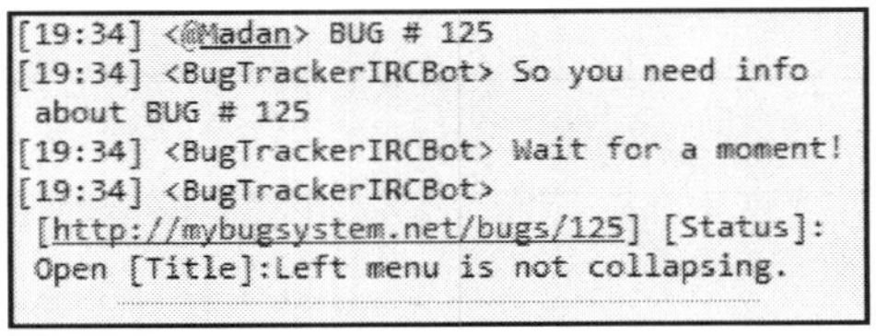

The bot replied with the URL of the bug-tracking system for a bug, and also **Status** and **Title** information.

Let's cross check in DocumentDB whether the bot is providing the correct information or not.

In DocumentDB, for `Bug # 125`, the following data can be seen:

If you enter a bug number that does not exist in DocumentDB, then the bot replies accordingly; refer to the following screenshot:

Here I entered `BUG # 12345` and the bot searched and could not find the bug, so it responded `No bugs found`.

So, we are able to extend our bot to meet our requirements. BugTrackerIRCBot can be further extended to assign bugs or even to create a new bug using appropriate commands such as `ASSIGNBUG`, `NEWBUG`, etc. I will leave it up to the users to extend our BugTrackerIRCBot that way.

Hopefully, you now have enough insight on how we can leverage IRC bots during development, and how we can provide an effective and efficient conversational experience to developers who are collaborating and communicating through IRC clients.

Summary

Every development team needs bug-tracking and reporting tools. There are typically needs for bug reporting and bug assignment. In the case of critical projects, these needs become very critical for project timelines. This chapter has showed us how we can provide a seamless experience to developers while they are communicating with peers within a channel.

Firstly, we created a very simple IRC bot in Node.js and verified how it can communicate within a channel using the IRC web-based client. Then, we extended our basic bot such that, based on a user's request, the bot will give us information quickly and easily while chatting itself. We also leveraged Azure-based cloud storage to store the bug database. This time we used DocumentDB – a NoSQL JSON database from the Microsoft Azure platform. We wired up DocumentDB libraries and IRC libraries in Node.js for our bot to function and had a great conversational experience.

In today's world of collaboration, development teams that use such integrations and automations will be efficient and effective while delivering their quality products.

In the next chapter, you will learn how to integrate Salesforce APIs and Kik's chat platform for the Salesforce CRM bot.

9
A Kik Salesforce CRM Bot

Kik Messenger, or simply Kik, is a free mobile messenger app. This is available on iOS, Android, and Windows Phone. Using this instant messenger app, users can send or receive messages, photos, videos, and so on.

Kik is mainly famous because it does not verify user information upon registration. This helps users to maintain their anonymity.

Kik users have their own code. Using these codes, users can connect with their friends quickly and easily. Users can scan the code of a user and start chatting right away. This is also applicable to Kik groups. Users can scan Kik codes for groups and join them easily.

The simplicity and ease of establishing a chat communication and, mainly, the anonymity, have made Kik a very popular chat platform among young people.

In this chapter, we will learn about how to create a basic Kik bot and how to enhance the same by integrating it with Salesforce CRM.

But before going into the details, let's understand more about Salesforce CRM.

What is Salesforce?

Salesforce is a cloud-based **customer relationship management** (**CRM**) software solution for sales, service, marketing, analytics, and collaboration. All these software solutions are prebuilt and run on a cloud platform. Salesforce does not need any IT person to set it up or manage. CRM users just need to log in to start using this platform.

Details of Salesforce can be found at `https://www.salesforce.com`.

What is Force.com?

Force.com is a **platform as a service** (**PaaS**). This platform consists of underlying components such as database, code, and user interface, on which developers can create and deliver powerful enterprise apps. With this platform, developers can deliver powerful apps just by using a few clicks or code. Even business users can develop and deliver app workflows just by dragging and dropping.

In short, Salesforce, with its products and solutions, is a customer success platform which changes the way people connect with their customers.

Kik mobile app

As mentioned in the introduction, Kik is a free mobile messenger app. This can be downloaded from the App Store (`https://itunes.apple.com/ca/app/kik/id357218860?mt=8`) or Google Play Store (`https://play.google.com/store/apps/details?id=kik.android&hl=en`).

For this chapter, I am assuming the Kik mobile app has already been downloaded and installed from the App Store or Google Play Store.

I have already installed the Kik app from the Google Play Store and also created my account on the Kik app. The following screenshot shows what the Kik mobile app looks like:

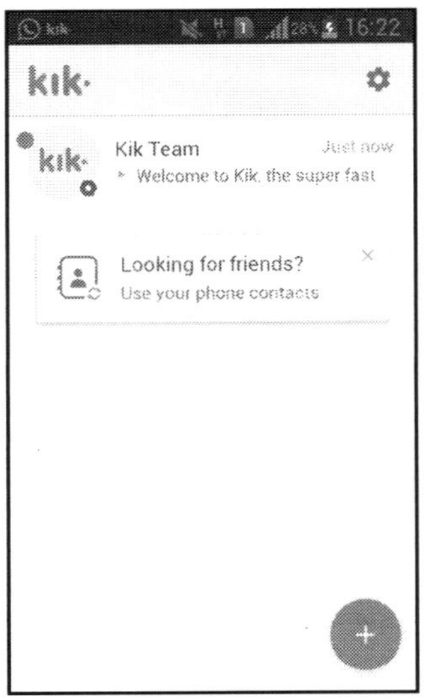

Kik does not have a web or desktop version for messaging so we will be using the Kik app from a mobile.

Kik bots

Kik bots are just programs that provide users with an automated conversational experience with the help of Kik APIs. Users can chat to these bots for fun, for any help, or for seeking information for entertainment. Kik has recently released a Bot Shop. Users can discover bots and connect them easily.

Our Kik bot

Our Kik bot will be based on the Salesforce and Force.com platforms, which I explained previously. At a high level, we will be following the following steps for our bot:

1. Developing a basic Kik bot
2. Enhancing our basic bot program for a more conversational experience as per Kik guidelines
3. Establishing a connection between CRM and our basic bot
4. Based on the user's requirements, getting CRM data from Salesforce and presenting the user data in the Kik app

Creating our first Kik bot

Just like Slack, Kik also helps us to create our bot using an automated agent, **Botsworth**. Let's follow the steps to create our first Kik bot.

Using the Kik dev platform on a browser

Visit `https://dev.kik.com/#/home`, as shown in the following screenshot:

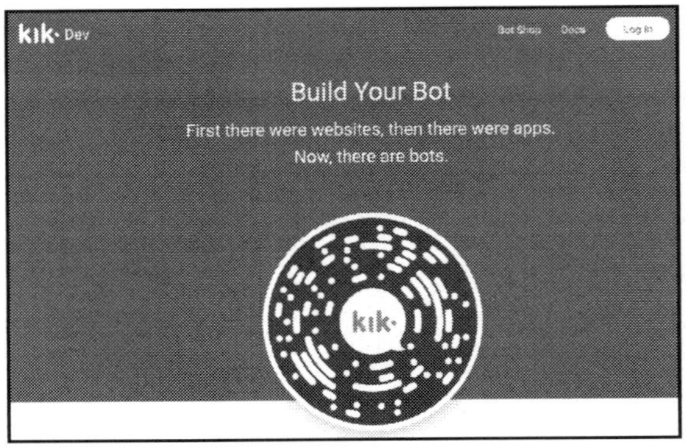

The URL opens the Kik developer platform, which helps us to create and configure our Kik bot. This screen shows a Kik code for creating a bot. This code needs to be scanned using the Kik app, which we have already installed and configured with our Kik account as well.

Using the Kik app from a mobile

Open the Kik app on a device and pull down from the top of your main chat list to open the scanner, as shownin the following screenshot:

Using the scanner, scan the Kik code from `https://dev.kik.com/#/home`.

This scanner can also be located from the Kik app's settings menu (a small gear icon on the top right) by selecting your **Kik Code** page from the menu items.

After scanning, Kik's trusty bot, **Botsworth,** will send a message, as shown in the following screenshot, on our app:

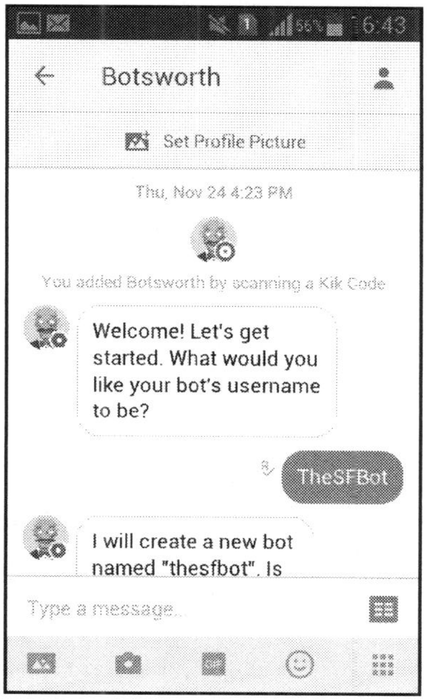

Now provide a unique bot name to **Botsworth** in the chat window itself.

Botsworth will create our bot and will also notify us of the same, as shown in the following screenshot:

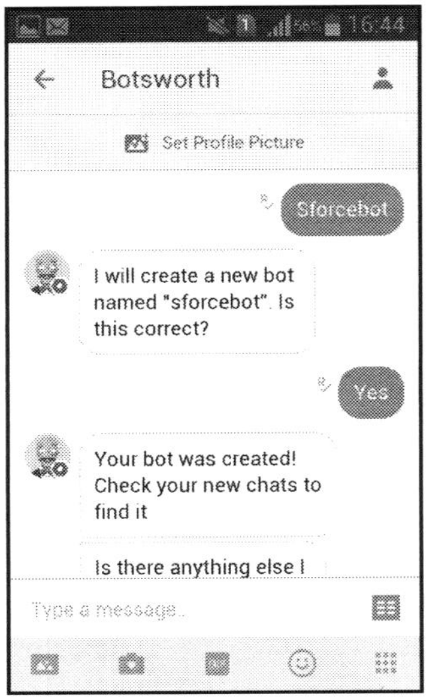

Now let's go back to our browser, where the `https://dev.kik.com/#/home` page is open. You will notice that the newly configured bot account has logged in to the platform and is showing bot properties such as **Display Name**, **Admins**, and **API Key**, as shown in the following screenshot:

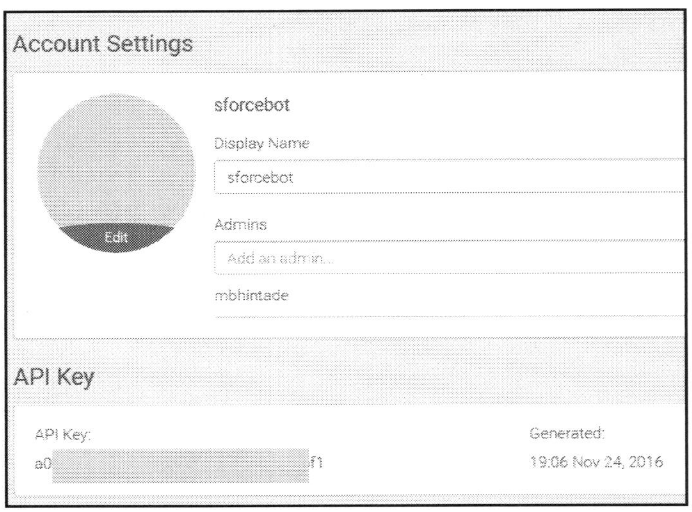

The bot name, **sforcebot,** and **API Key** will be used to wire up Kik APIs while building a conversational experience later.

To receive messages from users, our bot needs **Webhooks** integration. Before we set up Webhooks, let's create a Node.js server app for our bot on Azure in the next section.

Setting up our bot server in Azure

Let's log in to the Azure portal and locate App Services to create a Node.js-based bot server as `thesfbotsite`. This server app is based on the **Node JS Empty Web App** template. Refer to the following screenshot:

This will provision our `thesfbotsite.azurewebsites.net` server app in Azure.

To modify the basic bot program, first we will clone the template on our local filesystem using git commands. Then we will modify it and then deploy it to Microsoft Azure.

Let's start by creating a folder in our local drive in order to store our bot program from the Command Prompt:

```
mkdir thesfbot
cd thesfbot
```

Now clone the template to the local filesystem and change the remote git repository as well for this bot.

Detailed steps of how to clone the template to the local filesystem and how to change the remote git repository can be found in the *Setting up our bot server in Azure* section in `Chapter 7`, *Facebook Messenger Bot Who's Off – A Scheduler Bot for Teams.*

Kik bot configuration

Before our bot can start interacting with users, it needs configuration. To configure our bot, we will be making a POST request with a Webhook URL to which messages will be delivered. Also, any additional features for read receipts and receive typing can also be configured here.

This can be done by firing a URL command or by writing a JavaScript with the following code in a simple Node.js program:

```
request.post({
    url: "https://api.kik.com/v1/config",
    auth: {
        'user' : 'sforcebot',
        'pass' : '<YOUR BOT API KEY>'
    },
    json:{"webhook": "https://thesfbotsite.azurewebsites.net/incoming",
        "features": {
            "receiveReadReceipts": false,
            "receiveIsTyping": false,
            "manuallySendReadReceipts": false,
            "receiveDeliveryReceipts": false
        }
    }
}, function(error, response, body){
    if(error) {
        console.log(error);
    } else {
        console.log(response.statusCode, body);
    }
});
```

This code sets the `webhook` for our bot to the newly created site in Azure at the path `/incoming`.

Details of these configurations can be found at `https://dev.kik.com/#/docs/messaging#configuration`.

Wiring up our bot server with the Kik platform

In order for our bot to interact with the Kik platform, we will be using the Kik Node API library. This can be found at https://www.npmjs.com/package/@kikinteractive/kik.

Let's install the Kik API library and other libraries using the following command:

```
npm install @kikinteractive/kik  http  util --save
```

Let's update our server.js file as follows:

```
var util = require('util');
var http = require('http');
var Bot  = require('@kikinteractive/kik');
var request = require('request');

// Configure the bot
var bot = new Bot({
    username: 'sforcebot',
    apiKey: '<YOUR BOT API KEY>'
});

bot.send(Bot.Message.text('The SForceBot Started... '), 'mbhintade');

bot.onTextMessage(/^hi|hello|how|hey$/i, (incoming, next) => {
     incoming.reply('Hello,I am the SForce Bot. I provide your CRM
information just by chatting.');
 });


// Set up your server and start listening
var server = http
  .createServer(bot.incoming())
  .listen(process.env.PORT || 8080);
```

Understanding the code of our basic Kik bot

Let's look at basic code implementation from server.js.

We used the @kikinteractive/kik library with the following line:

```
var Bot = require('@kikinteractive/kik');
```

Using this library, we instantiated our bot by providing `username` and `apikey`:

```
var bot = new Bot({
    username: 'sforcebot',
    apiKey: '<YOUR BOT API KEY>'
});
```

When our bot is wired up successfully, this will show up in the Kik app. Also, our bot will notify the user `mbhintade` with the help of the following code:

```
bot.send(Bot.Message.text('The SForceBot Started... '), 'mbhintade');
```

When we say hi or hello to our bot, the bot will reply to us using the following code lines:

```
bot.onTextMessage(/^hi|hello|how|hey$/i, (incoming, next) => {
     incoming.reply('Hello,I am the SForce Bot. I provide your CRM
information just by chatting.');
 });
```

In the preceding code snippet, we are using the regular expression `/^hi|hello|how|hey$/i` to find out what user is messaging. The regular expression used precedingly can be described as follows:

Character	Description
/	Regular expression
^	Matches character `hi` and not from any character group
|	Matches any single word between two characters
$	Matches the end of the input

I hope this has given some basic understanding of our Kik bot and its code implementation. Now let's run our bot and see how it looks in the Kik mobile app.

Running our basic Kik bot

Let's deploy our modified `server.js` and installed Node packages using the following `git` commands:

```
git add .
git commit -m "First Change to server.js"
git push origin master
```

Once the code is deployed to Azure, hit the URL `https://thesfbotsite.azurewebsites.net` and see if there are any errors in the Azure log stream. If the code is successful, then the bot server will start and our bot will be shown in Kik chats with active status.

When the bot started, it showed us the message, **The SForceBot Started...**

When I greeted it by saying **Hi**, the bot replied with the message **Hello, I am the SForce Bot. I provide your CRM information just by chatting.**

Refer to the following screenshot:

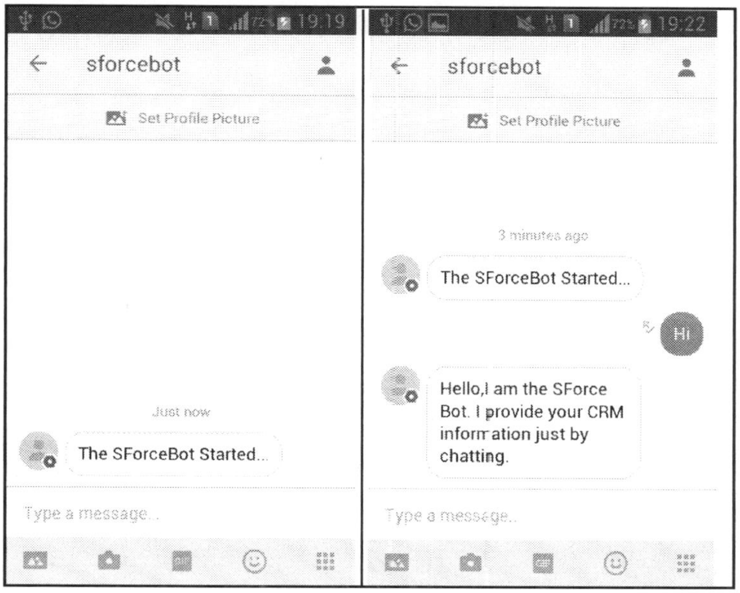

In the next section, we will enhance our bot for an interesting use case.

Enhancing our Kik bot

Having built a very basic Kik bot, *sforcebot*, let's enhance our Kik bot.

Typically, sales and marketing business users always need to keep track of their sales and marketing activities. They need to track their own leads and opportunities, and maintain campaigns. Now, to track these activities, they rely on CRM systems.

In the next section, we will actually look at how a bot can be effective in such business use cases. Our bot will be now integrated with a CRM system and will provide all the required information to the business users at their fingertips.

Let's assume you are one of the business users who work in sales and marketing. Now, you would like to see upcoming business opportunities quickly and easily. It is assumed that your organization is already on a cloud-based CRM. So you will be interacting with the Kik bot named sforcebot. During the interaction, you will request upcoming opportunities for the current month. The bot knows who you are and will look for opportunities owned by you for the current month. sforcebot will gather the information and will present opportunities in a nice readable format within a chat window.

Awesome!!

Salesforce and our bot

Let's assume we have our business opportunities data in Salesforce and we have already logged in to the Saleforce platform. Now, from our bot perspective, we are interested in showing opportunity data for the current month and the next month. In Salesforce, we get these views preconfigured for us.

Opportunities closing this month can be seen as in the following screenshot:

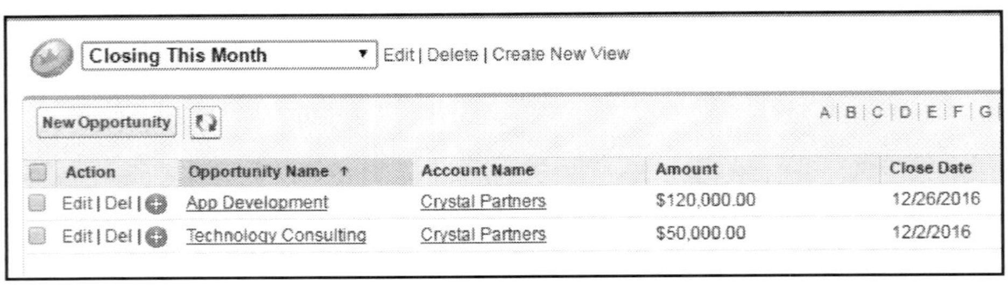

Opportunities closing next month can be seen as in the following screenshot:

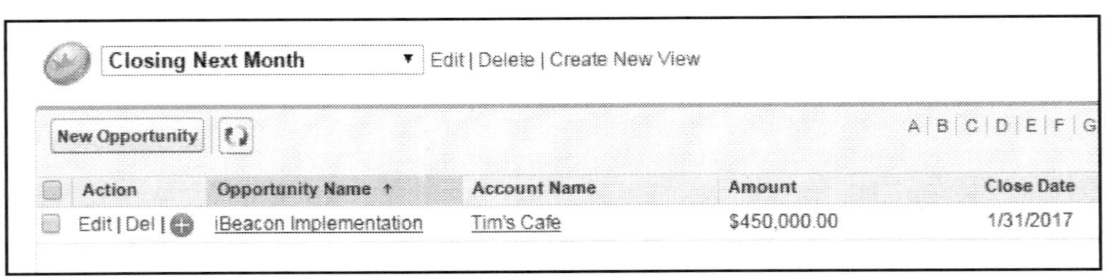

In our bot, we will be pulling the same data based on users' requests for information. So it's time to prepare for Saleforce and our bot integration.

Security token to access the Salesforce API

To access information from Salesforce, we need a security token. This token is a case-sensitive alphanumeric code which is associated with your password. Whenever we change our password, this security token is also reset.

Let's get our security token for our Salesforce API access, using the **Reset Security Token** menu option from Salesforce as follows:

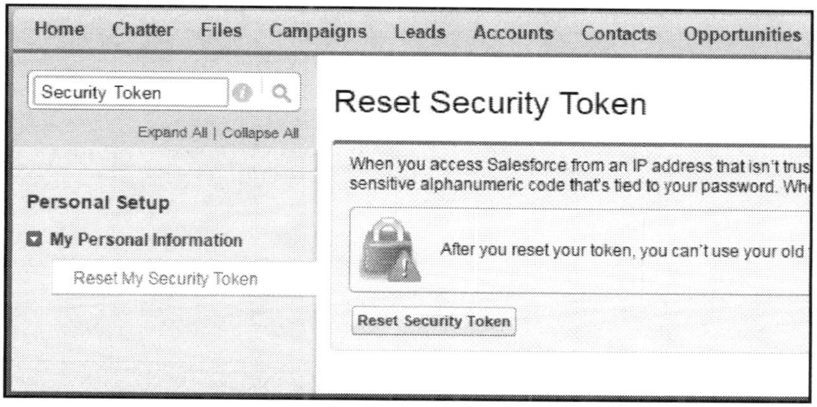

To quickly locate the **Reset Security Token** option, you can use the Quick Find/Search option from the left corner of menu options from Salesforce. In the preceding screenshot, I entered the words `Security Token` and searched for the option, **Reset Security Token**.

Click on the **Reset Security Token** button to get the fresh token for accessing Salesforce APIs. The new token will be sent to your registered e-mail ID.

Wiring it up all together

To wire up Salesforce and Node.js, we will be using the Salesforce API library JSforce. This can be located at `https://www.npmjs.com/package/jsforce`.

Let's install the `JSforce` library using the following command:

```
npm install jsforce --save
```

To wire up all the things together, let's modify our earlier `server.js` as follows:

```
var util = require('util');
var http = require('http');
var Bot = require('@kikinteractive/kik');
var request = require('request');

var username = "<SALESFORCE_USERNAME>";
var password = "<SALESFORCE_PASSWORD>";
var accesstoken = password + '<SALESFORCE_SECURITY_TOKEN>';

var fromUserName;

// Configure the bot
var bot = new Bot({
  username: 'sforcebot',
  apiKey: '<YOUR BOT API KEY>'
});


var jsforce = require('jsforce');
var conn = new jsforce.Connection();

bot.onTextMessage(/^hi|hello|how|hey$/i, (incoming, next) => {
  bot.getUserProfile(incoming.from)
    .then((user) => {
      fromUserName = user.username;
      incoming.reply('Hello,I am the SForce Bot. I provide your CRM
information just by chatting.');

      bot.send(Bot.Message.text('Select any option...')
        .addResponseKeyboard(['Closing This Month', 'Closing Next Month'])
        , fromUserName);
    });
});


bot.onTextMessage(/^Closing This Month/i, (incoming, next) => {
  incoming.reply('Opportunities for this month...!');
  conn.login(username, accesstoken, function (err, res) {
    if (err) { return console.error(err); }
    console.log(res.id);
    var records = [];
    var qry = "SELECT Account.Name,Name,Amount FROM Opportunity WHERE
CloseDate = THIS_MONTH ORDER BY AMOUNT DESC"
    conn.query(qry, function (err, result) {
      if (err) { return console.error(err); }
      rec = result.records;
```

```
        rec.forEach(function (d) {
          bot.send(Bot.Message.text(d.Name + ' for ' + d.Account.Name + '
worth ' + d.Amount.toLocaleString('en-US', { style: 'currency', currency:
'USD' }))
            .addResponseKeyboard(['Closing This Month', 'Closing Next
Month']), fromUserName);
        });
      });
    });
});

bot.onTextMessage(/^Closing Next Month/i, (incoming, next) => {
  incoming.reply('Finding your opportunities for next month...!');
  conn.login(username, accesstoken, function (err, res) {
    if (err) { return console.error(err); }
    console.log(res.id);
    var records = [];
    var qry = "SELECT Account.Name,Name,Amount FROM Opportunity WHERE
CloseDate = NEXT_MONTH ORDER BY AMOUNT DESC"
    conn.query(qry, function (err, result) {
      if (err) { return console.error(err); }
      rec = result.records;
      rec.forEach(function (d) {
        bot.send(Bot.Message.text(d.Name + ' for ' + d.Account.Name + '
worth ' + d.Amount.toLocaleString('en-US', { style: 'currency', currency:
'USD' }))
          .addResponseKeyboard(['Closing This Month', 'Closing Next
Month']), fromUserName);
      });
    });
  });
});

// Set up your server and start listening
var server = http
  .createServer(bot.incoming())
  .listen(process.env.PORT || 8080);
```

Understanding the code

We already have a code understanding for the basic bot. Let's look at the code step by step from a Salesforce integration perspective:

```
var username = "<SALESFORCE_USERNAME>";
var password = "<SALESFORCE_PASSWORD>";
var accesstoken = password + '<SALESFORCE_SECURITY_TOKEN>';
var fromUserName;
```

We have declared variables for the Salesforce username and password. We have also declared a variable, `accesstoken`. This is needed while accessing Salesforce APIs. The `fromUserNam` variable is declared for storing the username. This is used while replying to messages from the user who has started the conversation.

Now let's look at how we are wiring up Salesforce for our bot:

```
var jsforce = require('jsforce');
var conn = new jsforce.Connection();
```

These code lines use the npm package, `jsforce`, for connecting Salesforce.

Now let's see how we are enhancing the conversation experience for our bot. The following code lines help to guide the end user with possible input options:

```
bot.onTextMessage(/^hi|hello|how|hey$/i, (incoming, next) => {
  bot.getUserProfile(incoming.from)
    .then((user) => {
      fromUserName = user.username;
      incoming.reply('Hello,I am the SForce Bot. I provide your CRM
information just by chatting.');

      bot.send(Bot.Message.text('Select any option...')
        .addResponseKeyboard(['Closing This Month', 'Closing Next Month'])
       `, fromUserName);
    });
});
```

In the preceding code, whenever the end user says `hi` or `hello` or `how` or `hey`, the `bot.onTextMessage()` function is called and bot gets the username from an `incoming` message with the help of the `bot.getUserProfile()` function.

Once the name of user who is chatting is retrieved, the bot replies with an introduction to the user using the `incoming.reply()` function.

Along with this reply, sforcebot also shows a keyboard with suggested responses. This type of keyboard response is generated using the `addResponseKeyboard()` method with an array of suggestions such as `(['Closing This Month', 'Closing Next Month'])`.

To understand this in a better way, let me show you how the suggested responses can be seen in the Kik app in our case:

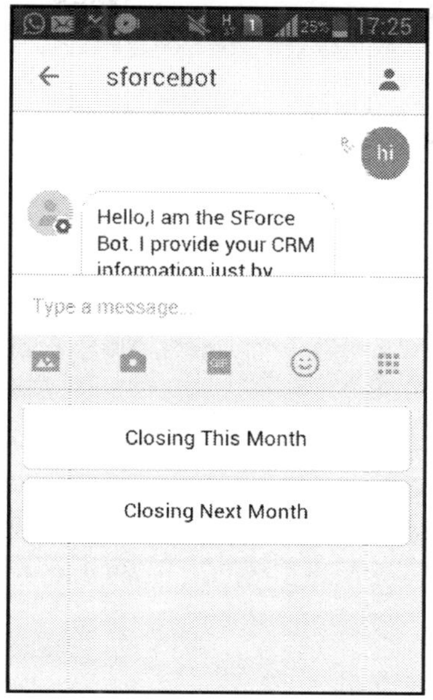

Closing This Month and **Closing Next Month** are appearing as possible suggested responses which the user can consider. This is really intuitive and helps the user to easily select options rather than entering keywords for further communication. The user can still enter these keywords and continue, but showing such a keyboard saves a lot of time for users. This also guides the user during the conversations.

In the next section, we will see code implementations for querying data from Salesforce.

Let's assume now the user has selected one of the options, **Closing This Month**. Our bot quickly captures with the help of the `bot.onTextMessage(/^Closing This Month/i, (incoming, next)` function and starts responding. There is a regex pattern matching done to understand what the user is selecting. Refer to the following code snippet:

```
bot.onTextMessage(/^Closing This Month/i, (incoming, next) => {
  incoming.reply('Opportunities for this month...!');
  conn.login(username, accesstoken, function (err, res) {
    if (err) { return console.error(err); }
    console.log(res.id);
    var records = [];
    var qry = "SELECT Account.Name,Name,Amount FROM Opportunity WHERE
CloseDate = THIS_MONTH ORDER BY AMOUNT DESC"
    conn.query(qry, function (err, result) {
```

```
        if (err) { return console.error(err); }
        rec = result.records;
        rec.forEach(function (d) {
          bot.send(Bot.Message.text(d.Name + ' for ' + d.Account.Name + '
worth ' + d.Amount.toLocaleString('en-US', { style: 'currency', currency:
'USD' }))
            .addResponseKeyboard(['Closing This Month', 'Closing Next
Month']), fromUserName);
        });
      });
    });
  });
```

Since the user has selected the option to see opportunities closing this month, the bot will log in to Salesforce and query the data with the help of the `conn.login()` and `conn.query()` functions.

While logging in to Salesforce, JSforce uses the SOAP login API, so we are using `username` and `accesstoken`. Once login is established, we execute the query on Salesforce and get the data. We iterate the results and formulate the message to be sent to the user identified by the `fromUserName` variable.

If you notice, the `qry` variable is the Salesforce Object Query Language (SOQL). You can find further details of SOQL at `https://developer.salesforce.com/docs/atlas.en-us.soql_sosl.meta/soql_sosl/sforce_api_calls_soql_sosl_intro.htm`.

In our query, SOQL has made it simpler for date operations. For getting opportunities for the current month from Salesforce, we just need to apply a filter using `THIS_MONTH` and `NEXT_MONTH`. This really made my life simpler while building these two use cases. SOQL is great!

Once this response is set to the user, the user might be interested in opportunities for the next month as well, so we are again sending suggested responses at the end.

The code implementation for **Closing Next Month** is on similar lines to **Closing This Month**. I have kept both the implementations in separate functions. This can be further optimized. I will leave this task to the readers.

Let's run our bot now and see how it interacts and provides us with a great conversational experience.

Running our enhanced Kik Salesforce bot

Deploy the updated code to Azure and start our sforcebot server. After successfully starting a bot, it will be shown in Kik. Or you can search by name and then add it for chatting. Once added, just say `Hi` and see how the bot is responding to us, as shown in the following screenshot:

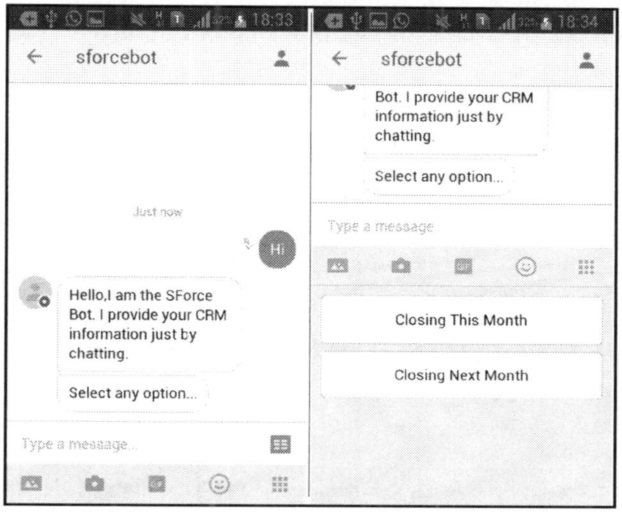

On selecting the option, **Closing This Month**:

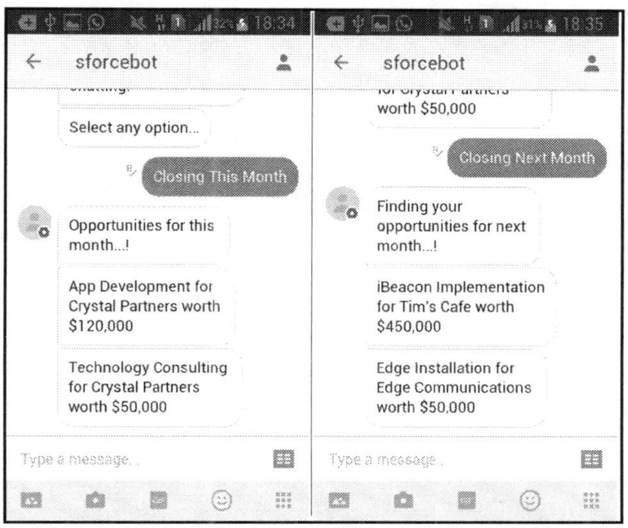

Hopefully, you have now enough insight on how we can leverage the Kik platform and Kik bots for better connection with your employees, users, and partners.

sforcebot for campaign management

So far, we have been retrieving opportunities data in messaging platforms; we can also retrieve Salesforce campaigns data. Assume that one of the universities is using Salesforce for their campaign management. This university would like to spread its campaigns across its students and to ensure there is a better connection and engagement between students and the university while running various campaigns.

Knowing students' presence on the Kik platform, this becomes a very effective way for connecting to students. Using the same sforcebot, this can be easily achieved. Instead of opportunities, now the data will be coming from campaigns. I am just illustrating this use case using the following screenshots:

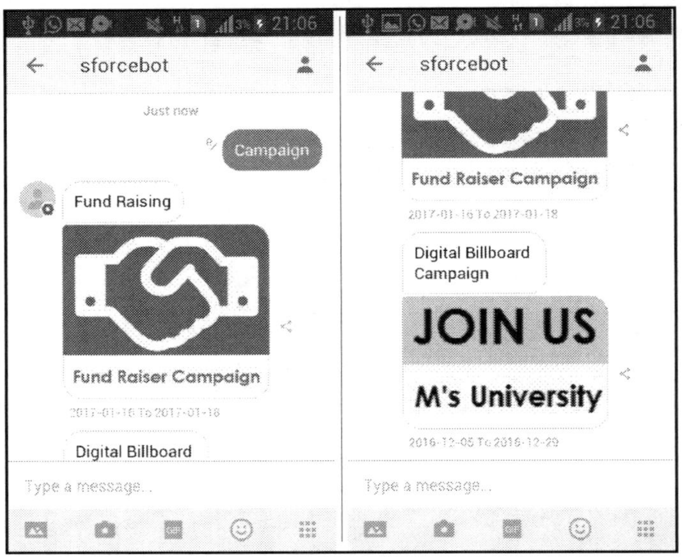

In the preceding screenshots, just by passing the `Campaign` keyword, sforcebot is displaying active campaigns from Salesforce. Since these are campaigns, we are not only showing text messages, but we are also showing pictures about these campaigns and their start date and end date.

This way, universities can establish a connection with students and improve their engagement and participation for such events.

Summary

Every enterprise would like to connect to their customers, employees, and partners. Knowing users' increasing engagement with chat platforms, these enterprises can leverage Kik-like messaging platforms for better connection.

In this chapter, we implemented the Kik bot sforcebot, assuming users' engagement with the Kik messaging platform. Sales and marketing users can collaborate as well as seeking the right information at the right time and tracking their sales and marketing activities easily and effectively.

Firstly, we created a basic sforcebot by scanning a code and implemented it in Node.js. Then we extended our sforcebot and wired it up with Salesforce. Now, based on the user's request, sforcebot provided information on the user's opportunities in the chatting interface itself.

We also saw a small example of how universities can use the Kik platform and Salesforce to connect to their graduating students. This way, universities can connect to their graduates and spread the word about campaigns they are running, during their academics.

I hope you had a nice Kik around with this chapter.

Index

A

B

C

M

N

P

Q

R

S

T

U

W